The Yog Of Th Bhagavat Gita

By

Sri Krishna Prem

Alight Publications

2022

The Yoga Of The Bhagavat Gita

By Sri Krishna Prem
New Edition Published in July 2022

Alight Publications
PO Box 277
Live Oak, CA 95953
http://www.alightbooks.com

Softcover ISBN: 978-1-931833-59-2

Printed in the United States of America

This Book Is Dedicated
To My Guru,
To Whom Alone
Is Due Whatever Truth Its Pages Contain

Table Of Contents

INTRODUCTION

THE Bhagavat Gita needs little introduction nowadays even in the West. Many have come to value it as one of the world's great spiritual classics and not a few take it as their guide to the inner life. Of its popularity in India there is no need to speak. Though its author is unknown (for we can scarcely adopt the orthodox view that it was, as we have it, spoken by the historical Krishna on the battlefield of *Kurukshetra*) it is revered by Hindus of all schools of thought, and is one foot of the triple base on which the *Vedanta* is founded, the other two feet being the *Upanishads* and the *Brahma-Sutras*. Every teacher who wished to claim *Vedantic* authority for his teachings was obliged to write a commentary on it showing that it supported his views.

In consequence of this we have commentaries written from many diverse points of view, monist and dualist, pantheist and theist. Enthusiasts for action, for knowledge (*jnana* or gnosis), or for devotion to a personal God, all find their special tenets in the Gita, and, though this universal appeal is proof of its catholicity, its authoritative status has had the drawback that the various commentators have often devoted more energy to special pleading and refutation of opponents than to straightforward inquiry into the real meaning of the text.

Into the views (equally diverse) of the Western scholars, with their incurably external method of approach, it is not proposed to enter. Garbe considered it a *Sankhya-Yoga* textbook overwritten by Krishna worshippers and then again by a Vedantist, while Hopkins held that it was a Vishnu-ite poem worked up in the interests of the Krishna cult. Nearly all of them object to what they term its philosophical inconsistencies and loose use of terms.

Let me say at once that I care nothing at all for these learned pronouncements. To anyone who has eyes to see, the Gita is based on direct knowledge of Reality, and of the Path that leads to that Reality, and it is of little moment who wrote it or to what school he was outwardly affiliated. Those who know Reality belong to a Race apart, the Race that never dies, as Hermes Trismegistus puts it, and neither they nor those who seek to be born into that Race concern themselves with the flummeries of sects and schools.

It is by such a seeker and for such seekers that this book has been written. Some may feel that the interpretation is a somewhat modernised one, but in answer to that I would only say that the words of an Enlightened One refer to eternal realities. Those realities are the same now as they were thousands of years ago, and the texts of the Gita should be interpreted in words that refer to those realities here and now, and not merely in words which did refer to them in mediaeval India or, for that matter, at the time when the book was originally written. To think otherwise is to mistake words for realities. As the Buddha teaches in the *Lankavatdra Sutra*: "Meaning is entered into by words as things are revealed by a lamp. . . . So, I, making use of various forms and images of things, instruct my sons; but the summit of Reality can only be realised within oneself."

The point of view from which this book has been written is that the Gita is a textbook of Yoga, a guide to the treading of the Path. By Yoga is here meant not any special system called by that name, not *jnana yoga*, nor *karma yoga*, nor *bhakti yoga*, nor the eightfold *yoga* of Patanjali, but just the Path by which man unites his finite self with Infinite Being. It is the inner Path of which all these separate yogas are so many one-sided aspects. It is not so much a synthesis of these separate teachings as that prior and undivided whole of which they represent partial formulations.

As such, it deals with the whole Path from the beginning to the end, from what Buddhists term "Entry in the stream" to the goal of Nirvana. It follows that the sequence of the chapters is of great importance, and that it is a mistake to do as some expositors have done and expound the teachings with no reference to the place at which they occur in the general scheme. For instance, stress has often been laid on Gita xviii, 66: "Abandoning all *dharmas*, take refuge in Me alone. Fear not, I will liberate thee from all sins," as though this teaching, which comes at the very end of the Gita, were capable of being practised in the early stages of the Path. All that results from such misplacing is emotional pietism. There is no short-cut to the Goal. The whole course has to be run by each disciple, and though, through having practised in previous lives, the early stages may for some be but a rapid recapitulation, each chapter has to be lived through in its proper sequence.

The Path is not the special property of Hinduism, nor indeed of any religion. It is something which is to be found, more or less deeply buried, in all religions, and which can exist apart from any formal religion at all. That is why the Gita, though a definitely Hindu book, the very crest-jewel of Hindu teachings, is capable of being a guide to seekers all over the world.

Recently the psychologist Jung, in the course of son sympathetic and interesting comments on a Chinese Taoi. book, found occasion to animadvert against those Westerners who practise Eastern yogas. It is quite true that much, probably most, of the so-called yoga practice indulged in by Westerners is foolish and misguided. That is, however, not because it is "eastern" in origin, but because it is not pursued for the right reason. Yoga is to be undertaken for the sake of Truth itself, for the sake of what the Buddha termed "unshakable deliverance of heart." To practise it, as many do, out of curiosity, in search of new sensations, or in order to gain psychic powers is a mistake which is punished with futility, neurosis, or worse. None should seek initiation into the mysteries from unworthy motives, or disaster will surely result.

In fact, though the particular dress in which it is presented in the Gita is an Indian one, the Path itself is neither "eastern" nor "western." It belongs, to no race and to no religion, being that on which all true religions were originally based. It is to make this clear that I have quoted so freely from other mystical literature, and in particular from Plotinus and Hermes Trismegistus. For the former I have used the translation of Stephen McKenna,[1] and for the latter that of G. R. S. Mead.

The parallels adduced should be sufficient to show that the Path is not a purely Oriental one having, as Jung would say, no roots in a Western psyche, but is something universal, to be found in all traditions, and fit to be trodden by anyone who has the will to do so. If a man has a healthy mind, a worthy aspiration, sincerity (including what is less common, intellectual sincerity), courage, and tenacity of purpose he need fear no serious danger on this Path. If a man approaches it from the scientific or philosophic side that is all that need be said. But if his approach is through some particular religion he will have to be careful to discard any idea that his own religion is a unique one and any clinging to authority in the shape of inspired scriptures. Failure to do this will result in delusions and blocking of further advance. He must, as the Buddha said, be his own Light and his own refuge. The only authority is within the Soul itself, and the would-be disciple must be ready to test everything and abandon his most cherished conceptions if they prove inadequate.

Superstition of any kind is a deadly foe and must be conquered at all costs. As it says in *The Precepts of the Gurus*:[2] "Reason being in every action the best friend is not to be avoided." While on the subject a few other aphorisms from the same source are so relevant that they may as well be set down:

"One should acquire practical knowledge of the Path by treading it and not be as are the multitude.

[1] Published by the Medici Society.
[2] Tibetan Yoga and Secret Doctrine, translated from the Tibetan by Lama Kazi Dawa-Samdup, and edited by Dr Evans Wentz. Oxford University Press.

"Weakness of faith combined with strength of intellect are apt to lead to the error of talkativeness.

"Strength of faith combined with weakness of intellect are apt to lead to the error of narrow-minded dogmatism.

"Desire may be mistaken for faith.

"Attachment may be mistaken for benevolence and compassion.

"Sense perceptions may be mistaken for glimpses of Reality.

"A mere glimpse of Reality may be mistaken for complete realisation.

" Charlatans may be mistaken for sages.

"A philosophy comprehensive enough to embrace the whole of knowledge is indispensable.

"A system of meditation which will produce the power of concentrating the mind on anything whatsoever is indispensable.

"An art of living which will enable one to utilise each activity (of body, speech and mind) as an aid on the Path is indispensable."

Those who seek after strange experiences, psychic powers, or the sweet-sounding consolations of religion had far better leave the whole thing alone or they will wreck their lives, and perhaps those of others as well. The path of Truth is a hard one, and the Inner Ruler will exact the last farthing of karmic payment for dallying with error.

The reader is recommended to have a copy of the Gita by him, and in order to facilitate references to the original the verses referred to have been noted in the margin. Where the interpretation seems to differ from generally accepted translations I can only say that the differences are not based on ignorance of the standard versions, but are the results of careful thought. A useful (and cheap) translation for the general reader is that of Mrs Besant, and for those who know even a little Sanskrit the edition by Mrs Besant and Bhagavan Das (T.P.H.), which gives the text and a word-by-word translation as well as the general one, will be found very helpful indeed. Another good translation is that by W. D. P. Hill (Oxford University Press), which also gives the text.

It is recommended that the Appendices should at least be rapidly glanced through before commencing serious reading of the actual book. Much explanatory matter that would have interrupted the general flow has been given there. A glossary of Sanskrit terms will also be found at the end of the book.

To him who reads with a view to treading the Path, however inadequately here set forth, I would only add:

"Thine own consciousness, shining, void and inseparable from the Great Body of Radiance, hath no birth, nor death, and is the Immutable Light."

Sri Krishna Prem

PROLEGOMENA
THE GENERAL SETTING

BEFORE starting to discuss the Gita itself it will be desirable to say a few words about its setting—namely, the events recorded in the *Mahabharata* which serve as the framework of the Gita. I am quite aware that many Western scholars consider that the Gita was not a part of the original *Mahabharata*, but, as most of them have yet to show any real understanding of either, I do not propose to discuss their views and will simply point out, with Telang,[1] that the Gita has been introduced into its setting in a perfectly harmonious manner, and, further, that a consideration of the events related in the *Mahabharata* can shed considerable light upon the inner meaning of the Gita.

For the sake of Western readers I will very briefly recount those events.

The Divinely-born Arjuna,[2] with his four brothers, was brought up with his cousins, the Kauravas, at the Court of the latter's father, Dhritarashtta, the king who, though legally disqualified by his blindness, had seized and held the throne. Not content with the seizing of the throne, the old king did not even hold the balance evenly between his sons and their cousins, the Pandavas, but constantly favoured the former. Hostility soon developed between the two parties and, after a brief attempt to divide the realm between them, the Pandavas were defeated at dice by trickery and made to wander for twelve long years in exile, followed by a thirteenth year in which their very whereabouts had to remain unknown. At the conclusion of this period the well-meaning but weak king found it impossible to persuade his headstrong and evil- minded son, Duryodhana, to restore to the Pandavas their share of the kingdom and, in spite of fruitless attempts

[1] See the introduction to his translation of the Gita in *Sacred Books of the East.*
[2] Arjuna's putative father, Pandu, was disqualified from having children by a curse, and so his wife, Kunti, bore the five Pandavas by five Gods, of whom Indra, the chief, fathered Arjuna.

11

to bring about a reconciliation by Sanjaya, Dhritarashtra's charioteer, by Bhishma, his wise counsellor, and even by the Lord Krishna Himself, war could not be averted, and the rival hosts faced each other on the field of Kurukshetra. It is at this point that the Gita commences.

Without going into the question as to whether all incidents of the *Mahabharata* have a symbolic significance and whether it is possible to trace a consistent symbolism all through the vast epic, it must be clear to all those who have eyes that there is an inner significance behind the events thus inadequately summarised. There is no need to ask the question whether the author of the *Mahabharata* had such a symbolism consciously in his mind. Many, perhaps most, great works of art are filled with symbolism that is often quite unplanned by the conscious minds of their creators, and sometimes this symbolism is truer and more profound from the fact of its having descended from a region beyond the realm of conscious thinking. It embodies not the head-knowledge but the soul-knowledge of the artist. If it were not so, then we should have to concur in Plato's rejection of art as being the shadow of a shadow.

Porphyry, the great Neoplatonist mystic, pointed out a wealth of symbolism in the epics of Homer.[1] It is true that most modern scholars reject all such interpretations as a mere reading into the texts of meanings that were never intended by the author; but such a view is entirely superficial and is based on an utter ignorance of the nature of great art, which is always symbolic, because it takes its birth in a realm whose only utterance is in symbol. If this is true of such a poem as the *Odyssey*, far more is it true of the *Mahabharata*, a poem in which all the culture, all the aspirations and all the traditions of an entire race found expression. Symbolism is, in fact, like beauty itself: either you see it or you do not. And if it is seen, then it is as irrelevant to inquire whether it was consciously intended by the author as it is to ask whether the beauty was consciously intended by him. It exists.

The skeleton interpretation that I shall indicate does not base itself upon the authority of scriptural texts, nor does it depend for its validity on anyone's ability to fit every event in the poem into the framework of this scheme. That may or may not be possible, and in any case is outside the scope of this work. Whatever value it may have for any reader will depend entirely on the light that it may succeed in throwing on the teachings of the Gita for him.[1]

In the first place we must notice that, though not the eldest, the chief of the Pandava brothers is Arjuna. He it was that won Draupadi at the

---

[1] It is not intended to claim truth for all Porphyry's interpretations.
[2] I may also add that no claim is made that these thoughts are original. Anyone who considers that they belong to him is welcome to take possession of them.

swayamvara,[1] and it was he alone that she really loved, and he who was the hero of the greates' exploits. Yudhisthira may excel in *dharma* and Bhima in feats of strength, but it is on Arjuna's heroic prowess that the Pandavas depend, and it was Arjuna who went to Kailash to get the magic weapons from Mahadeva Himself. It is Arjuna, again, who is the special friend of Krishna, and the latter confirms this view when, in the tenth chapter of the Gita, he proclaims Arjuna and not Yudhisthira as the chief of the Pandavas.[2] In the *Srimad Bhagawata* it is Arjuna who goes with Krishna to the abode of the *Purushottama* and is addressed by the latter as a second Krishna,[3] and, returning to the *Mahabharata*, it is Arjuna who is seen in heaven with Krishna, "those two foremost of all beings," by Yudhisthira on the latter's arrival there.

Arjuna and Krishna, the inseparable friends, are in fact well known to represent *Nara* and *Narayana*, the human soul and the Divine Soul, the *jiva* and *Atman*.[4] They are the two birds that are described in the *Upanishad*,[5] the two birds, eternal friends, seated upon the same tree, the body, of whom one, the human soul, eats the fruit, while the other, the *Atman*, is a silent witness. It is true that the terms *Nara* and *Narayana* are explained by a reference to the story of a dual incarnation of God in the form of two Rishis, *Nara* and *Narayana*, who performed *tapasya* and are believed to be still so doing, in the Himalaya. But this story is itself symbolic. The word *Rishi* means a seer, and in truth the only seer is the *Atman*. "That which sees through the eye but whom the eye sees not; that is the *Atman*." So says the *Upanishad*, and this story of the two *Rishis* is a symbol of the dual soul, human and Divine, incarnated in one body. It is significant that the very name of the place in which the two *Rishis* perform their austerities is *Badri*, the name of a tree bearing sweet fruits, thus bringing us back again to the Upanishadic birds who are seated on a tree which likewise bears sweet fruits (*swadu pippalam*).

The significance of Arjuna and Krishna having thus been indicated, we must next inquire into that of his brothers and cousins. We shall see that, in the sixteenth chapter of the Gita, Sri Krishna makes a division between two great tendencies or movements in creation which He terms the *Daivi*, or bright, and the *Asurik*, or dark. It is these two tendencies that are symbolised by Arjuna's brothers and by the hostile Kauravas respectively. Detailed treatment of these forces will come in its proper place;[6] it will be sufficient here to observe that the *Asurik* and *Daivi* creations, popularly identified

---

[1] A *swayamvara* was a sort of tournament at which a maiden of the warrior caste used to choose her husband. In this case the princess became the wife of all five brothers.

[2] Gita, x, 37.

[3] *Ityadishtau bhagawata tau krishnau pararneshthina.*

[4] See Appendix B.

[5] *Mundaka Upanishad*, iii, i, 1—3.

[6] Chapter XVI.

with vices and virtues respectively, in reality signify the "outgoing" and the "ingoing" forces elsewhere called "*pravritti*" and "*nivritti,*" the forces which tend to enmesh the soul deeper and deeper in "matter" and those which help and accompany it on its return journey to Spirit.[1] It is evident that the popular identification of them with the vices and virtues is but a rough approximation to their true meaning and one on a much lower plane of thought than that of the Gita.

It should be further noted that the Kauravas and the Pandavas are cousins. There is none of the ultimate dualism that has marred so much of Christian thought, no God and Devil standing as ultimate irreconcilables. The *Daivi* and *Asurik* forces both spring from the same Supreme Source and in the end both return to It.

It is not necessary to go into the question of the significance of the individual Pandavas (except of course Arjuna, who has already been dealt with) or Kauravas. The only other figures we shall discuss are Dhritarashtra, the blind old king, and Sanjaya, his charioteer. These two are of some importance, as they figure directly in the Gita.

The teachings of the Gita are spoken by Krishna, who is acting as the charioteer of Arjuna; they are overheard by Sanjaya as the result of the blessing of Vyasa, the author of the Scriptures, and who signifies the power of inspiration, and they are repeated to Dhritarashtra. This is the framework in which the teachings of the Gita are set. Who are these persons, and what is the significance of the two charioteers?

Krishna, we have seen, is the Divine Soul who imparts the life-giving Wisdom to the individual soul. The symbol of the charioteer is one that occurs in the *Upanishads* and also in the *Dialogues* of Plato. In the *Upanishads* the individual soul is described as the Rider in the chariot of the body, while "*buddhi*" a spiritual faculty that we shall have to discuss later, is the charioteer. In the Gita, however, the use to which the symbol is put is slightly different. True, the individual soul in the form of Arjuna is still the rider in the chariot, but the charioteer is, as we have seen, the Divine Self in the person of Krishna.

The difference between the Gita and the *Upanishad* on this point is more apparent than real. In tire first place, Krishna as charioteer stands for the *manifested Atman*, the great self (*Mahat Atman*), of which the *buddhi* is the purely cognitive aspect.[2] In fact, though in earlier texts, such as the *Kathopanishad*, the two are distinct, later writers fused them into one. When it is further noted that the *buddhi* is symbolised by the bright yellow robes in which Krishna is always depicted, it will be seen that the difference between the two views is very small indeed.[3]

---

[1] See Appendix B.

[2] See Appendix E.

[3] In *Maitri Upanishad* (2), a later *Upanishad* than the *Katha* but containing many significant teachings, the *Purusha*, that is the *Atman*, is given as the charioteer of the body.

It should also be stated that the individual soul, or *jiva*, here referred to is not an ultimate irreducible soul monad, but is the Light of the one *Atman* reflected in the vehicle (*upadhi*) of *manas*, the higher mind.[1] This *jiva* is what is referred to in the Gita as the *dehi*, or dweller in the body, the ego which passes from fife to life (sometimes termed *jivatman*). It is also referred to in the *Upanishads* as the person "of the size of the thumb," dwelling in the heart. This is not a piece of primitive superstition about homunculi souls, but a symbol of the *Atman* manifested in an appropriate size to fill the heart, considered as the seat of mind. Nowadays, no doubt, we think of the brain as the special seat of mind, but with the ancient peoples it was the heart, and moreover, however close may be the connection between the ordinary waking consciousness and the brain, it is a sheer fact that when the true ego, or *jiva*, makes itself felt it is in the heart (or at least within the breast) that it is perceived as an actual experience.

This identification of the *jiva* with *manas* may sound strange to those whose study of Indian thought has been based on the later and developed philosophical system. In the *Rig-Veda* the usual term for the individual soul is *manas*, while *Atman* is used for an impersonal breath, which is indeed the root-meaning of the word. There is a law, which may be termed the law of the degradation of spiritual concepts, by which terms originally used by Seers to express levels of supernormal spiritual experience become in the hands of later and purely scholastic exponents terms for elements in purely normal mental life. This law may be seen operating in most mystical systems, and its result is that further terms have to be invented or brought into currency from time to time to denote the higher levels.[2] It is by this process that the word *manas* ceased to signify the individual soul and became merely a name for the faculty of discursive thought.

Dhritarashtra, on the other hand, represents the empirical ego, the lower and transient personality which, blinded by egoism and foolish infatuation, wields a nominal sway over the kingdom of the body which it has unjustly seized, the word Dhritarashtra meaning one who has seized the kingdom. Although he arrogates to himself the title of King, yet his rule over the kingdom is merely nominal, for the real power lies with his *Asurik* sons, just as the human personality which so proudly says "I" is the sport of a continual succession of involuntary desires and passions which are the real rulers of the body it calls its own.

Sanjaya, the charioteer and adviser of the blind king, is the link

---

[1] See *Shwetashwatara Upanishad*, v, 8. The Light of the one Consciousness shining distributively on the pure mental level produces the multiplicity of individual souls. This will become clearer in the course of the Gita.

[2] Instances of this are the *turiyatita* (beyond *turiya*) state of the *Yoga-vasishtha* and the whole set of *suddha tattwas* in the Kashmir Saiva system. If told that the union with the *manas* is an important step, perhaps the most important single step in the spiritual ascent, many would reply: "Unite with *manas*? Why, I do that every time I have a thought or even correlate my sense impressions!"

between the higher and lower minds. The mind has a dual status in Hindu philosophy. "The mind is said to be twofold, the pure and the impure: impure by union with desire, and pure, completely free from desire." [1] The impure mind is Dhritarashtra, the empirical ego controlled by desire (Duryodhana), while the pure mind is Arjuna, the individual soul. Sanjaya is thus the link between the two.

It is not easy to give a clear account of the relation between these two minds, or better, perhaps, these two aspects of the mind. The higher mind, though individualised, is pure and detached, and sees in its own clear light, while the lower mind is stained by its union with the principle of desire. Failure to understand this is at the root of those modern views which plausibly urge that the mind is but the slave of the hidden tides, quiet or tempestuous, of the so-called "unconscious." Of the lower mind (which is what most men know as their minds) this is only too true, but the higher stands firm in its own being and is a rock of refuge in the surging waves of desire. It is of this that Plotinus has written:

"Even our human soul has not sunk entire; something of it is continuously in the Intellectual Realm, though if that part (i.e. the lower *manas*) which is in the sphere of sense be mastered ere and troubled it keeps us blind to what the upper phase olds in contemplation. . . . But there is always the other (the higher *manas*), that which finds no savour in passing pleasure, but holds its own even way." [2]

It is here that Sanjaya comes in as the link between the two. Plotinus speaks of the lower being loosed from its shackles and able to soar only when "it makes its memories [3] the starting-point for the vision of essential Being." The link should not be conceived as anything material, but as the purely mental connection between the two aspects of what is in essence one. When the lower thinks of the higher, the latter's knowledge shines upon the former and is manifest in the form of what Plotinus, following Plato, termed "memories," but what is perhaps more clearly described as perception of value—truth, beauty, or goodness. This is the root of what is usually termed conscience, though it must be carefully distinguished from the voices of social, family, and racial prejudices which are often dignified by that name. In some teachings it is termed *antahkarana*, "inward turning," though usually in Hindu philosophy that term is used, as meaning inner organ, for the various mental faculties taken as a whole. It is the drawbridge of the inner fortress, the gateway leading to immortality, the mediator through which the Voice of the Higher is heard by the lower.

Thus Sanjaya, though anchored in service to Dhritarashtta, yet reaches

---

[1] *Maitri Upanishad*, vi, 34.

[2] Plotinus, *Enneads*, iv, 8, 7.

[3] Memories in the Platonic sense of course: memories of what the soul (*manas*) knew and knows on its own level, not mere memories of life experience down here. Cf. Gita, xviii, 76, 77.

out to a faith in Krishna, and constantly counsels his master to abandon his weak egoism and submit himself to the latter. It is thus Sanjaya who, when aided by the inspiration derived from Vyasa, is able to "overhear" the dialogue between Krishna and Arjuna and so to form a link between the inner knowledge of the soul and the dark ignorance of the self-centred personality.

It may also be said that there is a correspondence between these four characters and the four states of consciousness taught by Hindu philosophy, the *jagrat, swapna, sushupti* and *turiya*, usually translated, more by way of analogy than of identity as the waking, dreaming, deep sleep and ecstatic states.[1] This correspondence, however, involves a different reading of the symbols and would only confuse the issue here.

We are now in a position to return to the outline sketch of the events that have led up to the delivery of the Gita. The Soul, leaving behind its Divine ancestry, became attached to a personality and lives amidst the conflicting forces that make up this world. The conflict, at first latent, as the *Daivi* and *Asurik* forces are not clearly differentiated, gradually increases in strength. Attempts at partition of their respective spheres of influence having failed, as indeed they must fail since all is one unity, and action and reaction must necessarily take place, the Soul and its associates are deceived by the illusions of the *Asurik*, or downward-tending forces, and are condemned to long wanderings in the wilderness. During this period, a period which in reality extends through long ages, the Soul wanders about from birth to birth performing actions and reaping their fruits. Reduced to powerlessness as it is, it yet slowly gathers wisdom as a result of its manifold experiences, and though exposed to countless hardships and perils, it is yet saved from utter disaster by the unseen power of its Lord, the Divine Soul. Experience, wisdom, and also powers are gained, for it is during this period that Arjuna gains his magical weapons that are later to be of such immense value to him. The *Asurik* forces rule the world unchecked and at length the thirteenth year arrives, the year of "*ajnata vasa*" in which the very existence of the Soul and its brothers has to remain unknown.

It is the darkest hour, the hour before the dawn, and the Soul, reduced to performing the tasks of a servant, is lost to sight altogether. The forces of materialism seem triumphant and the very existence of the Soul becomes a matter of doubt, or even denial.

But not for ever can the Soul be thus buried in darkness. The allotted period draws to its close, and the Soul emerges from its obscurity with all its flashing powers. Significantly enough, the first event is a battle in defence of the right, the battle fought on behalf of King Virata, in which the Soul, though still disguised, displays its prowess and puts to flight the powers of the Dark. So decisive, indeed, is the Soul's intervention that

[1] See Appendix C.

none can stand against it. All are aware of the rising star, and all foresee the terrible conflict that must now occur.

But the Soul seeks no autocratic power for itself. It is for its brothers, the dispossessed Bright Powers (*Daivi Sarga*), that it is prepared to fight, and even for them it claims no undivided sway. Knowing, as it does, that the *Asurik* forces are as much a part of the cosmic play as are the *Daivi* ones, it proposes only a just division of the kingdom, but this the Powers of the Dark will not grant.

Bhishma and Drona, the aged warrior counsellors, symbols of blind faith and of established Law and Order and ancient Tradition, foreseeing the disastrous conflict, plead for peace and reconciliation, as does Sanjaya, the conscience. Sri Krishna himself sets forth in persuasive words the advantages of harmonious peace, but all is of no avail. Duryodhana refuses to listen, and the old king professes himself powerless to control his headstrong sons. War is inevitable. The conflict of the *Daivi* and the *Asurik* can no longer be averted, and the rival hosts face each other on the field of Kurukshetra. It is at this fateful moment that the Gita commences. The opposing hosts are drawn up in battle array, and the long-expected conflict is about to commence.

Dhritarashtra said: "In the Holy Field of Kurukshetra what did they do, O Sanjaya, my sons and the Pandavas, gathered together eager for battle?"

CHAPTER I
THE YOGA OF THE DEJECTION OF ARJUNA

Too many readers pass by the first chapter of the Gita hurriedly as of no great importance, considering it a mere introduction to which no special significance need be attached. This, however, is a mistake. It is no doubt true that it is an introductory chapter, but introductory to what? Not merely to an historical situation or to a body of philosophic teachings that have been embedded in the epic poem, but to the Yoga itself, and, if properly understood, it has a great significance for us.[1] Like all the other chapters, it is termed a yoga, and is entitled *"Arjuna Vishada Yoga"*— the Yoga of the Dejection of Arjuna.

We have seen that the Gita commences at the point where the Soul, like one awakening from sleep, has emerged from the obscurity in which it lay buried. Arjuna, as the individual Soul, finds himself on the battlefield of Kurukshetra faced by Verses the necessity of a terrible conflict in which all his friends, relatives and former teachers are ranged against him, "eager for battle." On this field, significantly enough termed *"dharmakshetra"* the field of *dharma* or duty, the opposing forces of *pravritti* and *nivritti* stand face to face and, from a position to which it has been guided by the Divine Krishna, the Soul, stationed between the rival armies, surveys the situation. Verses 24-28

As long as the Soul remains hidden in the inner worlds, so long the conflict does not come to a head, and the individual passes from one experience to another in an apparently unordered fashion, as described in the introductory section. But this cannot last for ever, and after the intoxication of the awakening, symbolised by the triumphant battle fought on behalf of King Virata, has passed off, the Soul finds itself in a situation which may well inspire dejection.

It was easy to sound the war conches in defiance and to feel the thrill of anticipated battle with the *Asurik* forces of *pravritti*. But, suddenly, in Verse 14

---

[1] It is by no means intended to suggest that all the kings and warriors mentioned in this chapter have symbolic significance as individuals. Attempts to interpret them have been made, but such as I have seen bear an artificial stamp.

a flash of insight which comes while the Soul is poised inactive between the two opposing tendencies, Arjuna realises for the first time all that is involved in the struggle. Relations, friends of his childhood and revered teachers are also entangled amongst his enemies, and he realises that his own heart's blood is, as it were, arrayed against him. During the long ages of slumber the Soul has contracted all sorts of relationships and has submitted to the guidance of various ideals and traditions, and only now is it realised that all these relationships must be destroyed and all these ideals, ideals that have often seemed the very goal of life, must be ruthlessly sacrificed on the battlefield, since now they are seen to be leagued with the outgoing forces of *pravritti* and to be opposing the destined triumph of the Soul.

Up till now the individual has been content to live within the narrow circle of race and family, and bounded by the ties of kinship he has felt that it was enough if he fulfilled the duties that he owed to his society and nation, if he attempted to live according to the ideals of his *gurus*, the religious and ethical systems in which, by birth, he found himself. But societies and races are all temporary, while the Soul is eternal and, in the end, can rest on no support but Itself. The simple creed of "my country, right or wrong" lies in ruins, destroyed by conflicting loyalties, and the ideals which had uplifted him in earlier days are powerless to guide him any longer, as they are seen to be mere mental constructions, inadequate to the needs of the Soul.

Nor is the conflict to which the Soul is called merely one with outer ties, established institutions and recognised standards of conduct and belief. In the inner world, too, he is faced with the same situation. Arrayed against him he finds the army of his desires. Not merely those desires that are conventionally considered "evil" but many others too, the desire for "harmless" enjoyment, the desire to shine in society surrounded by friends, and the desire to lead a secure and comfortable life. All these and many more have taken the field against the Soul under the leadership of the various ideals that have been harnessed to their service. The call of the blood, the prestige of habit and established custom, the ideologies which had sufficed in the past are all arrayed against him, and perhaps the most bitter fact of all is the knowledge that the glittering ideals of patriotism, of family affection and of devotion to his religion have also "eaten the food of the Kauravas,"[1] and, though they served as guides and teachers in the past, are, like Bhishma and Drona, in arms against the Soul and must be slain.

This is the situation with which every aspirant is faced and through which, sooner or later, all have to pass. Small wonder is it that Arjuna is

---

[1] Bhishma explained his blind acquiescence in the injustice done to Draupadi in the Kaurava Court to his having for long eaten the Kaurava food. In other words, the power of faith had long been harnessed to ancient traditions now degenerated into superstition and so become forces of Darkness.

overcome with utter dejection and that his bow slips from his nerveless Verses 29-30
hand as he sinks down overcome by an intolerable sadness, a sadness that
is the inevitable experience of those who seek the Path. What will be the
worth of victory if "those for whose sake we desire kingdom, enjoyments
and pleasures" must first lie dead on the field? If all desire is renounced, Verses 32-35
will not the whole of life become an empty waste, a vast desert in the midst
of which the victorious Soul will sit enthroned in desolation, exercising a
vain and empty rule? For what purpose are we called to such a sacrifice
and, in the end, how shall we benefit by it? "Better to eat beggars' crusts in
the world than to partake of such blood-besprinkled feasts."[1] Better, that
is, to enjoy what simple enjoyments set out on this perilous path, a path to
an as yet quite inconceivable Goal, and of which the only certain thing is
that it leads over the dead bodies of all that we hold dear in life.

Moreover, a further doubt arises in the heart. "In the destruction of the
family the immemorial traditions perish and in the perishing of traditions
lawlessness overcomes the whole community." Will not the destruction of
all these desires— and, above all, of these ideals—cause great confusion
in the world? Society depends on the existence of the normal desires of its
members and is bound up with the one-sidednesses of current ideologies.
Can it be right to disturb in the name of the Soul's progress to an unknown
Goal an equilibrium which has at least stood the test of time? Will not the
aspirant, by his renunciation of desire, unfit himself to participate in the
everyday life of the world, to share in the joys and sorrows of his fellow-
beings, and by his shattering of the ideals enshrined in ancient traditions
will he not bring chaos into the world?

> " . . . Wilt thou dare
> Put by our sacred books, dethrone our Gods,
> Unpeople all the temples, shaking down
> That law which feeds the priests and props the realms?"[2]

Such, at least, are the doubts which present themselves in the heart,
some of them well founded, others ill, but all alike having their real though
unacknowledged source in the feeling of gloom which invades the heart at
the prospect of a life in which all desire for self will have to be renounced
and utterly slain.

Nor, at this stage, is the darkness lit by any ray of light, and although
the Divine Teacher is standing beside the Soul not yet has His Voice been
heard. Brought by its past evolution to the field of conflict, poised, as it
were, upon the very edge of battle, the Soul loses heart and sinks back
terrified at the desolate outlook, an outlook in which victory seems as

[1] Gita, ii, 5.
[2] *Light of Asia*, iv.

cheerless as defeat.

The real source of this desolation is, as has been said, the prospect of a life in which all desire and ambition will be dead. We arc so used to a life in which all action has its roots in desire that we can conceive no other, and sadly ask what would be the value of such existence. Not yet has the Soul learnt that, having Krishna, it has all; that it is not for their own sakes that parents, wives and children are dear, "but for the sake of the *Atman.*" [1]

Nevertheless, this experience of the *"vishada"* or sorrow, is a very necessary one, as we may see from the fact that the Buddha, too, as the first of His four Aryan Truths, set forth in eloquent words the essential sorrow of life.

The Voice of Krishna can be heard only in silence, and as long as the heart is filled with the clamour of desire the silver tones of the Voice cannot be heard. It is only when the outer world becomes utterly dark that the Ray of the Divine Star can be seen by us, for, although It shines eternally, yet it is only when the glaring sunlight of so-called life is eclipsed that we can at first perceive It.

Later, that Star will shine with such a Light that "if the splendour of a thousand suns were to blaze out together in the sky, that might resemble the glory of that Mahatma," [2] and not all earth's tumult will be able to deafen us to the majestic rhythm of that Voice, that Voice that reverberates throughout the Eternities as the tides of Being thunder upon the beaches of the worlds.

But the time for those glories is not yet. At first the Light is but a dim Star twinkling faintly within and the Voice is but the sound of a nightingale "chanting a song of parting to its mate." [3] Therefore it is that, before the bright Path of the Sun can be trodden, the aspirant must enter the valley of gloom, must close his eyes and ears to the light and laughter of life, and must realise in sorrow that all that he is and all that he has is nothing, before he can see and know in joy that within his heart is the All.

Verse 47   "Casting away his bow and arrows, Arjuna sank down on the chariot, his mind overborne by grief," and thus, in dejection and sorrow, closes the first chapter of the Gita and the first stage of the Path.

---

[1] *Brihadaranyaka Upanishad*, ii, 4.
[2] Gita, xi, 12.
[3] *Voice of the Silence.*

CHAPTER II
THE YOGA OF THE DISCRIMINATIVE WISDOM

"IF Emancipation means dissociation from all objects of pleasurable enjoyment for what reason would men cherish a desire for action? What do we gain by knowledge and what lose by ignorance?" These words of King Janaka to the *Sankhyan* teacher Panchashikha may serve as an introduction to the present chapter as they well describe the mood of Arjuna as the discourse opens.

Surrounded by desolation on all sides, the Soul has no alternative but to turn within Itself and seek there the Divine Teacher. Wherever else it looks it sees nothing but bitter emptiness, and even the appeal to a manly fortitude fails of its effect, for when all one's world is in ruins, manliness seems a mere posturing in the void.[1] In utter despair the Soul turns within to the Divine Krishna and, weighed down by wretchedness *(karpanyadosha)* a wretchedness in which self-pity plays a prominent part, cries out: "I am Thy disciple; teach me, I am Thy suppliant." Verses 2, 3 Verse 7

But not yet is the Soul really ready to abandon itself at the feet of the Teacher. True self-giving will only be possible later, for we see that there at the very feet of the Teacher to whom he has just proclaimed his submission Arjuna refuses to abandon his dejection, and cries out bitterly, *"na yotsya,"* I will not fight. Verse 9

Profoundly significant are these words, for they express the very fault we are always committing. The disciple appeals for teaching to the Guru, either to the Divine Lord within or to His embodiment in human form, and professes his willingness to serve Him utterly. But, spoken or unspoken, there always remains a reservation: "Lord, I am Thine and will do Thy bidding, but—ask not of me one thing, for that I cannot do. I will not fight!" This is why the appeal to the Teacher seems so often to bring no result and why many lose faith in His presence, feeling that, were He

---

[1] Compare Bertrand Russell's *Free Man's Worship*. His appeal for a Promethean defiance of the universe "based on the firm rock of unyielding despair," however thrilling it may be to the armchair agnostic, will scarcely nerve anyone who is actually in the abyss, and for all Russell's sincerity his glowing rhetoric rings false.

really there, they would assuredly hear His Voice.

But the impossible is not demanded and, slowly, if only there is patient perseverance, a new and Divine knowledge is felt obscurely stealing into the Soul and lighting up dimly the darkness within. For the true Knowledge is to be found within the Self; that which is merely derived from books or hearsay is no real knowledge. Outer teaching may be effective in helping to give clear expression to what is at first only dimly intuited, but it can form no substitute for the latter, and the work of any real Teacher is only to bring to birth that which already exists within, as has been well expressed by Browning in his poem, *Paracelsus:*

> Truth lies within ourselves; it takes no rise
> From outward things, whate'er you may believe.
> There is an inmost centre in us all
> Where Truth abides in fullness; and to KNOW
> Rather consists in opening out a way
> Whence the imprisoned splendour may escape,
> Than in effecting entry for a light
> Supposed to be without.

The first stage in the manifestation of this inner knowledge comes in the form of a perception that within the self is That which is immortal. This perception is of fundamental importance, because without it the spiritual life can find no lasting basis. Personal survival is not in question here, but unless the core of man's being is rooted in something immortal there can be no ultimate value in his life, since in the end all will be swallowed up in universal death.

"That man is the product of causes which had no prevision of the end they were achieving; that his origin, his growth, his hopes and fears, his loves and his beliefs, are but the outcome of accidental collocations of atoms; that no fire, no heroism, no intensity of thought or feeling, can preserve an individual life beyond the grave; that all the labours of the ages, all the devotion, all the inspiration, all the noonday brightness of human genius, are destined to extinction in the vast death of the solar system, and that the whole temple of Man's achievement must inevitably be buried beneath the debris of a universe in ruins—all these things, if not quite beyond dispute, are yet so nearly certain, that no philosophy which rejects them can hope to stand." [1]

Russell's call for the black hangings of tragedy is, however, not needed. Even at this early stage a dim perception of the Immortal rises up within the heart. At first this perception is likely to be clothed in the

Verse 13 somewhat crude theory of an unchanging soul-entity dwelling within the

[1] Bertrand Russell, *A Free Man's Worship.*

body. Time, however, will bring clarification, and in the meanwhile the crudity of the theory should not be allowed to blind us to the essential truth that it enshrines—namely, that within us is something that is Eternal.

We must not expect at this stage the clear vision that will come in due time, but, even now, the disciple should be able to realise that the Dweller within is something separate from the matter in which he dwells. Verse 14 The contacts of sense will come and go, but the disciple will feel that they are not himself, but things that happen to him, and he must set himself to "endure them bravely."

"Things themselves touch not the soul, not in the least degree. . . . Let the part of thy soul which leads and governs be undisturbed by the movements in the flesh whether of pleasure or of pain; and let it not unite with them, but let it circumscribe itself and limit those effects to those parts." [1]

Only he who thus resolutely attempts to withdraw himself from the Verse 15 life of the senses is worthy to realise his immortality, and to him, as he struggles, will come a perception that "this too too solid" world of names and forms is but a passing phantom show which veils from sight the true and unchanging Eternal Reality which is for ever unmanifest. "The Unreal Verse 16 hath no being; the Real never ceaseth to be." An echo of the same truth is found in Shelley's beautiful lines:

> The One remains, the Many change and pass;
> Heaven's light for ever shines, Earth's shadows fly.
> Life like a dome of many-coloured glass
> Stains the white radiance of Eternity.

With this perception comes a realisation that this Unchanging One, the Unmanifest in which all beings have their true selves, is indestructible. "Weapons cannot cleave It nor fire burn It, nor can any compass the Verses destruction of that Imperishable One." Just as the all-pervading light of 17-25 day is not destroyed with the perishing of the material forms in which it is reflected, but is either reflected in the new forms which have taken their place or remains in its own unmanifested nature, so the Unchanging One passes from one form to another, as a man changes a worn-out garment, and, though invisible, remains for ever even though the whole world perish.

This is no piece of theological dogma to be taken as an article of blind belief. The Gita is not concerned with beliefs but with knowledge, and the above is a truth that becomes clear to the disciple even at this stage, and a calm descends upon the Soul as it realises that neither can one slay nor is any slain. Forms and personalities come and go inevitably,

[1] Marcus Aurelius, *Meditations,* v, 19, 26.

but That which lies behind them all can neither come nor go for It for ever IS.

Verses 27, 28

Moreover, since all forms are the same in kind, whether they be forms of flesh and blood or forms of conduct and belief, the Soul learns not to grieve over the passing away of familiar social forms and cherished religious creeds, for it sees that the Reality behind them all, the Reality which gave birth to them, is the same for ever, and neither comes into being at birth of a new religion nor perishes with its decay. From the Unmanifest they take their rise, on the Unmanifest they float and into that Unmanifest they sink again. "What room then for lamentation," since all form is transient and must pass away, while all that is Real is eternal and perishes not throughout the ages.

Verses 29-36

Therefore, having perceived, if only dimly, that the Marvellous One is also the Dweller in the bodies of all, the Soul is exhorted to cease from vain lamentations over the disappearance of what is transitory by nature and to stand up and fight, fulfilling the duties that lie before it.

Verse 37

Should the disciple be worsted in the fight even then he will enjoy the fruits of heroic endeavour in the shape of better opportunities in the future,[1] while, if he is victorious, his will be the earth, for he is master of all manifested being. No longer a "procession of fate," as Hermes graphically puts it, but a king, throned in the Sunlight, ruling all that is.

This knowledge is what is referred to in the Gita as the wisdom of the *Sankhya,* but it should not be confused with the brilliant but purely scholastic version that is to be found in the much later *Sankhya Karika.* Partial accounts of the older *Sankhya* are to be found in the *Shanti Parva of the Mahabharata,* and suffice to make it clear that, while the later system was a frank dualism, the original teaching was monistic. The latter set out to explain the world as an evolution in a graded series of manifestations proceeding from one eternal Reality, referred to as "That," or the *Avyakta,* the Unmanifested. The duality between *prakriti* and *purusha* that forms the centre of the later system is here transcended, since both are but aspects of the *avyakta* and are ultimately absorbed in It.[2]

Thus we see that essentially the *Sankhya* was a body of teaching designed to give a coherent intellectual expression to the intuition of the Unchanging One that arises at the proper tune in the soul of the disciple

---

[1] Compare *The Voice of the Silence*: "For either he shall win or shall fall . . . and if he falls, e'en then he does not fall in vain; the enemies he slew in the last battle will not return to life in the next birth that will be his."

[2] See the teaching of Panchashikha, a pupil of Kapila and a traditional teacher of the early Sankhya, given in *Shanti Parva*, chapter 219. The soul (*Kshetrajna*) is said to "rest upon the mind" (cf. what was said in the introduction as to the Mind's (*manas*) being the higher ego) and to obtain emancipation or absorption into the Unmanifest Reality by complete renunciation of all that is manifest.

For other early accounts see *Shanti Parva*, chapters 311 and 312; also Caraka's account quoted in Das Gupta's *History of Indian Philosophy*, p. 213.

when stimulated into activity by the words of the Teacher.

It is, as Shankara rightly maintains, a system of *jnana yoga*, of yoga by knowledge, and, like all such partial systems, it suffers from a certain one-sidedness that Krishna makes it his business to correct. At the time when the Gita was spoken (as indeed now) there were several such yogas in existence, and we shall find that the first six chapters of the Gita (or rather chapters 2 to 6) contain expositions of the Path according to their various teachings, and also corrections of their deficiencies.

In this chapter we are taken along the path of the Sankhyan knowledge, because the first cry of the Soul when it awakens to a dim perception of the Eternal is for a coherent scheme of principles by which it may explain to itself its new knowledge. But there is a danger too in the demand for a detailed explanation, a danger that the original intuitive perception may be swamped by the clear-cut intellectual expression, a danger too that mere knowledge, divorced from the love and activity that are the other aspects of the Path, may be considered as the whole.

Many must have had the experience of seeing the flashing intuitions of the One *Atman* which come from a reading of the *Upanishads* fade and grow pale as the reader seeks to fix them by the help of even such a writer as Shankara, who made those intuitions the very corner-stones of his philosophy. The Soul flees just at the very moment when we seem to hold its gleaming splendour in our hands and all we are left with is one more dead butterfly to add to our mouldering collection.

Therefore the disciple has ever to keep in mind the fact that the clear intellectual grasp that he craves for, and may to some extent gain by the study of the "Sankhyan wisdom' is but a substitute, a symbol of the true knowledge which alone can bear the Soul upward on swift and flashing wings.

It is here that the one-sidedness of the pure *Sankhya* comes in. In proportion as the inner vision fades, the disciple endeavours to recapture its fleeing spirit and to galvanise it into life once more by a violent effort. Separating himself more and more from the world of action and emotion, he withdraws into a realm of abstractions and, bending upon them the whole power of his psychic energy, he often succeeds in imparting a kind of life to them at the cost of an ever sterner and more forcible warping of his nature. This "life," however, shows by its very lack of balance that it is not the authentic life of the Soul. Only in perfect poise and harmony can the Soul blossom and be developed, and not by any such forced and unnatural straining will the disciple reach the true Goal. Origen's act of self-castration did not enable him to attain that state that Hindu tradition terms " *brahmacharya*" and rigid isolation in a mountain cave will not bring about that inner detachment from the passing show of things which is the soil in which alone the flower of true Wisdom can grow.

The battle of life must be won and not run away from, and so, after

Verses
38, 39
a repetition of the injunction to gird himself for the fray, the disciple is instructed in the all-important *buddhi yoga* which is necessary to supplement the static analytic technique, the pure *Sankhya*. The latter attempts to gain its goal of pure emancipation *(Kaival*ya) by a forced isolation from the whole of the manifested universe which, even if at all practicable, can only result in a strained and unnatural attainment. The true Path aims at a detachment from the lower manifestations by a progressive union with the higher, and is as different from the former method as is the natural blooming of a flower from the forced opening of the bud.

What is therefore emphasised is the *buddhi yoga*, the *union* with the *buddhi* as a preliminary step to the utterly transcendent state of the goal. The *manas*, or mind, must cease to be, as heretofore, united to the senses, but must become *buddhi-yukta*, or united to that which is higher than itself, if the Path is to be really trodden and not merely talked about. For by climbing the ladder there is none of that loss of effort which is in store for him who attempts to leap in one bound to the roof of the world. Nor is there any transgression of the law that all that lives is one.[1] And at this point it is necessary to say a few words about the nature of *buddhi*.

Nowhere does the purely intellectual nature of the later *Sankhya* come out more clearly than in its account of the nature of *buddhi*, which it treats as simply one of the intellectual faculties, the faculty by which the mind comes to a decision after a period of doubt and hesitation. True it is that the *buddhi* is the faculty that gives determined knowledge (*nischay-atmika buddhi*), but the knowledge that it gives is no mere collection of intellectual propositions, but a living knowledge, better styled intuition, save that it has none of the sporadic flashings that we associate with that term, but, on its own level, bums with a steady radiance. In the *Kathopanishad*, *buddhi* is termed the *jnana atman*, and it is at once the knowledge of the Atman and the faculty by which that knowledge is attained. Symbolically it is the yellow cloth that is worn by Krishna, and its particular significance for the disciple lies in the fact that it is beyond the limitations of individuality.

On the level of the *manas* the Light of the One *Atman* is split up into a number of separate individualities, each standing on its own uniqueness. The *buddhi*, however, is non-individual, being the same for all.

Verses
42-46
This certainty-giving *buddhi* (*Vyavasay atmika buddhi*), which is one in all, is contrasted with the wavering and uncertain thoughts [2] of the ordinary man. It is the source of all real knowledge and, for him who can attain to it, it supersedes all the scriptures of the orthodox. Not that the latter have no value at all. Veiling in rites and ceremonies the eternal Truths

---

[1] The all-renouncing flight of the soul to the Unmanifest is in some sense a transgression of this law and it is for this reason that the Mahayana stigmatises the Pratyeka Buddhas (treaders of that Path) as spiritually selfish.

[2] The word buddhi in addition to being used of the super-mental level is also, as it were by courtesy and common usage, applied to ordinary mental knowledge. Hence the plural in the second half of the verse.

behind, they serve as guides to the great mass of men and furnish checks upon the grosser forms of desire; but they can do little for the serious Verse 45 aspirant for knowledge. "The Vedas deal with the three gunas," [1] says the Gita, while the disciple, steadfast in *sattva* alone, must reach out to what is beyond. The reason for their failure is that they depend on hope and fear (manifestations of *rajas* and *tamas* respectively), whereas only the *sattvik* devotion to Truth for its own sake can serve for him who seeks to tread this Path. The orthodox may thunder forth their dogmatic assurances, but all their books are, literally, as useful to the enlightened disciple (*vijanata* = possessed of *vijnana* or *buddhi*) as "a tank in a place overflowing with water on all sides." Hence the extreme importance of the *buddhi yoga*, for this union, when achieved, brings about a liberation from "the knots of the heart," the fetters which had bound the Soul within the prison of separate individuality. Only when this union with the super-individual *buddhi* has Verses 52, 53 been achieved will it be possible for the Soul to "escape from the tangle of delusions" and to "stand immovable," unshaken alike by the pleasures and pains of life and by the conflicting and partial views of reality that are all that can be achieved by the unaided *manas*.

Only he who is thus established in the *prajna* (a synonym for *buddhi*) will be able to make the final leap to the *anamayam padam*, the Sorrowless Verse 51 State, with any hope of success, and, in order to attain this union with the *buddhi*, the method recommended is skill in action (*karmasu kaushalam*), Verses 47-51 the maintenance of a balanced attitude, the same in failure as in success. The disciple is to keep his mind perfectly indifferent to the results of his actions while yet, in a spirit of utter detachment, performing such acts as are his duty. Acting in this way the disciple's actions will be guided by the impersonal knowledge of the *buddhi* and he will then transcend the limits of selfish good and evil.

This is the method of the *karma yoga*, whose theoretical basis will be gone into in the next chapter, of which it forms rhe specific subject. In this context it is enough to point out that its purpose is to gain control of the desire-prompted impulses of the senses and to harmonise the mind so as to render it possible for the latter to unite with the *buddhi* and enable the Divine knowledge to blossom forth. It is only through the *buddhi* that this knowledge can shine freely; below that level it is obstructed and broken up by the play of the separated individualities, and it is only when they are united with what is beyond them that the unifying Divine Wisdom can become manifest and the fetters of duality begin to fall away.

It is easy to say "unite the mind with the *buddhi*" but usually such words have but little meaning for the disciple, since he has as yet had no

---

[1] *Sattva, rajas* and *tamas*, the three *gunas*, or characteristics of *Mula-prakriti*, and so of all forms derived therefrom. Though not very easily translated, they may be rendered as harmonious purity, passionate activity and dark inertia respectively. See Chapter XIV.

experience of the *buddhi* and knows not what it really is. Moreover, the mind remains obstinately separate and will not suffer itself to be united with anything. Hence the supreme importance of supplementing the theoretic technique of the *Sankhya* by a practice designed to harmonise and control the mind in action. In reply to Arjuna's question about the characteristics of the man who has united with the *buddhi,* Sri Krishna describes how the disciple, uniting himself with the felt Reality within, must detach himself from the desire-life of the senses as a tortoise withdraws its limbs from contact with the outer world. Mere withdrawal is, however, not enough, for though the sense objects lose their power over the man who habitually practises restraint, yet the desire for them remains in his heart and dies only when something higher than the sense life is actually seen.

*(margin)* Verses 56-58

*(margin)* Verse 59

In the last resort, nothing but the vision of the *Atman* itself can cause the utter dying-out of desire, and therefore the disciple is instructed not to remain content with negative restraint but to centre his gaze upon the *Atman* within, unseen though yet it be. "Silence thy thoughts and fix thy whole attention on thy Master, whom yet thou dost not see, but whom thou feelest." [1] The slightest wavering, the slightest turning back in thought to that sense world on which the disciple has turned his back, will energise anew the desires which he is striving to abandon, and as the tension increases in his desire-nature (what some psychologists term the unconscious) they will burst out in a great flash of anger utterly devastating to his spiritual progress, shattering his inner perception and causing a loss of those "memories" [2] by which he hoped to mount.

(margin) Verses 62-63

It is not that the sense life is to be negated or outwardly discontinued, as impracticably taught by some *Sankhyas*. It is an inner withdrawal that is to be practised, a withdrawal to higher levels that will in itself bring that outer harmonisation which is essential if the *buddhi* is to be attained. In the old symbol of the chariot, the horses of the senses are to be held back *(nigrihita)* by the reins of the mind, but it is not intended that they should be unyoked from the chariot or that their movement should be stopped altogether. The aim of this practice is that the mind should, to some extent at least, be purified by the practice of selfless action and at least partially liberated from the thraldom of attachments, so that it may cease to assert its unique viewpoint at every moment. Then, as the wind of desire subsides, the disciple will feel a luminous peace and wisdom reflected in his heart, like the images of the eternal stars reflected in the depths of a lake, and he will have gained a preliminary perception of the actual nature of *buddhi* that will be a thousand times more useful to him than all the descriptions of the books.

*(margin)* Verses 65, 71

For the first time will the command to unite the *manas* with the *buddhi*

---

[1] *Voice of the Silence.*
[2] See Prolegomena, p. xxvi, second note.

begin to have a meaning for him, and only now will he be able to address himself to the task with any hope of success. Far overhead, Its blazing Light as yet a mere pin-point to his vision, burns the Star of the Supreme *Atman,* the Goal of all his efforts. Dimly It shines in the darkness and seems to flicker as Its rays pierce the unsteady middle air, but once seen It can never be forgotten, and offering himself to It, in utter devotion and Verse 61 worship, the disciple must press on, straining his vision to the utmost to pierce through what to him are the darkly throbbing abysses of non-being Verse 69 though to the fully awakened eye of the Seer they are a radiant pleroma of Light, the "Light that shines beyond the broken lamps," the glorious sunshine of the Eternal Day.[1]

"This is the *Brahmik* State, O Arjuna, which having attained, one is Verse 72 deceived no more," and though, as yet, the disciple has but a distant glimpse of that Farther Shore, and though the shadows will again and again return, blotting out the Light from his eyes, yet will its memory remain with him for ever, for he has "reached the stream" and the promise of final Salvation has been uttered: "Whoever, even at the final hour, is established therein attains the Supreme *Nirvana.*"

---

[1] Compare Plotinus: "The sphere of sense is of the Soul in its slumber; for all of Soul that is in body is asleep and the true getting-up is not bodily but from the body" (*On the Impassivity of the Incorporeal,* vi).

CHAPTER III
THE YOGA OF ACTION

THE third chapter commences with the disciple in doubt. "If it be thought Verse 1 by Thee that knowledge is superior to action why dost Thou, O Krishna, urge me to this terrible deed?" The Teacher has praised the wisdom of the *Sankhyas,* but had then urged the necessity of action, the thing which, above all, was shunned by the followers of the *Sankhya,* Lastly, He brought the discourse round once more to the praise of knowledge and described a state in which action would, at best, appear an irrelevance. Small wonder that the disciple is confused and begs to be taught clearly the one way to the Goal.

Nevertheless, the teaching is not confused; it is only that the disciple, in demanding a clear-cut intellectual presentation which shall be decisive and final, is looking for something which cannot be given. The method of a true Teacher is not to overwhelm the mind by demanding assent to an intellectual scheme clearly formulated once and for all. Such an assent, even if given, is entirely useless, as it does not lift the disciple above the level of the *manas,* the thinking mind. Rather, He aims, by setting forth apparently conflicting but actually complementary aspects of Truth, at forcing the disciple to transcend the ordinary levels of thinking by having recourse to the higher intuitive knowledge of the *buddhi* and thus bringing to birth in his soul a new and synthetic knowledge which shall be built into his very being.

If this is not sufficiently realised the reader is apt to make the mistake of thinking that the thought of the Gita is actually confused, or of picking out that aspect that most appeals to him and ignoring the rest. But the Gita is neither a confused eclecticism nor a one-sided sectarianism. It aims at setting forth the Yoga or Path to the Goal as a coherent whole, but, in so doing, it is inevitable that the mind, which loves to pursue one train of thought to its logical conclusion regardless of others, should be brought up sharply from time to time and made to grasp the other sides as well.

Verse 3   In answer to the disciple's query the Teacher states that since the beginning of time there have been two main types of aspirant, corresponding to the duality that pervades the manifested world. Modern psychology speaks of introverts, or those whose natural tendency is to occupy themselves with the subjective, and extroverts, or those whose natural flow of energy is directed towards the outer world. Corresponding to these we have the yoga of knowledge practised by the *Sankhyas* and the yoga of action of the *karma yogis*. Urged on by the lack of balance in their own natures, one-sided exponents always attempt to show that one of these is the chief teaching and the other only subsidiary. But the duality in the universe is not ultimate. In the end all is resolved into the unitary *Brahman,* and therefore no one-sided view can be the whole truth.

The doctrine of the *karma yogis* starts from the plain fact that a cessation from all action is simply impossible. Even a forcible abstention from the more obvious outer actions will leave the mental actions quite unchecked, and in fact more riotous because of the enforced outer inactivity. Psychologically it is certain that excessive and long-continued introversion will have disastrous results upon the psychic health and—as Jung, I think, puts it—the attempt to escape from all entangling outer relationships will result in an eventual domination of the ego by relationships of a neurotic and inferior type. "Not by mere cessation of activity shall the soul rise to the state of actionlessness," and therefore, since action is a necessity, we must make an effort to come to grips with it and prevent it from exerting its fatal binding power on us. Verse 4

For the great objection to action as ordinarily performed lies in its connection with results. We are bound by the results of our actions and must experience the consequences whether pleasant or painful. This so-called law of *karma* is apt to strike the Western mind as a mere unverified dogma or, at best, as a philosophical speculation. In fact, however, it is nothing of the kind, but a fact of nature which may be experienced by anyone for himself. Even on the ordinary levels of experience it is obvious that our destinies are largely shaped by our characters and they, in turn, by the sum-total of our past thoughts, and particularly those which have crystallised into actions. The man who thinks cruel thoughts usually proceeds to cruel deeds, and thus, becoming an object of fear and hatred to others, is at least extremely liable to meet with cruelty in his turn. Ordinary everyday experience can perhaps not take us much farther than this probability; but ordinary experience is not the final arbiter in these matters, and he who advances on the inner path, the Path of Knowledge, becomes immediately aware that it is no mere probability with which we are concerned but a perfect and unerring law—

"By which the slayer's knife did stab himself;
The unjust judge hath lost his own defender."

In the world of mechanics it finds expression in Newton's famous law that action and reaction are equal and opposite. The world of life is no less a unity than the world of matter, all lives being interlocked in one vast whole. It follows that any act—nay, any thought—sets up a tension in the whole which, however delayed may be the response, with utter inevitability brings about an "equal and opposite" reaction. I repeat that this is no mere intellectual speculation fitting only into the structure of some Oriental philosophy, but is a profound truth of experience, which may, like other natural laws, be disregarded only at one's peril. The same perception, quite divorced from "Hindu Philosophy," found expression in Christ's flashing words: "They that take the sword shall perish by the sword."

Thus, if action is inevitable, it is none the less a source of bondage, and, by tying the soul to its own position, whether good or bad, in the scheme of things, prevents that self-transcendence in union with the All that constitutes the Goal.

The method proposed by the *karma yogis* was that of scrupulous performance of the prescribed code of ritual actions which, according to Hindu custom, filled a Brahman's life and regulated his conduct down to the minutest detail. At the same time the yogi was to perform these actions without any desire for the fruit, in the shape of worldly prosperity and heavenly bliss, that the scriptures promised as the result of such actions. In this way they hoped to avoid the impasse created by the inevitability of action and its no less certain binding power. They rightly perceived that the binding power came not from the action itself but from the desire with which it was performed, and therefore taught that if the latter could be eliminated the poison fangs of the acts would have been removed.

"The righteous who eat the remains of the sacrificial offerings are freed from all sin, but those who merely prepare food for their own sakes verily eat sin."

This doctrine, literally understood, like the detachment of the *Sankhyas,* is not enough in itself. Taken literally and by itself it fails, because it reduces the vigorous creative life of action to a dead round of sterile ceremonies and smothers the spirit under a tedious formalism quite inapplicable to the ordinary actions of life. For them, action was but a necessary evil, inescapable while embodied, and they achieved peace only by making a desert, escaping desire by stifling it under tedium. To them, as to the typical follower of the pure *Sankhya,* this rich and wondrous life must have been no better than a ghastly mistake which had far better never have occurred.

This mean and ignoble view of action is by no means that of Sri Krishna. For Him, as for the *karma yogis,* action is a sacrifice, but one far different from the formal ceremonies of the Brahmans. The lower or sense mind is to be sacrificed to the higher and that higher to be united with the *buddhi,* as we have seen in the last chapter.

It is time now to say a few words about the actual process by which this is to be accomplished. We have seen (in the Prolegomena) how between Arjuna, the higher mind, and Dhtritarashtta, the lower, stands Sanjaya, the second charioteer, the voice of conscience speaking in the heart of the eternal values. Just as the *buddhi,* the Divine Knowledge, serves as a link between the individual ego and the One Life *(Mahat Atman),* so does Sanjaya on a lower plane serve as a link between the empirical personality and the true individual Self. By uniting with the *buddhi* the mind is raised into transcendence, and similarly, by making the empirical personality or lower mind the servant of the voice of Sanjaya, the personality is raised to union with its own true Self.

This is the reason for so much emphasis upon performing action as a duty. The lower self is not to be destroyed by self-mortification, but to be united with the higher by being trained to obey the voice of the higher under all circumstances. "Right action" is to be performed, the test [Verse 8] of rightness being its accord with the commands of that voice and not with any outer scriptural injunctions. The disciple must always listen for that voice, and having heard it must always act in accordance with it. By this means the lower self will be purified of its attachment to desire and will in time become united with the higher. This must be achieved before the next stage, that of union with the *buddhi,* the *dhyana paramita* of the *Mahayana* Buddhists, becomes possible.[1]

Having dealt with the practical importance of action, Sri Krishna next goes on to show its moral and cosmic significance. In a few rapid words He sketches the *yajna chakra,* the great Cycle of Sacrifice [2] that forms the manifested Cosmos, and shows how action is rooted in the Imperishable. Forth into all quarters of space streams in sacrifice the life-blood of the Supreme *Purusha.* But for that sustaining life the worlds would "fall into ruin," and ceaselessly does the Supreme pour Itself forth in action for the [Verses 10-16] welfare of all. Round and round circles this One Life through all beings in the worlds as It weaves unweariedly the pattern of the universe, and none can claim a proud independence of his brothers. The knowledge of the world that comes to us so easily today we owe to countless thinkers and discoverers of the past, and we cannot walk down the street of a town without treading on the bowed backs of the nameless toilers of dim bygone ages. Our intellects owe their every possibility of thought to those who

---

[1] See Chapter VI, which deals with this stage.

[2] It should not be supposed that verses 14 and 15 are pieces of archaic "rain-making magic." "Food" signifies the gross material world of which forms are built and "rain" the forces of desire which brings those forms into being. The sacrifice is the sacrificial self-limitation by which the many issue from the One and "*karma,*" action, is the Miila-prakriti from which all action issues (cf. Gita, viii, 3, and xiii, 29). While "*karma*" is the *Mula-prakriti* considered as the source of all action, " Brahma " (verse 15) is the same considered as the source of being, the great matrix (cf. Gita, xiv, 3), while the Imperishable is of course the supreme *Parabrahman.*

strove to grasp new conceptions long ago, and even our eyes are what they are only as a result of long and painful struggles of which no record now remains. No record, that is, but the debt inscribed in the imperishable characters of the book of *Karma*, a debt that claims our actions in return and from which not the proudest yogi in a Himalayan cave is free, though he may choose to ignore it. "He who on earth doth not follow the Wheel thus revolving, sinful of life and rejoicing in the senses, he, O Arjuna, liveth in vain."

Thus action is seen to be not only a mere physical necessity for those who are embodied. It is also a moral necessity, since out of sacrificial action spring the worlds and by sacrifices are they maintained in their ceaseless whirling around and in the Central Sun. Consciousness (the Gods) nourishes the forms, and forms in their turn sustain that Consciousness in manifestation. Thus is the whole universe linked in one stupendous Sacrifice, each separate element being related to all else that is.

It is important to realise, however—and that is why the instruction in the *Sankhyan* wisdom preceded the teaching about action—that without knowledge of the *Atman* the sacrificial action is not possible in the true sense. Until the One Self, or at least Its forth-shining Light, is known, the abandonment of all desire for the fruits of action is in no way really feasible and remains but a matter of grand words. The Light of the *Atman* must be known to some extent at least, and just in proportion as It is known, not as a matter of theoretic philosophy but as a vivid reality present in every moment of experience, will the disciple be able to discard any wish for _{Verses} the fruits of his actions. Rather will it be seen that the desire for fruits _{17, 18} is an utter irrelevance which will fall away of itself, though *only for as long as the disciple is thus centred in the Light*. When at last, after long and persistent struggles, this centring of life in the *Atman* is permanently established, when the disciple rejoices in the *Atman* and is content with the *Atman*, there will remain nothing further to be accomplished for himself and "no object of his will depend on any being."

_{Verses} Nevertheless, in thus escaping from "private" action, he has but united ₂₂₋₂₄ himself with the Divine and Cosmic action, and of him it will be said, as of Krishna Himself, that, though there is nothing in the three worlds that is unattained by him, yet he mingles in action unweariedly for the sake of the welfare of all. Note the word "unwearied." The Sacrificial Action, to a union with which the disciple aspires, is no tiresome carrying out of dull and spiritless acts such as are too often called up in our minds by the words sacrifice and duty. We saw how, at the beginning of the Path, the disciple was filled with despair at the thought of the joyless life which awaited him when all the desires which made life seem worth living should be slain. Verse 25 But this is an illusion which has to be dispelled. "As the ignorant act out of attachment to action, so should the wise act without attachment, desiring the welfare of the world." The glow which accompanies the desire-

prompted actions of the worldly, the enthusiasm and zest of youth and the tireless energy of the ambitious, must all be preserved and transmuted into something higher and not allowed to drain away into desert sands. The true "*vairagi*" is not a dull, dried-up, "holy" person of the type that has made the very name of religion a thing of nausea to so many of us, but a tireless fountain of joyful and inspired life based on the eternal *ananda* of the *Brahman* which overflows into creation out of Its own inherent fullness.

This, then, is the charter of action, the fact that the whole Cosmos is established on sacrifice; not on mere formal acts of ceremonial offering but on that of which these were but the outward symbol, the Great Sacrifice of which we read in the Vedas,[1] in which the One *Purusha* was offered in the fires of the worlds and His Limbs scattered like those of Osiris to all the quarters of space. This is the Sacrifice which the disciple is called to co-operate in. But, though he acts ceaselessly, yet is he not bound by *karma*, for his grounding in the *Sankhyan* wisdom has taught him that actions are performed by the modifications of *prakriti* alone. His bodies, gross and subtle, act, and the unwise are entangled in the acts, but he who has mastered the lesson of the previous chapter has learnt to see that the *Atman*, the True Self, is for ever but the detached Witness, serene and impartial. Actions can no more bind Him than weapons can pierce Him, and, clinging firmly to this knowledge in his heart, offering his actions to Krishna as the symbol of the Great Sacrifice, free from the fetters of selfish hope and fear, he engages with zest in the great battle against evil and sorrow, the evil of his own lower nature and the sorrow of his brothers.

Verses 27-30

For let none think that the battle is won at the first triumphant blare of the trumpets. The knowledge that has been given must be practised and built into the heart by constant struggle. Again and again must the battle be fought, and he who, shutting with subtle sophisms his eyes to the imperfections still existing in his lower nature, and his ears to the cry for help that sounds pitifully from suffering humanity, seeks to rest on his laurels is unworthy of the Wisdom he has received and is doomed to fall, however proudly he may carry things off for the time.

Doubts will assuredly come tormenting the heart with the suggestion that the struggle is useless:

"All things are vain and vain the knowledge of their vanity;
Rise and go hence, there is no better way
Than patient scorn, nor any help for man,
Nor any staying of his whirling wheel."[2]

---

[1] *Rig-Veda*, x, 90.
[2] *Light of Asia*.

Verse 33   All beings follow their own natures. The *Atman* is the impartial Witness of all; good and evil are but empty words and the fight against the latter is in vain. What shall restraint avail since actions flow inevitably from the workings of Nature and the Soul is but the passive witness of the phantom show?

But these deceiving half-truths must be conquered. It is true that the play of Nature follows fixed laws and that effect follows cause with unerring accuracy. Deeply embedded in the Cosmos is the power of attraction and repulsion by which all things move and change. From Verses the chemical elements with their "affinities," to men with their loves and 34, 35 hates, all are bound by this power within the iron circle of Necessity—all, that is, save he who has conquered desire and acts from a sense of duty *(swadharma)* alone. As long as the disciple does certain acts because he likes them and abstains from certain others because he dislikes them, so long must he whirl helplessly upon the Wheel; for, though he may be of a "virtuous" disposition, and so perform but "virtuous" acts, yet is he none the less the victim of his own nature.

But the *Atman,* the One Self, is for ever free in Its own being; Its apparent bondage comes only from the self-identification with Its lower vehicles, the mirrors in which Its Light is reflected. The higher the disciple climbs up the Ladder of the Soul, the more the inherent freedom of the *Atman* will shine forth and dominate the play of Nature instead of blindly suffering it.

Verse 42   He who acts from the dictates of the *manas* is freer than he who acts from those of the senses, and freer still is he whose *manas* is united with the *buddhi* and suffused by its Light, the Light of the glorious Flame Beyond. Therefore, instead of allowing himself to be guided by the likes and dislikes of the senses, the disciple must constantly strive, by acting from a sense of duty alone, to rise to higher and ever-higher levels of his being. Bound as he is by his nature at any given level, yet is he free with the inherent freedom of the *Atman* to choose whether he will act from his lower nature or from his higher. True the "higher" will ever recede as he climbs, and what is "higher" now will become "lower" in time; but at each stage his freedom will increase until he reaches the Unreachable and all desire is dead in that blazing Unity, slain like a moth at the threshold by the touch of the frosty air without.

Verse 43   "Thus understanding Him (the *Atman*) as higher than the *buddhi* restraining the lower self by the *Atman*, slay thou, O Mighty-armed, the enemy in the form of desire, difficult to be overcome."

Let the disciple dwell on this concluding verse, for in its few words is contained the secret that has baffled so many ascetics and philosophers, the secret of the conquest of desire. True, it is a secret that cannot be imparted in words, one which must be experienced in the heart; but he who has even partially understood the meaning of the words "restraining the lower self by the *Atman*" may know for certain that his foot is on the ladder, and that if he will resolutely put his knowledge into practice his further progress is assured, and neither gods nor men can hinder his ultimate attainment of the Goal.

CHAPTER IV
THE YOGA OF THE PARTIAL KNOWLEDGE [1]

"THE same imperishable yoga that I taught to Vivaswan[2] long ages ago I am again setting forth for thee to-day." Thus opens the fourth chapter, and in so saying Sri Krishna reveals the source and credentials of the teaching He has to impart. It is no "new" doctrine, the private property of a particular teacher, that is being set forth; nothing, either, that is intended to form a new sect, shut off by the fortress walls of dogma from the life all around, walls which will have to be broken with infinite pain before the imprisoned souls can escape.

It has to be clearly understood that there is no ownership in the realm of ideas. Ideas are not the property of individual thinkers. Rather is it the fact, as Plato rightly taught, that when we entertain a "new" idea we do but participate in something that is eternal, and that when two men "think" of the same idea they are united with each other by this very fact since both are participating in a particular facet of the Eternal Wisdom. Ideas are greater than any of the finite minds that think them and the Wisdom is greater than any particular teacher. Therefore it was that the Buddha made no claim to originality, being content to say that what He taught was but the echo of the teaching of all the former Buddhas, and therefore it is that Sri Krishna is careful to explain that the Yoga He is teaching to Arjuna is but a restatement of the Eternal Wisdom, for assuredly it was not as the personal Krishna that "He" taught it first to Vivaswan long ages before.

---

[1] This chapter, a mere literal translation of the title of which would be "the yoga of the section of knowledge" as distinguished from the full knowledge of Chapter VII, deals with knowledge as applied to the Sacrificial Action. Just as the theories of the *Sankhyas* and *karma yogis* formed the backgrounds of the two previous chapters, so the sacrificial theories of the *Mimansakas* form the background of this one.

[2] Vivaswan, Manu and Ikshvaku may be taken as standing for the Divine Kings of the prehistoric period. Even as late as the time of the *Upanishads* we find Brahmans going to Kshattriyas for instruction in the secret wisdom. In Egypt the same is true: above all the priests stood the Pharaoh. Rama, Krishna, Buddha were all Kshattriyas, rulers of the world—and of men's hearts.

Let none suppose, however, that by the phrase "Eternal Wisdom" is here meant some body of teachings set down in intellectual form in any books however old. The Wisdom is the wordless Truth itself as existing eternally in the Cosmic Ideation. It is the Norm by which all teachings must be judged, the Fount from which all great religions and philosophies have sprung, and being beyond the level of individuality it is utterly impersonal. It is *the Truth.* Fortunate is that man through whose mind even a ray of that Wisdom Light can manifest, for, though he still may make frequent mistakes, yet he has in his hands an Ariadne thread with which, if he will but follow it up, he can make his way safely through the labyrinth of theories and avoid the quicksands of doubt. It is this Wisdom which inspired the ancient Sages and the Divine Kings of whom the records of all Verse 2 the archaic peoples tell, and it is this Wisdom, or rather Its manifestation, that has " decayed here on earth through great efflux of time" as the warring schools sought each to imprison in its own system the gleaming splendour that shone in the words of its Founder. Vain their efforts, as of one who would seek to grasp the spirit of life by hermetically sealing up some living being!

Jnana yoga, Karma yoga, Bhakti yoga, Dhyana yoga, all are but one- Verse 3 sided glimpses, fragments of that mighty whole, the "imperishable Yoga," the imparting of which in its all-sided beauty is the aim of Sri Krishna.

Sri Krishna, in fact, *is* that Wisdom. Certainly He was also a living Teacher, one of those great Beings who, from time to time, incarnate on earth for the welfare of suffering humanity; but the "I" who taught Vivaswan, the "Me" to whom, throughout the Gita, attention is to be directed, is no mere historic figure, however great or splendid. It is the Divine Wisdom that is speaking, the *Mahat Atman* of the *Katho-panishad,* that which Plato referred to as the World of Ideas and which has here been termed the Cosmic Ideation.

It is the birth of this Wisdom in the human soul that is celebrated each Verses year at the *Janmashtmi* festival,[1] the Wisdom that destroys the demons 6-8 of ignorance and selfishness, the Wisdom whose other names are Love and Sacrifice. Though Unborn and Undying, yet does this Wisdom-Love manifest in human souls from time to time, and especially at times of great spiritual stress when materialism and the cosmic forces of disharmony arc straining at the personalities of men and forcing them away from their contact with the Inner Watcher. At such times a terrific tension is set up in the inner worlds, a tension which manifests itself in a psychic unrest in the heart of man, and also among the peoples of the earth, tossing them hither and thither in wars and revolutions like corks upon a sea of sorrow.

Then, like the lightning flash cleaving the night, comes at the dark Verse 9 midnight hour the great Mystery, the birth of the Birthless, the action of

[1] The Hindu Christmas, the birthday of Sri Krishna, occurring in August-September.

the Actionless, and once again the Light of the World is revealed to them that walk in darkness. Therefore does Sri Krishna say that they who know the *essential nature* of His Divine birth and actions wander no more in the cycles of suffering but attain to His exalted Being.[1]

But not only at certain seasons in the outer world must that Birth take place. It is not enough to look with longing backward-turned eyes at the Light which once blazed with such splendour in Muttra, at Buddha-Gaya, or in Nazareth. In the dark soul of every disciple must the Divine Krishna be bom, and throughout the ages many are those who, filled with the new-born Wisdom, the Slayer of the demons of passion, fear and anger, have passed along by the ancient narrow Path (the *anuh pantha puranah* of the *Upanishads*) and, piercing through the Darkness, have entered His Being.

Verse 11   "In all ways[2] men follow My Path," says Krishna, and, indeed, there is no other Path, *nanyah pantha vidyate 'yanaya*.[3] The only bridge that spans the sea of sorrow is the Bridge of Light, the many-coloured rainbow bridge, and though one may give what names one pleases to the various stages, and may use primarily intellect, emotion, or unselfish action as the stick by the help of which one essays the crossing, yet is it the same Path for all, the Ladder of Souls figured on many an Egyptian papyrus[4] and known to all the ancient teachers of the world, "the ladder whose foot rests in the deep mire of the disciple's sins and failings but whose summit is lost in the glorious Light of *Nirvana*." [5] Truly did Hermes Trismegistus say of it: "If thou but settest foot on this Path, thou shalt see it everywhere, both when and where thou dost expect it not."

But no mere theoretical knowledge of the Path will enable the disciple to tread it. It can be trodden only by *becoming* oneself its various stages. "In this Path, to whatever place one goes, that place one's own self becomes."[6] The consciousness must be raised step by step, and it is useless to think, as did certain *Sankhyas*, that if only action could be abandoned the soul would fly up at once, like a bird released from a cage. Useless, because, even if the more obvious outer actions be forcibly abandoned, the subtle actions of the mind will remain to bind the soul as firmly as ever.[7]

The only way to tread the Path in reality is by the knowledge of Krishna, of the *Atman* which is present as the unseen background of every action, the smallest as of the greatest, of the action that sends the pen Verse 14 across this page as of the action that hurls a million men into battle. Just as nothing can move except within the framework of space, so nothing

---

[1] See "Note on Avataras," Appendix D.

[2] "From all sides" is another translation, but both Shankara and Sridhara paraphrase "*sarvashah*" as "*sarvaprakaraih*."

[3] *Shwetashwatara Upanishad*, vi, 15.

[4] E.g. *Book of the Dead*, xcviii (Theban Recension).

[5] *Voice of the Silence*.

[6] *Jnaneshwari*, vi, 160.

[7] For discussion of the "four castes" (verse 13) see Chapter XVIII.

can take place except within the Light of the *Atman*, which yet is no more entangled in the actions than space is entangled in the movements of objects, and therefore Krishna says that those who know Him are freed from the bonds of action.

Such men are wise, for they see inaction in action and action in inaction. They see, that is, that while in the midst of all movements broods the motionless *Atman*, yet do all actions spring from that *Atman*, QT, rather, take place zuithin that calm and passionless Light. This is the knowledge whose fire burns up all actions, slaying desire for selfish fruits and making the man a Sage who, though his body and mind are for ever engaged in action, yet does nothing since he clings to naught. Verse 18 Verses 19-23

"Of one with attachment dead, liberated from bondage, with his thoughts established in knowledge, his works sacrifices, all action melts away."

For certainly the instinct which leads so many to reject the idea of an actionless life in spite of all arguments is a sound one. To reject action is to create a dualism between the *Brahman* and the universe, which leaves the latter on our hands as a vast cosmic folly, worse than folly, a monstrous cruelty that stinks to the heavens. But it is not so. There is no ultimate dualism in the Reality. It is not action that binds, for the surging tides of the manifested cosmos are as truly the manifestation of the supreme *Brahman* as is the calm bliss of the stainless witnessing Self. What binds us is a wrong attitude to action, the "knots of the heart" which, springing from ignorance, make us fancy that we are so many separate individuals, isolated from each other and "free" to perform actions for our selfish ends. This, and not action in itself, is what binds us, and therefore it is that Krishna returns again and again to the theme of unattachment to the fruits of action, for there is no freedom for the selfish actor any more than for a bird that is in the meshes of a net.

Let it, however, once become clear that the manifestation is also an aspect of the Supreme *Brahman* and it will be evident that there must be a way of action which does not bind the Soul. And this is the realisation that now begins to dawn in the heart of the disciple. He sees, though as yet but with his mind, for there is still a long and weary road to be traversed before the vision will permeate his whole being, that the action, the actor and the act are all so many manifestations of the stainless Eternal, and that if all action be but offered as a sacrifice in the consuming fire of that *Brahman* there can be no bondage; for the root-cause of the bondage, the ignorance which makes a dualism and a multiplicity where there is in truth but One, is now removed and, if not yet eradicated entirely, is at least seen for what it is, an unreal phantom, like the snake which is seen where in reality is but a rope. Verse 24

This knowledge has now to be applied if it is to be made effective, and so the Teacher proceeds to enumerate various types of practice by

Verses 25-30 which the knowledge may be made to pervade the whole life of the disciple. Some will practise restraint of the senses as a prelude to that more advanced stage in which the now controlled senses can be used for the service of the *Atman* which is in all. Others endeavour to serve with their wealth or learning, or with that concentrated force of character which is the result of self-discipline (*tapasya*). Others again devote themselves to yogic practices with a view to gaining that inner poise which will enable them to keep their balance in the whirlpool of activity and to hold out helping hands to others in due season.

Verse 33 All these strive to sacrifice themselves in various ways to the *Atman* who is in all, and all these sacrifices culminate in the wisdom[1] sacrifice, the effort to gain the life-giving wisdom, not, again, in order that oneself may be wise, but because in wisdom lies salvation for all.

Verse 34 All action and all efforts find their completion in the gaining of that Wisdom, but just as life springs only from other lives, so the flame of wisdom can be lit only by contact with those in whose heart it already shines. The disciple must resort to the feet of a wise teacher, one who is an embodiment of that Teacher Who is already in his heart, the Eternal Wisdom referred to before. Some will wonder why, if the Teacher is already present in the heart, there should be need for an external Guru at all. True, the Teacher is there, but we are so used to listening only to the trumpet tones of desire that the still small voice in the heart passes unheeded. Too often does the disciple mistake the promptings of desire and of unpurified emotion for the intuition which is the Voice of the Teacher, and therefore is it that he needs the guidance of one who, because his whole being has become one with the Wisdom, can speak with the same voice as that Teacher in the heart and yet do so in tones which can be heard with the outer ear.

Such Gurus are always to be found at the right time, for the earth is never without men who know the Truth, men who, however scattered and unlinked with each other they may appear, yet constitute a Race apart, a Race whose Light shineth in darkness though the darkness comprehendeth it not, a Race which never dies, for it is constantly renewed throughout the ages as the torch of Wisdom passes from hand to hand.

Verse 34 But it is not by wandering restlessly hither and thither, by searching out the remoter corners of the earth, that the Guru can be found. The Path which leads to the feet of the Guru, outer as well as inner, is an interior path, and only by treading the preliminary steps by oneself can one reach the outer Guide. It is only when this stage has been reached, the stage at which the disciple is ready to offer up his self in sacrifice to the Self in all, that the Guru can and does manifest himself: " When the disciple is ready

---

[1] See chapter xviii, verse 70, for explanation of the *Jnana Yajna*.

the Guru appears." [1] For him whose aims are selfish, however "refined" the selfishness may be, no teacher will be forthcoming, for he could be of little use, since his work is but to make more manifest the Voice in the heart, and until the disciple has learnt to listen always for that inner Voice a blind obedience to an external authority can do more harm than good, destroying self-reliance and so rendering fainter that which is too faint already.

When, however, the right stage of development has been reached and the disciple has found his Guru, he must, by the obedience of self-effacement, and the service which consists in putting the will at the disposal of the Teacher, so unite his being with that of the latter that the Wisdom which shines in him may light up in the disciple too.

Then will the disciple begin to *see* that all beings are within the Light of the One Self, just as all things exist within the matrix of space, and, by the raft of this Wisdom Light, he will commence to cross over to the Farther Shore. For, just as fire reduces fuel to ashes, so does the Wisdom Light destroy all sense of difference and multiplicity.[2] The actions which fatally bound the self are powerless to affect the Self, for action binds through ignorance and the Self is free through Wisdom. *Verse 35*

But though the Wisdom will save him who lays hold of it from bondage to his past sins, none should think that there is any room here for antinomianism, for none can serve God and Mammon, and he who is guilty of that egoistic self-assertion which is the essence of all "sin" is by that very fact far removed from the Wisdom whose heart is sacrifice of self.

True, the Wisdom is hidden in the hearts of all, "even of the most sinful," but it is only he who is "perfected in yoga," in sacrificial action, that finds It there in due season. For this the disciple needs faith *(shraddha)*,[3] not the blind belief of the sectarian creeds-men, but the firm aspiration of the soul which seeks to give itself, an aspiration which is itself a reflection of the Wisdom that it preludes. Not only must he have this faith. He must also have gained the mastery over his senses, else will they carry him away "as the wind hurries away a ship upon the waters," [4] and the sails of aspiration that were set for the voyage to the Deathless will but bear the Soul more swiftly to the black rocks of death. *Verses 36-39*

---

[1] Popular superstition has it that no Guru can give *diksha* (initiation) unless he is given *dakshina* (a fee). Corrupt as all such practices are, this is a symbol of a profound truth. Of all who seek a Guru the question is asked: "What do you offer and what will you give in return for the Wisdom that you seek?"
[2] Christians who are not too fettered by superstition may see here the meaning of the salvation of sinners by faith in the crucifixion of Christ. The blood of Christ is the Wisdom Light which is shed through the sacrifice of self for the sake of all. That Light, if clung to, has power by its very nature to save "even the most sinful of sinners."
[3] The nature of "faith" will be further discussed in connection with chapter xvii.
[4] Gita, ii, 67.

Above all must the disciple beware of doubt,[1] that creeps in like a dark fog over the sea, blotting out the guiding stars and filling the soul with despair. From time to time as he tries to advance will this fog of Verse 40 doubt enwrap his heart. The Light by which he has hitherto been guided will fade and be eclipsed, and all that he has accomplished will seem vain and a delusion. Then must he show of what material he is made, for if he wavers and loses heart he is lost indeed. Clinging to the compass of the Wisdom, an intellectual memory of which is all that remains to him in this condition, he must press on in confidence that the fog will lift in time and the familiar stars shine forth once more. For, in the end, it is only the Verse 42 Wisdom which can silence doubt. As long as there is any clinging to a separate self, so long is there fear for that self, since all that is separate must one day cease to be. Only the Wisdom which knows the Self as One in all can silence the whisperings of fear and cleave the fog of doubt. Only he shall live who feareth not to die, and such fearlessness can be his alone who, by the *buddhi yoga,* has united himself to the Light and, by the *karma yoga,* has offered up the self in sacrifice to Self. He alone will stand rock-like in the Self when selves are scattered like leaves by the burning winds of sorrow.

"Therefore with the sword of the knowledge of the One Self cleaving asunder the ignorance-born doubt dwelling in thy heart, be established in Yoga and stand up, O Arjuna."

---

[1] The doubt referred to here is not mere intellectual doubt, which is the usual precursor of any advance in knowledge; still less is it doubt of orthodox dogmas, for all clinging to dogmas must be destroyed, root and branch. It is the doubt of the reality of what has once been perceived, and springs from the inevitable pendulum swing of reaction after an advance has been made. If it is conquered further advance will come, but if given way to all progress is stopped.

CHAPTER V
THE YOGA OF RENUNCIATION

"RENUNCIATION of actions Thou praisest, O Krishna, and then also (*karma*) Verse 1
yoga. Tell me decisively which of the two is better."

The Wisdom which is now filtering into the consciousness of the disciple is not the intellectual knowledge of the schools, the knowledge which holds firm to the part as if that were the whole, but a unifying wisdom which fuses the broken lights of the mind into a living unity which the unaided intellect cannot reach. No one who has reached this stage can view the seated majesty of the Buddha without knowing in his soul that renunciation alone gives peace. But neither, when he contemplates the many-faceted figure of Krishna, warrior, statesman, lover, friend, can he refuse his soul's assent to that marvellous symbol of the Divine action, free and unfettered in the very midst of the cosmic whirl.

The interpreting mind asserts that these are incompatible ideals and Verses 4, 5
with facile logic seeks to lead the disciple to one side or the other; but he must cling, instead, to the inner wisdom of his soul, which will teach him how these seeming irreconcilables are in reality two aspects of the same truth. He truly sees who sees that the true meaning of the renunciation of actions that is taught by the *Sankhya* is the same as that of the action taught by the *karma yogis*. For, in truth, words are but fingers pointing to the moon, and though the mind clings desperately to its analytic hold upon the finger, the Soul reaches out intuitively to That which lies beyond.

True renunciation cannot be attained by any sudden wrench of the will, even though, when it does come, it may seem to appear with all the swift glory of the lightning. "Without *yoga*, renunciation is hard to attain to." As Verse 6
long as there is the feeling of a separate self, so long true renunciation is impossible, for it is the personal self which is the seat of attachment, being but the hypothetical or illusory centre of the bundle of attachments, likes and dislikes that make up the so-called self of man.

Psychologists can tell us how this "self" is gradually built up in the originally "selfless" infant, how it expands and becomes more complex with experience, how strains in the imperfectly integrated experience may sometimes distort and split it into two or more separate "personalities," and how these may be welded into one again by harmonising the conflicting stresses. Truly do they teach, as the Buddha taught long before, that in all this there is nothing immortal, nothing permanent, no hard changeless centre in the ever-changing flux of experience which could in truth be called a self. This self that we prize so dearly and to which we subordinate all is a mere emptiness, the empty heart of a whirlpool, a mathematical point which changes its position, not only from year to year, but even from hour to hour, as a man shifts from his "business" integration to that which is manifested at his home or his club.

Verses 7-9   Therefore does Sri Krishna teach that the disciple must utterly destroy the false sense of self, realising in all that he does, "speaking, giving, grasping," no self is involved; only "the senses moving among the objects of the senses."

But a whirlpool is real even though its centre be empty,[1] and Life is real though lives are devoid of permanent selves. There is a Life that is the Light of men, "a Light that shineth in darkness though the darkness comprehendeth it not." That Life, the *Atman*, is the Self of all beings, the very Breath of the Eternal, of which the *Rig-Veda* says: "The Only One, the breathless, breathed by Its own nature; apart from It was nothing whatsoever."

It is that One Life which is the life of all beings, that One Self, if it may be called a Self, which is the inmost heart of all. In that Life alone can immortality be achieved, and only when it is realised that it is in the bosom of that Ocean of Light that all these whirlpools of activity have Verse 10 their being, only then can the disciple "place his actions in the Eternal" and, in renouncing the illusory finite centre, achieve that renunciation of attachment which leaves the actions free and divine.

Verse 11   The disciple must, then, learn to divest himself of ego-centricity. He must no longer act for the separate self but for that Self which is in all, which means in practice that, seeking neither gain nor fame, he must work for the welfare of his fellow-beings. Body, mind and senses will act as before, but their actions must no longer find their meaning solely in the point within them, but in that mystic Circle whose centre is everywhere and circumference nowhere.

When he has achieved some success in this yoga of disinterested action the disciple will notice a change taking place within himself. Instead of the elusive personal centre, the empty and featureless point of reference, he will perceive a Light shining where before all was darkness, will hear a Voice where previously all was silence.

---

[1] Empty of any thing, that is. See Appendix B.

It is of this stage that the Chinese *Secret of the Golden Flower* writes: "When one begins to apply this magic, it is as if, in the middle of one's being, there were a non-being. When in the course of time the work is finished, and beyond the body there is another body, it is as if, in the middle of the non-being, there were a being. Only after a completed work of a hundred days will the Light be real, then only it will become spirit-fire. After a hundred days there develops by itself, in the middle of the Light, a point of the true Lightpole (*yang*). Suddenly there develops the seed-pearl. It is as if man and woman embraced and a conception took place."

"Having renounced all (desire-prompted) action with his mind, the Inner Ruler sits blissfully in the nine-gated city of the body, neither acting nor causing to act." Verse 13

For the centre within is only illusory when considered as an independent self, a monad separate from all others. In reality the "point" within is a window, a point of view *through* which the Eternal One as subject looks out upon Itself as object. Just as a window, empty in itself, is yet a focus through which the all-pervading sunlight can illumine the world of objects, themselves but other forms of the energy we know as light, so is the self a focus through which can shine the Light of the One Consciousness illumining the objective world which is the other aspect of the *Great Atman* or Universal Mind (*Mahat Atman*).

This Light, differing in no way from that which shines through the innumerable other foci which constitute the world of beings, is the real Self, and, as stated in the text, it dwells blissfully in the body, neither acting nor causing to act. Serene in Itself, It is untouched by the good and evil deeds of the personality and constitutes a fortress in which the disciple can take refuge, unharmed by the tides of battle, and yet in no selfish isolation, for he will be one with all that is. Verses 14, 15

This inner Self, however, as is shown by the use of the word "*vibhu*" the all-pervading one, is not to be regarded as an eternally existing monad, separate for each disciple. In all the worlds there is nothing eternal but the one *Brahman*, and to consider the "inner point" as a permanent separate self, even if a "higher" one, is to attempt to repeat on a higher level the unwisdom which sets oneself over against others.[1] Verse 15

As long as this delusion of separateness exists, so long is "wisdom enveloped by unwisdom." When, however, this clinging to separate existence is abandoned, the disciple is able to pass through Verses 15-17

---

[1] This is the great heresy of *satkayadrishti* against which the Buddha directed so much of his teaching, the theory that there are permanent soul monads, eternally separate. What has here been described as the higher Self, the true Ego, constitutes no doubt a relatively permanent individual centre, but it is in reality only a focus of the One Self and not a separate entity. Its separateness lies only in its content, not in itself. Strictly speaking, even the One Universal Self (the *Mahat Atman*) is not permanent, since it is part of the manifested Universe and is withdrawn at the universal dissolution (*pralaya*) into the *Parabrahman*, which is alone eternal in the strict sense of the word.

the inner door of the heart and to enter a realm in which he is one with all, and in which the wisdom light of the one *Atman* shines forth unobstructedly, revealing the Supreme, the nameless Eternal. All names are based on the discriminating analysis of the mind, and how should names be given to that which is one and indivisible in all? Therefore have the sages referred to It merely as "That," that Reality "from which the mind turns back together with the senses, unable to comprehend." [1]

This is not the first knowledge which the disciple has had of "That." Long before, in chapter two, he had his first intuitive glimpse of It, though, at that time, It presented Itself to him merely as the Unmanifest, the unchanging background of all that is. Again, at the stage represented by chapter four, he perceived It a little more clearly as the mysterious source of all the action in the world. Thus, circling round in spiral progress, he gets ever nearer to clear vision, and now, peering through the open "inner door" he sees that the Eternal is the same in all, in learned Brahmin and in despised outcast, in animals as in men. Stainless and equal in all is the Supreme Eternal *Brahman*, and the disciple who has seen that Light *sees* that it is the merest folly to suppose that It can be affected by the good or evil deeds of men. As the pure sunlight is not affected by the foulness of objects that it falls upon, so the *Brahma* Light is not touched by the differences in the bodies which It illumines. This is a plain fact which all who care may see for themselves, and he who has seen it will of necessity look with a very different eye upon his fellow-beings. Behind all the masks, beautiful or repulsive, is the one Clear Light, and no longer can he think of men as beings to be praised, criticised, or condemned. His gaze centred on the Light, his one thought will be how to help It to shine more clearly through the obstructing bodies, and, acting with that in view, he will gradually achieve in practice that abandonment of self-prompted action which constitutes the true renunciation.

Verses 18, 19

On this Path action and vision go hand in hand, and that is why the teachings of the Gita alternate between knowledge and action in a way so baffling to the purely intellectual man. Purified and disciplined action opens the inner eye and grants the vision of the highest that the disciple is yet capable of seeing. But that vision must not remain a mere private ecstasy. It must be translated into action, and so built into the personality before another range of vision can present itself to the inner eye and the way be opened for yet another cyclic advance.

A casual reading of this section (*e.g.* verses 17 or 24) might suggest that the full attainment is being described or, at least, that it is now possible for the disciple to go "straight through," as it were, by the longed-for

---

[1] *Taitiriya Upanishad*, II, iv, 1.

short-cut. But it is not so. The disciple at this stage is as one who has got his head through the inner door but whose body is too big to follow. Once again the vision must be translated into practice. His body, the personality, must be so refined by vision-lit action that it will cease to be an obstacle to his passing right through, and, though these verses may describe the condition of attainment, yet are they meant but to encourage the disciple and to help him to keep before his mind the Goal to which tend all these weary strivings and disciplinings of the self.

And so, firmly attached to the Light that he has seen behind the phantoms of the senses, he must strive to live in the Eternal, to realise in practice the stainless balance of the Reality and cease to be whirled away by the pleasant or painful "contacts of the senses." *Verses 21, 22*

Sensations will still come and go as before, but the inner vision he has achieved will give him a new power of withdrawing from them even while experiencing their pleasure and pain. What characterises pleasure and pain *Verse 23* is not any quality in the sensations themselves so much as the psychic attraction or revulsion that takes place within. When, through his grasp of the Light of the Eternal, the disciple is able to master this inner revulsion, he finds that the pain sensations, though unchanged in themselves, have, in some quite indescribable way, become "different," have lost their power to storm his being or to lead him to blind reaction; though of rational and controlled response he is more capable than ever before. No longer are they masters, smashing their way brutally into the consciousness, demanding instinctive reaction as a right, but mere phenomena to be observed, studied and deliberately attended to at will.

The teaching about the control of desire that was given at the end of the third chapter now begins to bear fruit. Previously the disciple had no means of dealing with unwelcome sensations but Stoic endurance of them, and no method of resisting the surging waves of desire but the method of the personal will, a method which must have failed him many times and which is inadequate at best. Now, however, the position is different. He has only to use his will to establish himself in the inner fortress and, for the time being at least, desires will drop dead before his eyes like butterflies killed by frost as they emerge from a warm house. True, they will rise again from the dead, and again have to be faced, but a great gain has been achieved in that, instead of the grim setting of the teeth of the personal will that was before necessary, only that relatively small effort of will is needed which may enable the disciple to take up his position in the fortress, and, once he does so, victory is assured.

But any surging up of personal pride at this stage will ruin all. Great as is the achievement that has been attained, the power of slaying desire at will, much has yet to be accomplished before the *Brahma-Nirvana*, the utter "blowing out" of personal desire in the calm Light of the Eternal, is reached, before the disciple will become a *Rishi* and be able to echo the triumphant words of the Buddha:

"Now art thou seen, O Builder. Never again shalt thou build house for me. Broken are all the beams and sundered lies the ridge-pole. My mind is set on the Eternal; extinguished is all desire." [1]

Pride implies duality, and all duality must be rooted out for ever. Therefore the disciple is reminded that it is not as a personal refuge from the sorrows and pains of life that he must enter the fortress. The *Brahman* is One and the same in all, and only he who has developed the all-embracing compassion of a *Bodhisattva* can attain the Supreme Enlightenment of a *Buddha.*

Nevertheless, great is the achievement of him who has got even so far as this. If only personal pride can be suppressed the disciple's further progress is assured, for "the *Brahma-Nirvana* lies near to those who know the *Atman*" and who are able in consequence, by the method outlined, to "disjoin themselves" from desire and anger. The next chapter will indicate a method which will enable the disciple to leap his consciousness across the gap that still separates his conscious mind from the Ocean of Light beyond. Here it should be noted, however, that it is only to him who has reached this point, to him who has seen through the inner door to the Light on the Other Side, who has mastered his lower self and who is "intent on the welfare of all beings," that the *Brahma-Nirvana* lies near at hand." [2]

For him who has not trodden faithfully the Path so far, it is quite useless to attempt to flash the consciousness into Enlightenment by any meditative *yoga* for, if anything at all results from his premature practice, it will only be in the nature of dangerous mediumistic psychisms, neurotic dissociations of the personality, perhaps even insanity itself.

Verse 28   But for the fit disciple, for him who has mastered senses, mind and *buddhi*,[3] who is free from all selfish aims, who has cast away desire, fear and anger, desire for any enjoyment, fear of any consequences and anger against those who obstruct his progress, who has seen, though as yet only

---

[1] *Dhammapada, 154.*

[2] Verse 27 does not refer to sitting in trance with the eyes turned upwards (as practised by some *hatha yogis*) but to the habitual attitude of the disciple at this stage. Externalising the outer (sense) contacts— that is to say, considering them as something external to himself—the disciple transfers his eye, his centre of vision, to the symbolic spot between the eyebrows. Seeing with the ordinary eyes stands for the ordinary sense vision, seeing with or in the heart for the eye of the individual Self, the nianas, while seeing from the spot between the eyebrows symbolises seeing with the third eye, the eye of spiritual knowledge, the calm, all-illumining knowledge of the *buddhi*. Compare the symbolic description in the *Mahayana* scripture, the *Saddharma Pundarika* (introduction): " And at that moment there issued a ray from within the circle of hair between the eyebrows of the Buddha. It extended over eighteen hundred thousand Buddha fields . . . and the beings in any of the six states became visible without exception." See also *The Voice of the Silence*: "Then from the heart that Power shall rise into the sixth, the middle region, the place between thine eyes, when it becomes the breath of the One Soul, the voice which filleth all, thy Master's voice." *Buddhi* is, as it were, the breath of *Mahat*, the One Soul.

[3] The reference to the mastery of the *buddhi* should be understood as anticipatory in the context. It will occur before liberation (*mukti*) is attained.

through the "door," that eternal Krishna who is the One Self of all, the One for whom the Cosmic Sacrifice was undertaken, the Great Lord of all the Verse 29 worlds, the *Lover of all beings*, for such a one all doors stand open, his further progress is assured, and speedily will he attain the Peace, the Peace that only Enlightenment can give.

CHAPTER VI
THE YOGA OF MEDITATION

By some mystics the Path has been divided into three stages, called respectively the Way of Purification, the Way of Illumination, and the Way of Unity. The first six chapters of the Gita correspond to some extent with, the Way of Purification. This sixth chapter marks the transition to the Way of Illumination, for, as was mentioned in the last, it sets forth the technique of a mental discipline which is meant to transfer the consciousness unbrokenly from its ordinary waking condition to those higher levels which, up to this point, have been working, as it were, behind the scenes, glimpsed perhaps in occasional flashes of inspiration, but always as something beyond, something outside the dominion of the will, coming and going with the apparent caprice that veils an unknown law.

This technique is called "*Dhyana yoga*" the yoga by meditation, and it corresponds, more or less, with the method systematised by Patanjali in his *Yoga Sutras*. But, at the very outset, it should be clearly understood for whom this practice will give results and for whom it will not. This is vitally important, since there are many who consider the practice of meditation as *the* yoga *par excellence* and eagerly seek to practise it without, having trodden the all-important earlier stages. As stated before, nothing but dangerous mediumistic psychisms or neurotic dissociations of personality can result from the practice of meditation without the qualifications mentioned at the end of the last chapter.[1]

Verse 1   It is not he who gives up the fire and rites that symbolise his social duties in order to plunge into meditation in some Himalayan cave who is the true *yogi* or *sannyasi*, but he who performs such actions as are enjoined by duty without any selfish desire for fruit.

Verse 2   It is not work which has to be renounced but the "*sankalpa*," the

---

[1] This warning against the premature practice of meditation refers only to the deliberate attempt to scale the Ladder of the Soul by a meditative technique. Meditation on the symbol of the Supreme or on the figure of the Teacher, reflection on the eternal truths about the Soul and the world, and the calm analysis of one's character are practices which are useful and desirable at all stages of the Path.

formative will which seeks its own aims, an attitude that is found in too many would-be yogis who seek in yoga, not the *Atman*, but an enhanced power of moulding the environment to a pattern more pleasing to the personal self.

For in truth it is in action, disinterested selfless action, that the way to yoga lies. Forcible opening of a bud will not produce a blossom, and it is only when the disciple is "*yoga-rurha*," is firmly established in the Path, that the serenity of meditation can be a means of further advance. Verse 3

It is easy and common to fancy oneself already at this point, but, in truth, the stage is a very high one. Only he may be said to be established in the Path who feels no more attachment to the objects of the senses nor to self-seeking activity, and who has thoroughly renounced the above-mentioned desire to impose his own formative will upon the course of events. Verse 4

Before the practice of meditation can be available to flash the consciousness now centred in the lower or personal self across the gulf which separates it from the *Atman*, or higher Self, it is essential that there shall be a harmony between the two. If the self is in harmony with the Self, if it ceases to exert its personal will, if its impulses are under control and it is able to offer itself as an instrument through which the Self can work, then the *Atman* is its friend, a source of inspiration and guidance, the Inner Teacher of whom mention has previously been made. But if the self is allowed to sink down in inert depression, if it pursues its own aims and stands proudly upon its own individual uniqueness, then, indeed, the *Atman* is felt as something hostile. No more a source of inspiration, It makes itself known as the mysterious source of misfortunes and sicknesses, of those "blows of Fate," in short, which are the teachers of the Law that all life is one.[1] Verse 5 · Verse 6

In order that the disciple may know whether he has truly arrived at this stage or not, certain signs are given in the text and, impartially scrutinising his own mind, he must see whether they are present or not before he ventures farther. If the self is really controlled and harmonious, then the Higher Self will be felt always as a calm background to all the activities of the mind. The "pairs of opposites" that torment other men will have no power to disturb that inner serenity. The gratifications of honour and the death-like sting of dishonour, those infallible testers of claimants to the yogi's title, can have no effect on him whose only honour is the approval of his Teacher, whose only dishonour is the shame of having subordinated Self to self. Wealth is nothing to him who feels within him the living water of the sacred wisdom, and the distinctions that mean Verse 7 · Verses 8, 9

[1] It was perhaps some realisation of this truth (though from a different angle of vision) that prompted the words of Jung: "Only when in disharmony . . . do we discover the Psyche; we come upon something that thwarts our will, which is strange and even hostile to us."

so much to others are absurd in the eyes that have caught a glimpse of the One Life which is in all.

Now comes the time for the practice of meditative yoga and, accordingly, the Gita proceeds to give some teachings about the technique to be pursued. Essentially the method consists of gaining such control over the mind-processes that they can be stilled at will, thus enabling the consciousness to perceive the Truth like a calm lake reflecting the eternal stars above.

Only brief indications are given in the text because the full process cannot be set forth in writing. It varies for each disciple and must be learnt from the Guru, who, as explained before, is always available at this stage. It is true that there are books which apparently give full instructions about the practice, but their apparent fullness is misleading. It is easier to become an artist by the study of a manual of oil-painting than to become a yogi by the study of books on meditation, whether those books were written yesterday or whether they were written five thousand years ago.

The few notes which are here given are intended merely to help the reader to follow the text and by no means as a sufficient guide to practice.

Verses 10, 11   The first necessity is a quiet place in which he may practise meditation undisturbed by friends or visitors, whose presence would be apt to agitate the disciple's mind with thoughts of what so-and-so is thinking of him. This too is the meaning of the phrase that the place should be "pure," that is to say, it should be free from any features likely to give rise to aesthetic irritation or to distraction. Certain natural surroundings, such as the banks of rivers, the tops of mountains, or the open sky, are particularly helpful, as such surroundings exert a calming influence on the mind and have, moreover, a symbolic reference which works powerfully even if not consciously attended to.

The directions about the seat (*asana*) are of an entirely practical nature. The seat should not be so high that there is risk of falling if trance (or more likely sleep!) supervenes, nor so low that there is danger from poisonous insects such as scorpions. The other specifications are that it should be soft enough to give ease of body and of such a nature that it will keep the yogi off the damp ground, hence the use of a leather skin in days when waterproof materials were unknown. More important than these technicalities are the instructions that the disciple should make his mind calm and free from hope and greed, that is to say, from that attitude of wishing to grasp things to and for oneself which is characteristic of the lower mind.[1]

---

[1] Compare the Buddhist practice of removing the five "Hindrances" (sensual passion, ill-will, sloth and torpor, worry and perplexity) from the mind before beginning the meditation (jhana) proper. Note also the Buddhistic emphasis on the "Middle Path" in verses 16 and 17. It is needless to say that the purpose in adducing these and other parallels is not to suggest "borrowing" but to point out that the true yoga is the same wherever it is found.

The next point is posture (also called *asana*). The postures used in this *yoga* have nothing to do with bringing pressure to bear on centres in the body, whether nervous or "occult." The essential is, as Patanjali said, that Verse 13 it should be steady and pleasant. By pleasant, however, it is not meant that it should be an arm-chair sort of attitude, as that would be more conducive to sleep than to meditation. It must be one which can be maintained for a long stretch without sensations of cramp or fatigue, and at the same time it should be one which is conducive to mental alertness, hence the traditional instruction to keep the spine straight.

The direction of the gaze is another point on which there is often confusion. A wandering gaze means a wandering mind, and therefore the eyes are to be kept fixed in one direction. In practice it has been found that the best way to do this is to direct the eyes along the line of the nose and then to half-close the eyelids. This should not be confused with the fixing of the gaze between the eyebrows which is often referred to, and which means that the centre of consciousness should be transferred to the *buddhi* which is often symbolised by that spot (see note on page 45 of the previous chapter). "When one fixes the *thought* on the mid-point between the two eyes, the Light streams in of its own accord." [1]

Though not mentioned here (it has been mentioned in the previous chapter) the breathing is also to be kept regular and smooth, as there is a vital connection between the flow of thoughts and the rhythm of the breath. To quote the same Chinese book: "Because breath comes out of the heart, unrhythmical breathing comes from the heart's unrest. Therefore one must breathe in and out quite softly so that it remains inaudible to the ear." That is all: elaborate processes of holding the breath and of breathing through alternate nostrils (*pranayama*) find no place in this *yoga*.

All these are the preliminaries and can be understood by anyone. The heart of the *yoga* is more difficult and is what cannot be taught in words. It is the "checking of all the modifications of the mind," the "holding of the heart to the centre of the midst of conditions," the "making of the mind one-pointed" and its direction towards Him, the *Atman*, the Light that "streams in of itself between the eyebrows." This is the essential thing, and produces the detachment from the desire nature and the union with the *buddhi (buddhi yoga)* that gives Enlightenment. The state is not one

---

[1] *The Secret of the Golden Flower*, a Chinese Taoist book of yoga, translated by Wilhelm. Compare also the following quotation from the same book: "Therefore the Master makes especially clear the method by which one enters in the cultivation of life, and bids people look with both eyes at the end of the nose, to lower the lids, to look within, sit quietly with upright body and fix the heart on the centre in the midst of conditions [the "point of view" or central reference-point, the higher ego]. Keeping the thoughts on the space between the two eyes allows the Light to penetrate. Thereupon the spirit [*buddhi*] crystallises and enters the centre in the midst of conditions. The centre in the midst of conditions is the lower Elixirfield [the lower immortal or higher ego], the place of power [that is, the seat of will]." The words in brackets have been added.

of mental vacuity, as represented by some critics, and still less is it one which is produced by some "occult" mechanism or other. The centre of consciousness withdraws its attention from the world of outer phenomena, whether of sense or of thought, passes through the central point, which is itself, and emerges in the spiritual world of the *buddhi* which is in deepest truth the same world seen in a different manner. It is the same world because in truth all "worlds" are but illusions. All that exists, exists within the One, and what we see as a world depends upon the point of view from which we see; that which we see is One. As the *Maitri Upanishad* puts it: "Thought is verily the world and therefore should be purified with care. As one's thought is, so one becomes; this is the eternal mystery." [1]

It is no use attempting the specious clarity of an explanation in modern terms. The process will be clear to him who is ready for it. "This is the pathway to Brahman here in this world. This is the opening of the door here in this world. By it one will go to the other shore of the darkness. When the five sense knowledges cease together with the (lower) mind, and the *buddhi* (here the higher mind) also stands motionless, that they say is the highest Path." [2]

Verse 14   Two absolute essentials are *brahmacharya*, or control of the sex-impulse, and utter purity of aspiration. *Brahmacharya* must not be confused with mere ascetic celibacy. It is the *control* of the sex-impulses that is meant and not their mere inhibition, a control that will take varying forms under differing circumstances. There is no merit in the sexlessness of the eunuch, whether his castration be a physical or a mental one, and Hindu tradition is right in affirming that the householder whose sex-life is controlled is as truly a *Brahmachari* as the ascetic who observes the vow of total sex-abstinence. In any case it must be borne in mind that the inner world of sex-phantasy is as important as the outer one of procreation. Without control of sex, in both its inner and its outer manifestations, it is safer to play with dynamite than to practise the *yoga* of meditation.

Turning now to the other essential, the aspiration must be purely directed towards the One Self, as, under any other circumstances, the
Verse 14 practice of meditation will give rise to visions and hallucinations which will mislead the disciple and plunge him into a whirlpool of psychic illusions that may even delude him into fancying himself an *Avatara*, or other great personage. [3]

Purity of aspiration and the proximity of a *wise* Guru are the only

---

[1] *Maitri Upanishad*, vi, 34.

[2] *Maitri*, vi, 30. Compare also the words of Hermes: " Whenever I see within myself the Simple [*i.e.* unitary as opposed to multiple] Vision brought to birth ... I have passed through myself into a Body that can never die. And now I am not what I was before but I am born in Mind. The way to do this is not taught" (from the *Secret Sermon on the Mountain*. The part in brackets is added).

[3] Such delusions are common in India and elsewhere, and are by no means always due to deliberate imposture. Often the *Avatara* is his own first victim.

safeguards against such delusions. It must never be forgotten that visions and other psychic experiences prove absolutely nothing whatever. True knowledge is possessed by the *Atman* alone, and no dualistic knowing can be relied on, whether the senses which mediate it be the outer or the inner ones. It is the grossest folly to suppose that a vision, say, of the crucifixion of Jesus, or the birth of Krishna, is, as such, any testimony to the historicity of those events. Even if it were, it could prove nothing of importance, as it could no more reveal the inner significance of those events than could the physical vision of those who witnessed them with their bodily eyes. In all events it is the *Atman* that is of importance, and it is the knowledge of the *Atman* alone that is the true knowledge. Therefore is it said that he alone is safe "who sees Me, the *Atman*, in all beings and all beings in Me."   Verse 30

Hence all the emphasis on the Self, the *Atman*. The yogi must be united with the *Atman,* with thought fixed on the *Atman,* absorbed in the yoga of the *Atman,* seeing the *Atman* by the *Atman.* It cannot be too emphatically stated that no true yoga is possible by the unaided personal will. Thought may be stilled to the point of trance, but unless the self is surrendered to the *Atman* there can be no yoga in the true sense of the word. True, the preliminary effort at concentration is made, from the lower level, but the complete stilling of the mind by sheer will is like balancing a pyramid upon its apex, a feat of balance which, even if accomplished, is so precarious that no useful result can be achieved.

The true concentration comes when the disciple is able to surrender himself to, and identify himself with, the *Atman,* that Self which is present as the unchanging Witness of every thought and of every sensation. It is only when this is achieved that the mind of the yogi becomes steady "like   Verse 19 a lamp in a windless place," [1] a state which, to anyone who has seriously tried to concentrate from the lower level alone, will always seem an almost fantastically difficult feat of mental acrobatics. The true process is certainly hard enough, but it is infinitely easier than the lower one, failure to achieve which is a source of depression to so many.

It is because of this impossibility of achieving success in meditation without some perception of the Higher Self that it is only in this sixth chapter that instructions for its practice are given. Up to   Verse 3 this point "action is called the means," that is to say, the means of getting a preliminary perception of the higher level of consciousness, the *buddhi*, by which the yoga is to be achieved. [2]

"Little by little let him gain tranquillity by means of *the buddhi,* firmly   Verse 25

---

[1] The point of this simile—evidently much older than the Gita—is often missed. It is useless to try to make the flame steady in a windy place. The mind must withdraw to a region where the winds of desire no longer play before it can become more than momentarily steady.
[2] See Chapter II.

adhered to," and thus, securely seated in the *Atman,* to which *the buddhi* is a bridge, it will be possible for him to bring all thoughts to a standstill and yet remain in a stable state of serenely blissful consciousness, "which Verse 22 having attained, he thinketh that there is no greater gain possible," and which all the assaults of pain and sorrow can never shake.

Verse 23   "That should be known as yoga, this disconnection from the union with pain." Profound words, which gain an added profundity when we remember the teaching of the Buddha that *all* experience is *(in itself) dukkha,* painful by reason of its finite and transitory nature. This "disconnection" from Verse 25 union with all finite experience is the secret of successful yoga, or rather, it is half the secret, the other half being the *atma sanstha,* the abiding in the *Atman.* The two processes, negative and positive, go on side by side, as a man climbing a ladder loosens his hold on one rung while simultaneously attaching himself to the next.

    These two processes are the "detachment and practice" referred to in verse 35. Without their aid there is no possibility of stilling the restless and fickle mind and of climbing up the ladder. For countless ages the mind has been turned outwards and has been given a free rein to attach itself to objects of desire, and it is not to be expected that it will be possible to wrench it away from them at once. A bamboo that has long borne a weight will not be straightened merely by its removal; strenuous effort will also be required to neutralise the acquired bend. So with the mind; long bent by the forces of desire, it must first be detached from them and then, by constant practice, united with that which is higher than itself.

    This practice is not a matter of an hour, or even of several hours, of daily meditation. Throughout the day (and even, in a sense, throughout the hours of sleep as well) constant effort must be made to retain in the consciousness as much as possible of the detachment and insight that were achieved during the meditation period. Throughout the day the disciple must hold on firmly to whatever degree of realisation he was able to gain in those calm hours, for a short period of uncontrolled thought, an hour of despondency, or even five minutes of anger, will undo all that he has accomplished, and, like the web of Penelope, what was woven in the morning will be unravelled by next day.

Verse 37   It is a long and uphill struggle, and one which, to the disciple, will often seem hopeless. Progress is slow and attainment looms far away. The night of Death may come before the haven is reached, but he must not Verse 45 despair, for the Path is one that must be trodden through many lives, and he may repose serenely in the arms of the Cosmic Law, knowing that not Verse 43 the slightest effort is ever wasted, and that, like a man completing on the morrow the unfinished task of to-day, he will be able to begin in his next life at the point where he left off in this.

    If only the effort is steady his ultimate triumph is secure, and at last, Verse 44 like a tree long bound by winter frosts, bursting suddenly into glorious bloom, the arduous struggles of many lives will bear fruit and he will burst into the Light and attain the *Brahma-sansparsha*, the contact with the Eternal, no longer sensed as a vague background, no longer even glimpsed fitfully through the inner door, but felt in actual contact, contact that will drench the soul in bliss. Verse 28

Gone is the sense of a separate finite self, with its individual gains and losses, its personal hopes and fears, and in its place comes the experience of the One *Atman* abiding in all beings, of all beings as eddies in that all-pervading ocean of bliss. Verse 29

This stage may be reckoned as the third great landmark on the Path. The first was the Entry on the Path; the second, the consciousness of the Divine Birth in the heart; and now, with the overwhelming perception of the unity of all life in the One Self, the third, termed in some traditions the Mystic Marriage, may be said to have been accomplished. It is the fifth (in some traditions sixth) or *Dhydna Paramita* of the Buddhists, after which the shining path of *Prajna* lies open before the disciple's feet. Thrice great is he who has travelled thus far. The bridge which separated self from Self has been crossed, and now no obstacle remains to prevent the Divine Light from irradiating the personality with Its wondrous rays.

Wherever he may be, and whatever he may be doing, the yogi is now established in the ever-living Divine Unity. The touch of the Eternal Krishna has awakened the flame of love in his heart, love the great liberator, the breaker-down of all barriers. Borne out of himself on its rushing wave, he sees no more himself or others, but everywhere and in all things the blue form of Krishna flashes forth. Beneath the frowning brows of his foe no less than within the smiling glances of his friend he perceives the gleaming eyes of his Divine Lover, and he pours himself forth in utter worship of the Unchanging One seated within the hearts of all. Verse 31

Worship is a word which conjures up before us ideas of hymns and formal offerings, of churches and temples and of rewards in heaven; but the worship which the disciple now offers is something quite different. It is the worship which gives itself because it can do no less, the worship of self-forgetful service compelled by the sovereign power of love.

What need has he of temples when every form enshrines his Lord, and how shall he withhold his service when he sees the Divine beauty distorted by the gloomy ugliness of the world, the Divine bliss masked by the myriad sorrows of men?

Great is the *tapasvi*, the ascetic who disciplines himself; great the *Jnani* standing firm in the calm knowledge of Reality; great, too, is the man of action, for he is the instrument, albeit unconscious, of the unresting cosmic tides. But greater than all is the yogi, for he combines in himself all three. United with the Divine Lover in his heart, he sees Him as the One Self in all and, offering his disciplined personality on the altar of self-sacrifice, he serves unrestingly the Wisdom-Love that ever plans the Verse 46 welfare of the worlds. "*Sa me yuktatamo matah*—He in my opinion is the greatest yogi of all."

CHAPTER VII
THE YOGA OF KNOWLEDGE

WITH this chapter the Way of Illumination, the *Prajna* Path of the Buddhists, commences, and the glorious Knowledge dawns on the disciple's inner eye, the Knowledge "which, having known, there is nothing more here Verse 2 that needeth to be known." It would be a mistake, however, to suppose that the actual Knowledge is or can be described in the verses that follow. As a two-dimensional photo is to its three-dimensional original, or as a map is to the actual countryside, so is this or any other description to that wondrous Knowledge, and none should fancy that a grasp of the statements set forth is the same thing as the illumination itself.

At the very outset it is desirable to dwell for a moment on the extreme Verse 3 rarity of this Knowledge. The vast majority of men know nothing of its existence, and though a few by strenuous effort have succeeded in establishing themselves upon the Path that leads to it, yet, at any given time, only one or two gain it in its fullness. This is not said in order to depress the disciple, but in order to keep him humble now that he is on the Path of Illumination. Let him not fancy himself a God because he has attained a measure of Light, nor think that he has scaled the eternal Snows because he stands upon a foot-hill peak.

What is this wondrous Knowledge that is now to be described? It is the knowledge of Krishna, the Undying *Atman*, the Stainless Eternal Being that lies behind all change. This should be borne in mind in all that follows, for though there are many who worship Krishna as a personal God, yet, though they may be on the Path, they are of those who "know not Me in essence." Who or what Krishna in essence is, is what is attempted to be set forth in this and the four succeeding chapters. Here, more than ever, must the disciple beware of words, for, as the *Upanishad* says: "It is not known by him who knows It though known by him who knows It not." [1] The knowledge that can be expressed in words is not the true Knowledge. The description that is given is useless if interpreted by the intellect alone,

---

[1] *Kena Upanishad*, ii, 3.

and its words are but a shining curtain through which the disciple must pass to "That from which all words, together with the mind, turn back unable to attain."

Before the disciple can attain to the comprehension of that Supreme Unity he has to understand the twofold nature of the Manifested Universe. In all that is manifested, whether gross or subtle, whether living beings or what we call "dead" matter, there are two aspects which must be understood. These are the ever-changing forms and the unchanging "consciousness" which supports them. Whether the forms of matter, the "five elements," [1] or whether the more subtle forms of thought, all form is but a transient play that is upheld in the light of consciousness, the higher or living (*jiva-bhuta*) nature. Apart from this witnessing consciousness no forms could exist at all.

But, it may be asked, what about "brute matter," as it is sometimes called, the sheer "stuff" of which the world is made? The answer, an answer more acceptable to the ordinary man now that even physical scientists have reduced matter to "waves of probability," is that there is no stuff in that sense at all. Analyse matter to its furthest limit and it evaporates, as it were, or is resolved into something incomprehensible but non-material. It is in fact true, as Plotinus said, that matter in itself is sheer negation; it is the unmanifest sub-stratum of the ever-changing forms in "consciousness."

This is a subject that will have to be further dealt with later, but here it is sufficient to know that these two, consciousness and form,[2] are the womb in which all beings are born. But beyond this duality is That with which Krishna here identifies Himself, the Marvellous, Incomprehensible One, not the blank absolute unity of intellectual philosophy, but the rich and unspeakable Infinite Wonder which is the ground of all, of consciousness and form alike, on Which all this is threaded like pearls upon a string.

This is the essential being of Krishna, to which He says so few attain. Words fall away, useless and empty labels, and even the mind, the line and plummet of the universe, dizzied in ceaseless whirlings, sinks and is dumb before that viewless Wonder, the Void which is the Full, the Full which is the Void. The lips of those who have known It are sealed with reverent awe. Knowing they know It not, they cease "to sink the string of thought into the Fathomless." Let us bow down in awe before that Sacred Mystery and keep our words for realms where words can live.

But since it is just this fathomless Mystery that must be known, some ladder must be found, some means of knowing That which the mind cannot reach. And so Sri Krishna goes on to teach that, though the manifested

Verses 4, 5

Verses 6, 7

---

[1] On "consciousness" see Appendix A; on "matter" Appendix B; and on the "five elements" Appendix H.

[2] United on the level of the *Mahat Atman*.

cosmos is illusion, yet is it a Divine illusion, and at its throbbing heart stands He Himself.

The disciple must in all things—in earth and fire and water, in sun and moon and in all splendid things, in men, strong, wise, ascetic, and in all living beings—seek for the Essence, for that which makes them what they are. Undistracted by the accidents of outer form, the passing phantom shapes which are the great illusion, he must hold firm to that essential nature of which the forms are crude embodiments. For those essential natures are the Divine Ideas, Ideas which live for ever, shaping all things from within, "moulding blind mass to form." [1] *(Verses 8-12)*

The eye of flesh sees but the changing forms, and, holding fast to them, is utterly deluded by the false shows of things. Like Plato's dwellers in the cave, men see only the shifting shadows on the wall. They cannot see the Light, nor yet those truer forms from which the shadows come. This Divine illusion is indeed hard to cross, because long ages spent in grappling with material things have taught our minds to dwell exclusively on what is without. A doctor, trained to view all bodies in terms of health and disease, cannot with ease see with the artist's vision, and we, who owe our mastery over nature to this fidelity to outward fact, cannot at once pass to the higher vision and reverse our customary modes of thought. *(Verses 13, 14)*

This reversal is the *jnana-yoga*, and, as the *Katha Upanishad* says, "some few wise men, seeking the Immortal, with eyes turned in, saw the Undying *Atman*." The disciple must avert his gaze from the manifold illusion. In its place he must see "Me" the Divine idea of Fire in all things fiery, "Me" the Divine Strength in all things strong, "Me" the Divine Life in all that fives and breathes.

Only by turning thus to the Eternal *Atman* can the illusion be crossed. Those who look outward, who embrace the illusions, the treaders of the *Asurik* path,[2] can find no foothold in the cosmic flux and are tossed hither and thither on its unresting tides. *(Verse 15)*

In contrast to these are those who tread the inner Path, they who serve[3] Krishna. They are divided into four classes, graded according to the degree of perception they have attained. First come the "*arta*," those who have seen that all life is but sorrow. *(Verse 16)*

> Ache of the birth, ache of the helpless days,
> Ache of hot youth and ache of manhood's prime;
> Ache of the chill grey years and choking death
> These fill your piteous time.[4]

---

[1] *Light of Asia.*
[2] The *Asurik* path is the outgoing "pravritti " path, of which more will be said later. See Chapter XVI.
[3] *Bhajate*, usually rendered worship, comes from the root *bhaj*, to serve.
[4] *Light of Asia.*

Seeing that life is transient, that all things pass and die, they turn from them in sorrow and seek consolation from That which is beyond all suffering, the Undying Krishna, beyond the reach of change.

This is the first stage, the first of the Buddha's four noble Truths, but it is the first only because it is based on mere recoil from suffering. Insight has shown the disciple that life is shot through and through with sorrow, its so-called joys mere cheats, and so he sadly turns away his eyes. Were life to be more joyful he would not thus have turned his face to Krishna.

The next class is the *"jijnasu"* the inquirer, the seeker after knowledge. Knowledge gives mastery and power, and, seeing that life is sorrow, he seeks the understanding that shall master it, the knowledge of the causes of men's woe.

Next comes the *"artharthi,"* he who seeks the Real.[1] Knowing that it is the outgoing forces of desire that are the sources of all sorrow, knowing, too, that all manifested life is transient by its very nature, he turns his back on all desire for anything that is manifest and seeks the *anamayam padam,* the Sorrowless State of Liberation, lifted on high above the bitter waters of life.

Verses 17-19 But beyond this stage there lies another, the stage of the *jnani,* the Wise One, he who treads the Path of perfect knowledge. For the seeker after Liberation there is a dualism between the world and the *Nirvana* and he rejects the one to cleave unto the Other. But the *jnani* is one who sees that all duality is false. "Here," as "There," his opened eyes see nothing but the One. He seeks no liberation for himself "beyond the flaming ramparts of the world," for he has seen that "all is *Vasudeva"* [2] and, in the words of the *Upanishad,* he knows that "what is There is here; what is not here is nowhere at all."

This glorious realisation, as rare as it is wonderful, comes as the fruit of countless lives of effort. Noble are all who tread the Path, but noblest of all is he, for bis realisation leads him to unite himself with the One Self in all, and, seeking no selfish gain, he rejects not the bitter waters of sorrow but rather seeks to sweeten them in service of his Lord. Not his own self but the One Self is dear to him, therefore he is supremely dear to Krishna. Because he knows that naught but Krishna is, he seeks no gain or Goal but to serve Him. Like Krishna Himself, he pours himself forth in sacrifice and love. He is made one with Krishna's very *Atman,* and, knowing himself to be the One in all, he is established in the highest Path.

Verse 20 Few there are who reach these lofty heights. To give oneself utterly,

---

[1] This term *"artharthi"* is often misunderstood and applied to him who seeks for wealth or worldly objects. The order of the words in the verse is sufficient to show that this is not the true meaning. The artharthi is not he who seeks for the *artha* (wealth) which is *anartha* ("illth"), but he who seeks the true Wealth, the *Paramartha,* which is *mukti* or liberation.

[2] A patronymic of Krishna, but here signifying "the Light which dwells in all."

caring for no reward, is not for those whose hearts are clouded by desire. The worship of the majority of men is not the worship of Krishna even though they use the name of Krishna in their prayers. Seeking to gain some good for their own selves they worship various gods "according to their natures."

What are these gods and what the nature of their worship? In all manifested nature there is, as we have seen, duality of life and form. Nowhere is there life without some form and nowhere, also, form without the Life. The powers of Nature, which to modern eyes are but so many dead "forces," are in truth embodiments of that one Living Power which wields the universe in Its unceasing play. They are not "persons," but in ancient times they were given personal form to symbolise their living nature. *Indra*, *Agni* and other Vedic gods are the personified symbols of the Living Power ensouling Nature's "forces," a Power no more to be identified with the physical embodiments than is the Life ensouling us to be identified with our physical frames.[1]

Modern man seeks to gain benefit from these Powers of Nature by an understanding of their outward being's laws, but ancient man sought the same ends by different means. By various rituals he attuned his consciousness to the Life that ensouls all Nature and sought to control her powers from within by lending his human imagination and will to then-living but will-less being.

Acting in this way, it is possible to obtain from the "gods" the benefits desired, but that is so because beneath the varied powers is the One Power, the Cosmic Harmony known in the Vedic age as "*rita*." Krishna it is who, from behind the scenes, makes steady the faith of such worshippers and by His Eternal Laws secures to each the fruits of all his deeds. Verses 21, 22

All things are possible of attainment if the right means are known, but, though all things are possible, yet must their price be paid, for in all things the law of *karma* rules and action and reaction are inseparable. Therefore it is said that the fruits of all such worship are but finite and "to the gods will go their worshippers; My devotees come unto Me." Verse 23

Let it not be thought, however, that this "Me" is but one God among the gods. Krishna is the Unmanifest Eternal, imperishable, supreme. Useless to set up some one Figure, even His Figure, as Supreme when all the time conceiving Him as one among the many, thinking that, since He is "our" God, He must be chief of all. All that is manifest is, in the end, illusion. In the manifested plurality all interact, none is Supreme. The One is never Verse 24

---

[1] The modern notion that because the winds and waves move according to law they are therefore "dead" is wrong. Do not our own bodies move by law as well? The fact is that nowhere in all the universe is there any form that is not subject to Law, and nowhere, either, is there anything that is "dead"; for all forms move and have their being in the one all-pervading Life.

The Vedic gods have also another aspect, in which they are the symbols of the various levels of the Consciousness, but that is not the aspect with which we are here concerned.

Verse 25 manifest, though fools may think It so, but dwells for ever hidden, unborn behind the ever-changing many. Not in the manifested world can He be found. Deluded by the great illusion of plurality, men seek Him fruitlessly, saying "Lo here! Lo there!"—but all they find is some one thing among the many, searching in this way they can never find the One.[1]

Seeing only the "pairs of opposites" men walk the earth deluded. Whirled about by the forces of attraction and repulsion, seeing only the many, they go "from death to death." They cannot know the Deathless Being of Krishna, for none save the One can ever know the One.

Only by the *jnana yoga*, the yoga that seeks the One *within*[2] the many, can He be found, and, as the *Upanishad* says, "having known Him, one crosses beyond all death, there is no other Path for going there." [3] Fire of the fires, Life of the lives, Light of the lights, He stands beyond all forms; past, present, future—all are one to Him.

Verse 28 This knowledge, however, can only come to him whose sins are at an end. Sin does not mean the infringement of any arbitrary code of morals worked out by human reason or set forth in "holy" books. Sin is the assertion of the separate self, the making of difference where, in truth, none exists. Sin is the central ignorance which sees the separate, personal self as real and seeks its own gain though the whole world perish.[4] To this assertion of the personal self all sins are due, and only he can win the Truth who has renounced such sin and whose pure selfless deeds are all directed to the service of the One in all.

Verses 28-30 They, the selfless ones, refuged in the One Self, strive for the liberation of that Self from matter. They are the true mumukshus, or seekers after liberation, for they scorn to seek a liberation for their own selves alone, knowing that all that lives is One. They also are the truejwdws, for they know the primordial Unmanifested Trinity, the one Eternal Brahman and Its aspects, *Adhyatma*, the Unmanifested Self (the *Shanta Atman* of the *Kathopanishad*) and the Unmanifested *Mula-prakriti*, here referred to as the totality of (potential) action.[5]

But this knowledge is not enough in itself. The Three are eternally the same. They dwell beyond the "Abyss" which separates the manifest from the Unmanifest, and he who treads the "selfish" Path seeks but to lose

---

[1] Compare the saying of Eckhart: "Some people expect to see God as they would see a cow."

[2] Note the contrast between *among* the many and *within* the many. Even the word "within" is not strictly correct, for, as we shall see in Chapter IX, He is not within the many but the many within Him. Nevertheless, at this stage, it is as within them that He will be perceived.

[3] *Shwetashwatara Upanishad*, vi, 15.

[4] This is the meaning of the Buddha's teaching that as long as there is belief in *atma* (here meaning separate self) there can be no *Nirvana*. Christians also teach that salvation from sin is found only in Christ, the meaning of which is clear to those who know that Christ is the One Self in all, and therefore is it said that "No man cometh unto the Father but by me."

[5] For explanations of the technical terms used in these last two verses see the next chapter.

himself for ever in their unchanging timeless bliss. Not so the follower of Krishna, he who treads the Path of Sacrifice and seeks to gather up in the Treasure-House (*cf.* chapter ix, v. 18) the pearls which have been buried in the Cosmic Ocean, to reunite the scattered limbs of the dismembered Osiris.

For him the knowledge of the transcendent Eternal is not enough. There are not two realities, *Nirvana* and the world, for all is *Vasudeva* and what is "There" is likewise "here" as well. He who would tread the Path and knows the Self, not in its own eternity alone but here amid the changing play of life and form, sacrificed here upon the cross of matter, becomes one of the "fishers of men" spoken of by Christ. Others may scorn the world as mere illusion, and, at the death hour, wing their way across the blackness, alone to the Alone. He, however, the fully harmonised one, seeing the One here in the midst of the many, knows no black gulf of death, but in full Light of Consciousness garners the fruits of the Divine Adventure, and, in the words of the *Isha Upanishad*: "*Avidyaya mrityum tirtva, vidyaya'mritamashnute*—Having crossed over death by knowledge of the many, by knowledge of the One he gains the Deathless State." Verse 30

CHAPTER VIII
THE YOGA OF THE IMPERISHABLE ETERNAL

THE farther the disciple proceeds upon the Path the clearer the Light that comes flooding into his heart. The last chapter ended with the mention of some technical terms which are now seen to refer to the Ladder of Being, the Rainbow Bridge, down which the Soul has come and up which it must return. This Ladder has been described in various terms in all the ancient traditions, for instance as the Sephirothal Tree of the Kabala, but the disciple who has reached this stage can read the various symbols that the Teachers have employed, for the reality behind them all is one.

Verse 3   Beyond all and alone stands the Supreme Eternal, the Imperishable *Brahman*, dark in Its utter mystery, the Root of all that is, was, or shall ever be. Neither subject nor object, neither knower, knowing, or known can exist in the unspeakable Being of That which is beyond all names.

All manifestation springs from the self-limitation of that *Brahman*. *Brahman* as subject sees Itself as object and thus we get the first though still unmanifest duality. The essential nature (*swabhava*) of the One as transcendent Subject, here called *adhyatma*, separates out, as it were, leaving the other aspect of the *Brahman* to stand as the eternal Object, *Mula-prakriti*,[1] This *Mula-prakriti*, the unmanifest basis of all objectivity, is, from its very nature, the source of all the manifested Many. Reflecting as it does the Light of the One *Atman*, It is the root of all plurality. In Its dark being lie all the seeds of action, seeds that, under the Sun's bright rays, will shoot and grow into the great World Tree.[2]

Because it is thus the root of all action, the Gita terms it "*Karma,*" but it should be borne in mind that it is not any sort of primordial "brute matter" existing in its own right, as speculated on by nineteenth-century scientists, but merely the objective aspect of the *Brahman*, the unmanifest Substratum in which forms live and move and have their being. It cannot stand alone apart from the *Brahman* of Which it is an aspect. It was a

---

[1] For a fuller account of this cosmic evolution see Chapter XIII and Appendix F; see also the diagram in Appendix E.
[2] For an interesting parallel in the Kabala see Appendix F.

failure to perceive this that led the later *Sankhyas* into dualism. Remove the dualistic knowing [1] and the *Mula-prakriti* collapses into the *Brahman* of which it is but the appearance. If the *Brahman* is to appear as an object at all it is only as the *Mula-prakriti* that It can so appear.

Passing now to the manifested Cosmos, we find that the interaction of   Verse 4 these two, the Unmanifested Subject and the Unmanifested Object, gives rise, on the one hand, to the changing world of forms, the "perishable nature" (*adhibhuta*), and, on the other hand, to the witnessing Consciousness, the One Life, the *adhidaiva*, termed in the *Kathopanishad* the Great or *Mahat Atman*.[2]

Then comes the *adhiyajna*, the Mystic Sacrifice by which Krishna, the One Life, unites Himself with the passing forms. Just as the Unmanifested Two find their unity in the Supreme Unmanifested *Brahman*, so do the manifested Life and Form find union in the sacrificial act of Krishna. This is that Mystic Sacrifice mentioned in the *Rig-Veda* in which the *Purusha* was dismembered to create the world of beings, and this the crucifixion of the Christ, pouring out His life-blood on the Cross of matter, redeeming thus the duality of the world.

The One Self, seeing Itself reflected in the myriad forms, willed by Its mystic yoga to identify Itself with them and share their limitations. Thus were the individuals formed, the central being of men, sometimes termed (higher) manas, sometimes *ahankara*,[3] the scattered limbs of the Divine Osiris. These are the Immortal Sparks, the Shining Threads, dying in myriad forms and yet, unseen, passing from life to life in age-long immortality.

This "Sacrifice" has also been described in the *Poemandres* of Hermes Trismegistus:

"He (the Cosmic Man), beholding the form like to Himself existing in Her water, loved it and willed to live in it; and with the will came act, and so He vivified the form devoid of reason. And Nature took the object of her love and wound Herself completely round Him, and they were intermingled; for they were lovers. And this is why beyond all creatures on the earth man is twofold; mortal because of body, but, because of

[1] This dualistic "knowing" is, however, not individual but cosmic. It springs from that mysterious extra-cosmic Something called by various schools the Will of God, *lila* (the Divine play), Eternal Law, or *Maya*. All these names express some aspects of it, but, being beyond the manifested Cosmos, it is beyond the reach of words. Its nature is too mysterious to be speculated on, but its reality is proved by the fact of manifestation having taken place at all. In attempting to describe it Shankara was forced into paradox and contradiction, while the Buddha preferred to keep silent altogether.
[2] Also known in some traditions as the third Logos.
[3] *Ahankara*, literally the I-maker, is a term that can be applied either on the level of the personal self or on that of higher Self, the true individual. In later writings it is usually employed in the lower sense, but in the Gita manas is generally used for the lower self and *ahankara* for the higher. The term higher *manas* is not used in the Gita, though, as previously mentioned, it is referred to in *Maitri Upanishad* (vi, 34) as *suddha* (pure) *manas*. The term *ahankara* has the same significance, but emphasises not its cognitive but its ego nature.

the essential Man, immortal."

Verses
5-7

On account of this twofold nature of man it is of great importance that the disciple should at all times, and especially at the critical hour of death, identify himself with what is immortal in him, with the Undying Krishna within and not with the mortal form which constitutes his body. Imagination is the power which wields the universe. From imagination sprang the dualism of the Cosmos and through imaginative union came about the Mystic Sacrifice. As a man thinketh, so shall he become. Therefore is it of such supreme importance how the disciple uses his imagination. Identifying himself in thought with the perishable body he shares the latter's death, while if he can unite himself with what is Deathless he will partake of immortality.

There is no appeal here to the authority of ancient texts.

It is plain fact of which, as the Gita says, "there is no doubt at all." To him who doubts it only needs to say: "Make yourself ready, try it and reap the fruits." Try it and see; you are the immortal Spirit: "Thou wast not made for death, immortal bird! No hungry generations tread thee down."

Verse 8

But, as in the ancient myth, the elixir of immortality must be churned from out the Cosmic Ocean. How will the Soul's immortality benefit him who thinks he is the body? It is useless to rely on any mere death-bed thoughts. Only he who in life "strives with continual practice" to know himself as that which is immortal can meet the illusions of the death hour with unruffled mind and place his being in the Deathless Spirit, treading the Bridge of Souls to the Eternal.

Verse 9

Five are the stages on the Rainbow Bridge, five gates of consciousness through which the soul must pass. First comes the Ancient Seer,[1] the world creator, *Brahma* the Demiurge, red-coloured with desire. It is the Light we know as the desire-consciousness, the Light that shines through the senses, inner as well as outer, for this it is that makes the world of beings, and from this point must the ascent commence.

Next comes the Inner Ruler, smaller than the small. This is the inner "Point" mentioned in chapter five, the Higher Self, shining in the pure Mind. He sows the field and He reaps the harvest; happy the man ruled by that Inner Lord!

Above this comes the *Buddhi*, All-Supporter, the luminous Sea in which the separate Sparks are all united in one Living Flame. It is the

---

[1] The use of the word "*kavi*," seer or poet (also applied to the poet-seers of the *Vedas*), shows how essentially the creative process is conceived as one of imagination. This level is the same as that of the Gnostic Ilda-Baoth. The word *Brahma* is also used in another sense (e.g. verse 16 of this chapter), where it stands for the highest level of manifested being, the plane of the Creative Word, the Cosmic ideation. There need be no confusion about this double use. Both signify the creative Power, in the one case on the level of unity, the *manifested* unity; in the other case on the level of plurality, the plurality which is the world of beings. There is a reference in *Shwetashwatara Upanishad* (v, 2) to "the reddish-coloured seer who was engendered in the beginning." On the five levels see Appendix E.

Light that shines above the Mind, uniting individual points of view in one all-seeing Wisdom. It is the vestibule that leads beyond to the Great Being of unimagined form, the Cosmic Ideation which is Krishna,[1] the farthest edge of manifested being. This is the Plane of the Creative Word, and he who has attained this lofty height can hear the thunders of the mystic Sea that ebbs and flows throughout the Universe, "and hear its mighty waters, rolling evermore."

Beyond it lies the dark unfathomed mystery of Unmanifested Nature, and beyond again burns the White Light, the Sun beyond the Darkness, the calm and peaceful Light of the Unmanifested *Atman*.

Beyond once more is the Supreme Eternal, the Nameless Mystery symbolised by the one-syllabled *Om*[2] He who can tread the Path of Consciousness, sinking the senses in the mind, the mind in *buddhi, buddhi* in the "Great Self," and then go on Beyond, enters the bliss of that Supreme Eternal and comes no more to birth.

This description of the Path has been taken from the *Katha Upanishad*, but the same thing has been stated here in more symbolic terms. The gates of the senses are to be closed by withdrawal of the consciousness from them and the lower personality (the mind) to be merged in the higher Self, here called the heart. Then, as Shankara puts it, "ascending through the subtle path to the head," the yogi is to establish himself in the *buddhi*, here termed the "breath of the *Atman*." From here, contemplating the symbol of the Eternal, he performs the Great Passing-On (*samparaya*). Verses 12, 13

Between the Unmanifested and the manifest lies an Abyss which thought can never cross. Up to the farthest edge of manifested being, the Great Self or Cosmic Ideation, here referred to as the world of *Brahma*, all things are transient, even though they last a thousand ages. From out the dark Unmanifested Nature they issue forth at every Cosmic Dawn. They last for untold ages, but the eternal rhythm of Day and Night is on them and, at length, there comes a time when, like plants that have flowered, they sink back in the Unmanifested Root of all. In that dark matrix of the Universal Mother the seeds of all that has been lie in latency through the long Night till the next Cosmic Dawn. This mighty rhythm of Cosmic Day and Night, towards an idea of which modern astronomers are perhaps dimly groping, was clearly known to the great ancient Seers. They knew that nothing Cosmic lasts for ever and that even the Unmanifested Verses 16-21

---

[1] Only in one aspect of course. Throughout the Gita, Sri Krishna identifies Himself with different levels at different places.

[2] A lot of nonsense has been written in the West about *Om* and its "vibrations." Some of it is now filtering back to India and I read in a Hindi religious magazine of how a "Western scientist" had shattered a glass tumbler with the vibration aroused by chanting *Om* and only just stopped in time to avoid disintegrating the Bank of England or some such place! The true meaning of the word should be studied in the *Mandukya Upanishad*. H. P. Blavatsky, who was not averse to writing about "vibrations" when it suited her, when asked by her pupils as to the correct pronunciation of Om replied: " *Aum* means good actions, not merely lip-sound. You must say it in deeds."

Mother, Mula-prakriti, sends forth her shoots again each Cosmic Dawn. Therefore they sought to live in the Eternal, in that Supreme Unmanifested *Brahman*, the Indestructible, the Highest Goal. Beyond the Cosmic Tides, That stands for ever, the Great *Nirvana*, the Supreme Abode. Those who attain It know nor Day nor Night. Like seeds destroyed by fire, no Cosmic Dawn can bring them forth again to worlds of sorrow. Of them naught can be said save the great mantra of the *Prajna Paramita*: "*Gate gate paragate parasangate bodhi swaha!*—O Wisdom gone, gone to the Other Shore, landed on the Other Shore, *Swaha!*" [1]

Verse 22   This is the Goal reached by the Rainbow Bridge; what of the means by which to tread that Path? It is one thing to know of the different levels of Consciousness but quite another to be able to raise oneself at will to higher levels. The best means to accomplish this is "unswerving love and devotion to Him in whom all beings abide, by Whom all this Cosmos is pervaded." Let there be no misunderstanding here. This is not said in the spirit that has marred so many of the *bhakti* schools of India, the spirit of rivalry with those who teach the Path of Knowledge. Knowledge is indeed the very Path itself. The Path is made of various levels of Knowledge and we have seen the *Jnani* described as Krishna's very Self. But this Knowledge is not the knowledge found in books. It must be gained by making the ascent to higher levels; and how in fact may that same rising be accomplished? Who is there that has tried to tread the Path and does not know what is referred to here? Above our heads, like the full moon, shines forth that higher level of our being. We see it there, drawing our hearts with beauty, and yet, for all our efforts, inaccessible, beyond our reach.

The best and easiest means to make the ascent is for the disciple to give himself in love and devotion to that which is above his present level. Loving devotion is the easiest way by which man can transcend his limitations. This is the great force which will carry the disciple out of himself.[2] One's self is dear to all, but he who loves or worships with unswerving heart loses his self to find a higher Self in the Beloved or the Worshipped one. Thus does he find himself upon the level which, up till then, had gleamed beyond his reach. Thus does he tread the Path and "sink

[1] *Swaha* is the mantra with which offerings are made in the sacred fire. In this, the *Brahma yajna*, the self has been offered and consumed in the fire of the Eternal.

[2] The reason that love and devotion have this power is that they have their roots in the *buddhi* and so beyond individuation. It is true that, as we find them in ordinary life, they manifest through and in association with the strong currents of the sub-mental desire-nature—hence their mixed and sometimes unsatisfactory nature in common experience. Nevertheless their roots are in the *buddhi*, and thus they have the power to pull the disciple right through the "dead-centre" of the higher ego where so many others stop, subtly magnifying self with every effort to diminish it. Hence also the fact that these higher emotions, as we may call them, have a definite cognitive aspect and give a knowledge that is beyond the analytic knowledge of the mind. Compare the words of Jung: "Intellect does in fact isolate the soul when it tries to possess itself of the heritage of the spirit. It is in no way fitted to do this, because spirit is something higher than intellect in that it includes not only the latter, but the feelings as well."

the senses in the Mind," and so on till he reaches the One Self, the Shining *Atman* within Which all live.

This *Atman* may be symbolised for him as his own Teacher or as some great *Avatara*. But, through the symbols, he should ever bear in mind it is the One Great Self of all he worships, for, as it says in *Brihadaranyaka Upanishad*, not for the son or husband are son and husband dear but for the *Atman* which is dear to all. For though one cannot scale at once the heights of being, yet one can reach them step by step through love, giving oneself to that which stands above one, climbing in this way till the Goal is reached.

It is true that there are other ways of making the ascent. Plotinus said that only he attains the One who has the nature of a lover or philosopher. The disinterested passion for Knowledge, which was what he meant by philosophy, is also capable of lifting man out of his personality, of making him forget all self in contemplation of the universal Truths. But few are they whose feet can tread this latter Path. Many, no doubt, desire Knowledge intensely, but of them, most seek it for the power it confers and not for its own sake. It is in that rare case alone where knowledge is desired for Truth's own sake that man can lose all self in its pursuit.

Love is, in any case, the power by which we rise, whether that love be of the True or of the Beautiful or, best of all, of the One *Atman*, Krishna, Who shines through everything men love or worship. Truth of all truths, Beauty of all things beautiful, Soul of all things beloved, to Him at last all come, losing themselves to find their Self in Him.

> "Lamp of Earth! where'er thou movest
> Its dim shapes are clad with brightness
> And the souls of whom thou lovest
> Walk upon the winds with lightness
> Till they fail as I am failing
> Dizzy, lost, yet unbewailing!"

These lines of Shelley describe, as no words of mine can ever do, the rapture of the Soul, dizzy with loss of self as it soars towards the Light.

There are two Paths, two everlasting Paths; by one or other must all souls go forth. "By the one he goeth who returneth not, by the other he who again returneth." These are the "Way Above" and the "Way of Death" of Hermes Tris-megistus; probably also the Two Paths, one through the sky and one beneath the earth, mentioned by Plato in his *Vision of Er*. These Paths, the Path of Light and the Path of Darkness, have been veiled in symbolism throughout the ages. This particular symbolism is far older than the Gita, and these so-called "times" are no times at all. It does not matter when a man may die; if he has Knowledge he will tread the Upward Path, if not, the Path of Gloom to birth and death.

Verse 23

Verse 24   These "times" are stages on the Paths that Souls must tread; the one, the Bright Path of the Consciousness, the Path Beyond, trodden by him who knows the Self in all; the other, the Dark Path of Matter, trodden by the ignorant. He who goes by the first climbs the steep inner Path from flickering firelight to the Sunshine of Eternal Day. Rising from Light to Light in ever-widening splendour, he treads the trackless Swan's Path till the blazing Goal is reached.[1]

Verse 25   The other is the Path of gloom and sorrow. Here the only Light is that reflected in the Moon of matter, and the traveller in that pale radiance, taking foes for friends, losing himself in forms which are illusions, knowing not the Immortal, goes from death to death.

Verse 27   The man who knows these Paths has, as it were, a compass with which to guide his steps at every instant, in death as in life. For let it not be thought that these teachings are for this life and world alone. Man is a citizen of many worlds, and not here alone are dangers and temptations to be faced. Dire illusions await man in the realms beyond the grave. Those who believe that all has been achieved if mere "survival" can be demonstrated, those who accept the fantasies of mediums as the Truth, expose themselves to dangers which no "spirit-guide" can save them from.

There, in those worlds, the mind, freed from the dragging fetters of a gross material body, treads its own path, the path prepared for it by its own thoughts and actions, done while yet "alive." Either it shines serene in its own Light or else it burns in self-enkindled flames of hatred, greed and lust, the "threefold gate of hell" (chapter xvi, verse 21). This hell is no less real because it is a mind-created one. Fierce illusions[2] will beset the soul and he who knows not the Paths will be whirled irresistibly away. Turning his back upon the Fearless Stainless Light of the One *Atman,* he will embrace the seeming beautiful but horrid phantoms of his own desires. No sooner does he do so than the phantoms change. The beauties vanish, leaving horrid pits of shame, through which the soul descends to birth again and treads once more the weary path of sorrow.

Much that is written in ancient tales of magic is a reality in this enchanted realm. Sir Gawain, awearied of his questing for the Grail, finds a silken pavilion in a field and merry maidens in it,

". . . but the gale
Tore my pavilion from the tenting pin
And blew my merry maidens all about."

---

[1] See Appendix G.

[2] A good account of the after-death illusions is given in the *Tibetan Book of the Dead*, translated into English by Lama Dawa Samdup and edited by Dr Evans Wentz. In reading it allowance must of course be made for purely Tibetan imagery, and also for errors which have crept into the text through its having fallen into the hands of professional death-bed priests.

These illusions work their fell magic from behind the veil even in this daily life of ours, but after death they burst upon the disembodied mind with all the vividness of ancient myth. Those who yield to them echo the cry of Tennyson's Gawain, whose ghost cries out to Arthur at the last:

> "Farewell! there is an isle of rest for thee.
> But I am blown along a wandering wind.
> And hollow, hollow, hollow all delight."

Two are the Paths, there is no third for man. Cleave to the Self in *yoga* or lose yourself in matter. Brief is the choice, yet endless, too, for at each point the Way is forked: one can go up or down. Now should the choice be made, while yet the heart is flexible with life, for in that After-State the mind is fixed, fixed like a death-mask, by its previous thoughts. There but Verse 28 a ghostly shade of choice remains. Sped by its former thoughts and deeds, the soul will either sink through dread illusions to rebirth in matter, or it will rise past heavenly realms of Light, stopping at none till it attains the Goal, the Deathless and Supreme Eternal State.

CHAPTER IX
THE YOGA OF THE ROYAL SCIENCE AND ROYAL SECRET

"The One Swan is in the heart of the world;
He verily is the Fire that has entered into the Waters.
Having known Him one crosses over Death;
There is no other Path for going there."
Shwetashwatara Upanishad.

THE Royal Secret is not one that can be told in words. Throughout the world runs a tradition of a wondrous Secret sought under different names by men through all the ages. The Philosopher's Stone, the Elixir of Immortality, Verse 1 the Holy Grail, the Hidden Name of God, all these have been the objects of men's quests, and all are one if rightly understood. Many have "followed after wandering fires," and others have sold their quest for gold or fame, but throughout all ages there have always been a few who trod the Path and found the Shining Secret.

No pen can ever write down this Secret, nor can any lips reveal it, but it is written in the inmost heart of man and has lain there through countless ages, awaiting the day when the disciple, tearing aside the veils of ignorance, perceives its blazing letters in his heart. There is no man, however mean or sinful, in whose heart it is not written, but few there are who read its life-giving words.

Verse 2 This is the meaning of the statement that it is *pratyakshavagamam* to be directly known. On this Path there is no such thing as blind belief. The various faith-mongering creeds urge their adherents to take everything on trust, to believe without question what is written in "revealed" scriptures. But the Gita proclaims man's inherent freedom from all such fetters. The man who treads the Path sees for himself the Truth, not in some promised heaven after death, but here in this very life. Here are no books demanding blind unreasoning obedience, no priests waving the keys which unlock heavens and hells. The Truth, once seen, shines by its own resplendent Light, and he who drinks of its waters "shall never thirst again."

Verse 3 No doubt faith is required to reach this Knowledge, but that faith is not an intellectual belief in any set of dogmas nor in the efficiency of any priestly rites.[1] The faith required is the inner conviction that sent the Buddha on His lonely quest, the faith that " Surely at last, far off, sometime, somewhere, the veil will lift for his deep searching eyes" [2]; that somewhere there is a Knowledge that will save the world from sorrow, and a determination to rest not till that Knowledge be attained. This is the faith and this the will that has sent out the Seekers of all ages. Its life is rooted not in intellect but in the inner Knowledge itself, and thence its rays shoot out, though dimmed by matter, to draw the hearts of men towards the Goal.[3]

How far this Knowledge soars beyond the reach of words is shown by the contradictory descriptions cast on the beaches of our lower worlds. The Upanishadic Seers termed it the knowledge of the Full, the *Atman*; the Buddhists, knowledge of *Anatman*, of the Void. Yet both descriptions were attempts to express the same transcendent Truth, Truth that was known to both but which, when dressed in words, appears in these conflicting forms.

The Gita, too, has recourse to paradox, the paradox that all beings dwell and yet do not dwell in the One Supreme. In order to understand this at least partially, for full understanding comes only with direct knowledge, it should be borne in mind that throughout the Gita Krishna speaks from different levels. In verse 4 He is speaking of His Great Unmanifested Form (*avyakta murti*), the *Parabrahman*, Rootless Root of all. By that Supreme all this world is pervaded; Itself rooted in naught, all beings dwell within Its bosom. *[margin: Verses 4, 5]*

Of it Plotinus writes: "Generative of all, the Unity is none of all, neither thing nor quality, nor intellect nor soul; not in motion, not at rest, not in place, not in time; It is the self- defined, unique in form or, better, formless, existing before Form was or Movement or Rest, all of which are attachments of Being and make Being the manifold it is." [4]

But in verse 5 Sri Krishna speaks from a "lower" level. We have seen in the previous chapter how from the One spring forth the Two, the Unmanifested Self or Subject and the Unmanifested Root of objectivity. It is the interplay or union of these two that constitutes the Sovereign *Yoga* (*yogamaish-waram*), and in neither of them can "the beings" be said to dwell. Not in the *Mula-prakriti* for, though that is indeed the support of beings, itself stands not in its own right but is the appearance of the *Parabrahman* "seen" by the One Unmanifested Self. Like space, It is the great container of all beings and yet, like space, It is not touched by them.

Neither can beings be said to dwell in the Unmanifested Self. That Self is the "nourisher of beings," for, by Its creative gaze (*ikshana*), It brought

---

[1] In fact, as the Buddha taught, faith in rites and ceremonies is one of the fetters that has to be thrown off by the disciple on this Path.
[2] *Light of Asia.*
[3] See the notes on the higher emotions on p. 74 of the previous chapter.
[4] Plotinus, vi, 9.

Verse 6

them forth from the unmanifested matrix and holds them in existence; yet they are no more rooted in It than the forms we see are rooted in the sunshine which illumines them. Like space again, It holds them all and yet is touched by none.

Perhaps the best way to gain some understanding of the mystery is to remember the Hermetic axiom and study the creative process in the microcosm, for, as it says in the *Zohar*, "esoterically the man below corresponds entirely to the Man above." Consider a creative writer in the act of creation. If we look into his "mind" we can see there a number of figures playing their parts with semi-independent life, each with his separate character and deeds, all issuing from a dark unconscious matrix, all lit up by the light of consciousness. These beings seem to live their independent lives though over all a certain moulding power wields sway. Their creator cannot kill them off at will, nor shield them from the consequences of their acts. They take their being from the seeds of past experience, personal or racial, buried deep within the dark unconscious matrix which is the stage on which they play their little parts. But that dark stage is not their real root. The dark is but the appearance which the root puts on when watched by consciousness, and veils the deep reality which is alike the source of forms and witnessing consciousness.[1] But it is time to return to the Macrocosm. By a Mystic Union, the *yogamaishwaram* of verse 5, the Unmanifested Self unites, as it were imaginatively, with the Unmanifested Nature, the *Mula-prakriti*. The Self leans on or "embraces" the Dark Nature, and at that embrace the seeds of plurality buried within from previous universes shoot into life and the Great Descent begins. This Descent is a graded perception of increasing objectivity. As the Self "gazes" at each level a further objectivisation takes place, resulting in plane after plane of being. Through the mystic union with these levels[2] the whole Cosmic Machine, down to the so-called gross objective matter, whirls and revolves with the indwelling Life, for, as Hermes says, "not a single thing that is dead hath been or is or shall be in this Cosmos."

Verse 8

Verses 8-10

Nor is this process one which is accomplished once and then remains for ever. Again and again, as described in the last chapter, the mighty Outbreathing takes place and all the countless beings thread their tangled ways throughout the worlds, to be absorbed again at the next Cosmic Night, in which "only the One breathes breathless by Itself."

---

[1] It is not intended to assert that this account of the microcosmic creative process is true for all artists (though it is for some, *e.g.* R. L. Stevenson), and it is only meant as a suggestive outline. Neither is it intended to equate the *Parabrahman* with the collective unconscious of some modern psychologists nor with the metaphysical unconscious will of Schopenhauer or Von Hartmann. The higher levels of being seem dark to us only because their Light is too intense to register through our brains, just as a room blazing with ultra-violet light seems dark to our eyes though not to a camera. Compare also the words of Hermes: "And if thou wouldst in practice understand this work, behold what taketh place in thee desiring to beget" (*Hermetic Corpus*, xi, 14).

[2] "Having entered into union (*yoga*) with principle (*tattva*) after principle" (*Shwetdshwatara Upanishad*, vi, 3).

"This is the Truth: As from a blazing fire thousands of sparks of like form issue forth, so from the Imperishable, O friend, manifold beings are produced and thither do return." [1]

All that has here been written, all that can be written, is but a web of words, a ladder by whose help we seek to scale the ramparts of Eternity. Viewed by the eye of Wisdom all this clash of world with world, the Sparks which fly from the Eternal Anvil, are but a vast phantasmagoria. Nothing is outbreathed nor anything descends to rise again. All are the visions of the Eternal Mind; the changing finite centres that are us ourselves being but the countless points of view within that mighty Whole, "for there is naught in all the world that is not He." [2]

But few there are whose souls are of such stature that they can look upon the highest Truth and live. In him who sees before his soul is perfect, love and compassion die, killed by that freezing Knowledge, and all the strivings of a million lives are lost, and he who might have been a lamp to suffering men chooses *Nirvana* and is lost to us as though at no time had he ever been.

Let us take up our web of words again lest too much knowledge, like the Gorgon's head, should freeze us where we stand. Though the One Self projects the Cosmic Wheel and fills it with Its life-blood, yet is that Self not bound upon its whirling spokes. Filled by the One Life, countless beings strive, enjoy or suffer, die and come to birth again, and yet that One Verse 9 Life is for ever free, " seated like one indifferent, unattached to actions."

" I saw the King of Kings descend the narrow doorway to the dust, With all His fires of morning still, the beauty, bravery and lust, And yet He is the life within the Ever-living living Ones, The Ancient with Eternal youth, the cradle of the infant Suns." [3]

Men sin and suffer, act and reap the fruits, and yet the *Atman* seated in their hearts, the Self whose life moves all that is, impelling all to action, feels not the sting of death but lives for ever, free and unattached even in the very web of deeds. This is the mystery of the Divine Action; he who knows its secret comes not to birth again (chapter iv, verse 9). The little figures on the writer's inner stage, ensouled by him, made of his very being, weave out their destinies, bound by their own past acts, and yet his contemplative consciousness is free. [4] So is the *Atman* free though through

[1] *Mundaka Upanishad*, II, i, 1.
[2] *Hermetic Corpus*, v, 9.
[3] From A. E.'s poem *Krishna*.
[4] Those whose hearts may feel tempted to revolt at the idea of the free Self calmly watching the bound selves should remember that it is not any personal extra-cosmic God who is here spoken of, but *our own* true Self, seated within *our* hearts. Were He not ever free we could not break our bonds. In Him alone is freedom, truth and immortality. The analogy of the writer should not be made to yield the inference of a personal Cosmic Author. Even here, genuine artistic creation springs from a level quite beyond the author's personal self.

Its life the Cosmic Wheel revolves. "He ever is at work, Himself being what He doeth. For did He separate Himself from it, all things would then collapse and all must die." [1]

Two types of men are found in the world. The first are those who Verse 12 unite their being with the deceitful outer nature (*mohini prakriti*), the ever-changing world of transient forms. These are those foolish ones who Verse 11 disregard the shining *Atman*, seeing only the perishable bodies which It ensouls. Therefore are they said to be empty of hope, for there can be no hope in forms that come and go; and empty of deeds, for deeds can have no meaning save as the service of the One Eternal Life.

Verses 13-15 In contrast with these are the wise ones who unite their being with the *daivi prakriti*, the Divine Life which flows like *Ganga* through the triple world, ensouling all the forms, the stainless living Radiance streaming from the Imperishable Source of all. Ever united with that living Light, firm in the vow[2] which offers self in service of the Self, they turn their gaze within and see the radiant Source as One beyond all forms and yet as manifold within the hearts of all.

Verse 19 From that Source, the Father, Mother, All-supporter of the Cosmos, comes forth the fire of life and the creative waters of desire. All that is manifest, as well as what is still unmanifest, comes from that wondrous Treasure House (*nidhanam*).

The higher up the Path of Light a man ascends the more gloriously radiant are the forms which It ensouls, and there are always many who climb a certain height only to lose themselves in heavenly enjoyments.[3] Verse 20 But, if this temptation is yielded to, the energy of the ascent is dissipated among those fair creations and, when it is spent, the pilgrim soul is carried down by the unresting cycles and must, in circumstances good or ill, start on this earth once more its upward climb. The seeds buried in the darkness of earth shoot up and bear their fruit in the free air, the corn seven cubits high that grew in the Egyptian fields of *Ahloo*, and then return as seeds once more to earth.

Though this is called the Path of Darkness in the previous chapter, yet Verse 21 is it only such in contrast to the glorious Path of Light. It is the normal cyclic path of human life throughout the long ages of evolution, during which the souls lured by desire (*kamakama*) must know and suffer all before they take the Homeward Path.

It is only for the grown soul of the disciple that this path becomes a snare to be avoided, for he is one who has renounced desire and may not without shame yield to the lure of heaven. His duty is to offer up

---

[1] *Hermetic Corpus*, 11-14 (Mead's translation).
[2] Compare these "firm vows" (verse 14) with the vow of the Bodhisattvas, "as the chain of births is endless, so long shall I live the holy life for the well-being of all creatures" (*Shantideva*).
[3] At the time when the Gita was written this gaining of heavenly enjoyments after death had come to be considered the path taught by the *Vedas* (verses 20 and 21).

himself in sacrificial service to the One Great Life that is the Lord of all; Verse 24 all other worship is an obstacle for him. Forms in the psychic world, spirits of the blessed dead, the shining gods themselves, all these exist beyond the world of men, and all have drawn the souls of men in worship. But the result of worship is assimilation to the being who is worshipped, and no God, limited himself by name and form, can give the Soul that State which is beyond all limitations. These shining forms may serve to lead men upwards and make them blossom in the higher worlds; but blossoms fade and must return to earth, this drab but wondrous earth in which alone the plant of life can grow.

The Path of Liberation is for men alone. The gods are stopping-places on the way, fair forms for most, but veritable Moloch mouths for him who Verse 25 treads the Homeward Path, since, once assimilated to their being, there is no onward path save through the womb of earth again. The disciple at this stage must leave the forms and see the Light that shines through all, for it is by that Light that all are glorious. The worshippers of gods are ignorant, for they see but the forms and not the Light of that Unknown Eternal without which they are nothing.

But, comes the question, how can that Light be worshipped? Stainless, serene, eternally transcendent, "That from which speech turns back, together with the mind, unable to attain,"[1] how can we soar to that Eternal Krishna? The Way to Him is not through any complicated rites Verse 26 or ceremonials but through sheer giving. The disciple must reverse that process of grasping which builds up a personal self and strive to give away instead of getting. First with symbolic gifts of leaves and flowers and fruit, but afterwards with gift of self, the consecration of all acts to Him. Nor Verses should any think his gifts are not accepted. All gifts, however small, are 27, 28 "accepted," because all giving is a breaking-down and weakening of the barrier which, like some iron egg-shell, cuts off the soul from the wide life outside. The smallest act of giving is a step upon that Path and leads the soul by easy steps to that sublime stage where the whole personal life, with all its acts and thoughts and feelings, is dedicated to the service of the One in all, where acts can bind no more since self is dead, and naught remains that can be bound by them.

The Way is taught, but each must tread it by himself. "The same am I Verse 29 to all beings; there is none hateful to Me nor dear." No special privileges can be found upon this Path. He who seems to climb with glorious ease to-day is not a favoured darling of the gods but one who reaps the fruit of arduous struggles yesterday, while he whose breath comes hard upon the mountain path may know for certain that, if he persists, a time will come when he too will gain the athlete's grace and mastery.

There is no other way to Krishna than giving of the self to Him in

---

[1] *Taittiriya Upanishad*, II, iv, 1.

service. By his own efforts each must climb the Path, but always Krishna stands within the soul and none who seeks to offer up himself can be refused the chance. Though he must climb in weary loneliness, striving alone with his own heart, yet is that loneliness a mere illusion, for there, unseen, "closer to him than breathing, nearer than hands and feet," stands his eternal Friend and inmost Self. Nothing interposes between him and his inner God except the veil of egoism which he himself has made, and which is thinned and weakened by each unselfish act of giving.

Verse 30 Therefore is it said that even if the most sinful of men turns to Him and serves Him with undivided heart, he too must be accounted righteous, for he too has entered on the Homeward Path. True, the self-assertive acts that constitute the evil of his past have left him with a legacy of tendencies that he will have to struggle hard to overcome, for nothing can annihilate deeds once they have been done. To seek to have their consequences washed away by any magic or by any prayers is merest superstition, but even so, no man is ever fettered utterly. A man may sin a thousand times, and by those acts so strengthen his lower self that it is almost certain he will sin again next time. Almost, but not quite certain, for in everyone shines the free *Atman*, and where That exists no bondage can be absolute. Always a man *can* turn and climb the upward path, for the Divine Freedom that is in his heart can never be annulled, and even the very power by which he sins, traced to its source, springs from the Stainless One.

Verse 31 Once the resolve is made *and kept* to act in future for the higher not the lower self, progress is speedy,[1] and the Path is entered on which leads at last to the Eternal Peace. Though there will many times be fallings off and failures, yet once the link with the Divine Self has been established the disciple cannot fall again into the utter darkness. Something has awakened within him which will never let him rest again in matter, and, though at times he may even fight against it, the inner pull will ever and again be felt, and like a big fish held on a slender line he will eventually be brought out of the stream to land, for, as Krishna says, "know thou for certain that my devotee perishes never."[2]

Verse 32 The *Atman* dwells within the hearts of all and therefore is this path open to all without distinction of race, caste, or sex. The *Vedic* path needed a wealth of learning and therefore was inevitably closed to those, such as women and the *Sudra* caste, who were debarred by social rules from *Vedic*

---

[1] The word speedy must be interpreted relatively, since we know from chapter vii, verse 19, that the Path is one which takes many lives to tread. The process is called speedy here in contrast to the age-long wanderings in the wilderness of self. This is of course all past history for the disciple who has reached the stage represented by this chapter.

[2] The symbolism of the soul caught on the line of the Divine Fisher is found in many ancient mysteries and underlies the statement of Jesus about "fishers of men." For details see Eisler's *Orpheus the Fisher.*

study.[1] This Path, calling only for sincere self-giving, needs no scriptural or philosophic learning and so is available for all, since all the Knowledge that is needed comes of itself to him who gives himself.

Therefore the Teacher sums up all that He has said in one brief verse, a verse whose great importance may be seen from the fact that the same verse (with an insignificant variation) is used to sum up the completed teaching at the end of chapter eighteen:

"On Me fix thy mind; give thyself in love to Me; sacrifice to Me; Verse 34 prostrate thyself before Me; having thus united thy whole self (to Me), with Me as thy Goal, to Me shalt thou come."

The disciple must with his pure mental vision see Him, the One in all, and with his heart offer himself in love. His active powers he must use in sacrificial service and, as prostration, see the personal self as naught before that mighty Whole. Thus in balanced union, avoiding any one-sided intellectualism, emotionalism, or activity, head, heart and hands all fixed on Him, filled with Him, transmuted to His nature, he treads the Royal Path on which the Soul, dying to self, rising again in Self, knows the Eternal Swan and, having known, crosses beyond all death.

---

[1] Verse 32 must not be taken as sanctioning the relegation of women to an inferior place in society. When the Gita was written (as to a large extent even now) women were *in fact* depressed and practically deprived of the advantages of education. Sri Krishna is not supporting this but pointing out that, even with these handicaps, this Path is open for them. The phrase "womb of sin" refers to the fact that the *karmik* penalty for wasted opportunities is loss of opportunity in future, and so a birth in one of those sections of society which, *at that given time and place*, suffer in fact from lack of freedom and opportunity. It should not be taken as justifying such a state of society.

CHAPTER X
THE YOGA OF THE PERVADING POWERS

SEEKING nothing, give thyself utterly to Me. These words will serve to summarise the teaching that has now (in Chapter IX) been given. But who is it who thus claims allegiance from the Soul? "Worship thou Me," says Krishna, and His words find echo in the saying of Christ: "No man cometh to the Father save through Me." Sectarian creeds in East and West have fastened on these sayings and urged the personal and unique greatness of their own particular Teacher, Son of God or very God Himself, incarnate in the world to save the souls of men. For either we must think these Great Ones were deluded in thus proclaiming themselves the sole Way to the Highest, or else we must suppose, which is indeed the case, that it is not the personal Krishna who is speaking, Krishna the son of Devaki and Vasudeva, the Kshattriya hero, wise and passionless,[1] but the unborn beginningless Eternal, the *Brahman* in which all abide, "by which all this is pervaded."

It is the knowledge of this One Eternal that, from the seventh chapter onwards, is growing in the heart of the disciple. This is the knowledge which "having known, naught here remains to know."[2] It is not enough to know the personal Christ or Krishna, for though their garments are embroidered with the mystic symbols of the *Atman*, yet He who must be known is the Supreme Eternal Whose Voiceless Voice finds utterance through their lips. Failure to see this truth leads to those facile dilemmas with which religious apologists confront their public, saying that such and such a Teacher must be considered God or else a liar and impostor.[3] Such men can never see that though the Teacher is man by birth and body, radiantly man, the shining crown of countless lives of effort, yet is He, too,

---

[1] See *Chhandogya Upanishad*, III, xvii, 6. See also Appendix D.
[2] Gita, vii, 2.
[3] The ordinary exoterically religious man has the same type of mind as the anti-religious materialist. Both have the same naive attitude to verbal propositions, the same childish conception of what constitutes reality. Their quarrels are family ones, hence their bitterness. Hence too their common dislike of the mystic, who moves in a world unknown to both of them.

beyond all human limitations. Step by step he has climbed up the ladder of the Soul until his consciousness is now united with the All, and now, down that same ladder of perfected vehicles (upadhi), shines forth in manifested glory that Unmanifested One, showing with human limbs the action of the Actionless, uttering through human lips the Voiceless Wisdom of the Eternal Brahman.

It is thus not a person who is speaking in the Gita but the great *Brahman* out of Which all beings come and into Which all will in time return. Its secrets are for ever hidden in that uncreated Darkness. Nor God nor Sage can know Its rootless being, for from It all come forth, and he who plunges in to know Its utmost mystery is God or man no more, his being all dissolved in blazing Light that yet is darkness to the highest dualistic knowing. _{Verse 2}

All we can know is that all separate qualities, the various Verses states of mind, some positive, some negative, exist in unity as moments of that blazing Darkness and from It issue forth to shine in men as separate states of being. Verses 4, 5

The seven great Lights,[1] which are the planes of being, all issue forth as previously described (chapters viii and ix). These seven Lights or planes are here divided into three main classes. First come the "previous four,"[2] the four high levels of being (two of them "unmanifested") beyond all individuation. These have been symbolised as four eternal, chaste, ascetic youths, the four *Kumaras*, who refused to create offspring, preferring to remain in contemplation of the One. The truth behind this symbol is that these four planes are planes of unity in which the separate individualities have not been formed. Verse 6

Below these come the "*Manus*" here the separate individuals (*jivas*) the "points of view" within the all-seeing Light.[3] From them, the age-enduring points, issued "this race of men," dying and being born on endless wheels of change.

These "*Manus*" are the central or, as it were, neutral points of the whole manifold creation; on them as on a pivot all is balanced.[4] The two higher levels (for we can leave aside the "unmanifested" two as no

---

[1] Verse 6. In addition to the meaning of sage or seer the word "*rishi*" means light or ray. And it is in this latter sense that the word has been used. Here, as so often, the ambiguity of the Sanskrit language has been used to symbolise abstract truths in personal forms, the seven sages of mythology.

[2] Some read "the four previous *Manus*" but there were more than four previous *Manus* according to the *Pauranic* account and commentators are reduced to various ingenuities to explain why four are mentioned. These four levels are referred to in the *Kathopanishad* as the *Shanta Atman*, the *avyakta* (*Mula-prakriti*), the *Great Atman* (*Mahat*) and the *Jnana Atman* (*Buddhi*). See diagram in Appendix E.

[3] This use of the word "*Manu*" may be seen in the *Vaishnava Pancharatra Agama*. See Schrader's *Introduction to the " Pancharatra."* This level corresponds to *manas*, the (higher) mind or, in other systems, *ahankara*.

[4] This level is sometimes also referred to as "*sthanu*" the fixed or stable, and is the same as the *adhi-yajna* of chapter eight.

part of the manifested cosmos) are mainly inward-turned, so to speak centripetal, and hence are symbolised as chaste ascetics. The lowest two,[1] the changing worlds of beings, are outward-turned or centrifugal in their tendency, while between both, as points of equilibrium, are found "the *Manus*" standing firmly in themselves. Of them, or "through" them, come the changing beings, the sons of *Manu* known as *manavas* (men). These *Manus* are the Sons of God and no man goeth to the Father save through them alone. "Know thyself," ran the inscription at the Delphic Oracle, and he who would attain the wider being beyond must find and enter through the narrow door within the heart.

Verse 7 On all the planes of cosmos is the One as immanent pervading Power (*vibhuti*) united with the forms by mystic *yoga* (see previous chapter), and therefore it is said that he who knows in essence this pervading power and *yoga* of the Supreme unites with Him in firm unwavering yoga.

Verse 8 "I am the source of all," says Krishna, "by Me all revolves." As *Mula-prakriti*, He is the Source of all the forms and, as the One transcendent Self, it is His *yoga* that throws them into motion. The ordinary man sees nothing but the passing forms, in them he puts his hopes, in them is fixed his being. Forms come and he feels happy; they go and sorrow overwhelms his mind, for never can it be that forms shall stand for ever. But the disciple, seeing thus the source and life of all as one, is rooted in that One and remains blissful though all the forms around him change and pass.

Verse 10 To such as can thus root themselves in Efim, serving Him ever with the worship born of love, He gives the *buddhi-yoga*, that union with the *buddhi* by which they go to Him. The *buddhi* is the wisdom which sees the One in All; it also is the faculty by which that vision is acquired. We have seen how the individual self is balanced between the centrifugal and the centripetal forces. United to the lower levels the self flows outwards into forms and dies, as it were, with them, while united to the higher it is carried Homewards by the inflowing cosmic tides.

Verse 11 "Out of pure compassion for them, dwelling within their Self, I destroy the ignorance-born darkness by the shining lamp of Wisdom."

It should not be thought that this compassion is something capricious, something given or withheld at will like a Maharaja's favour. The sun's rays shine on all alike; without them all would die. But he who would feel their warmth upon his skin must leave his shut-in cave and seek the open air. Similarly, he who would experience the Divine Compassion in his soul must leave the cave of self and seek the wider being. He must strive upwards, outwards from his self, breaking the barriers till the Homeward-flowing tides are felt and sweep him off his feet.

---

[1] The desire-nature and the physical world referred to in the *Kathopanishad* as the *indriyas* (senses) and their objects. This structure of the universe is one meaning of the well-known ancient symbol of two triangles standing point to point (*cf.* the *damaru* of Shiva), the upper triangle, the worlds of being; the lower one, the worlds of flux and change, reflected worlds of *Maya*'s shifting play.

These Homeward tides that sweep the upper planes of being, and not some capricious "grace," are the Divine Compassion which will bear the soul up to the One Eternal, but, before they can be felt, the disciple must strive desperately with all his might to cling to Krishna, and by his own unaided efforts break down the prison walls.

To him who says "show us the Lord and it sufficeth us" comes the reply "that which is highest in thyself is Him, as much of Him as thou canst see as yet. Cling then to that and thou shalt go to Him."

Clinging thus to Krishna, the mind becomes irradiated by the Light of the One *Atman* shining serenely through the *buddhi* overhead. The effect of this irradiation is that the intellectual knowledge of the mind is vivified and rendered luminously certain by the *buddhi*'s direct intuition. This is shown very clearly in the Gita in the twelfth and following verses.

"Thou art the Great Eternal, the Great Light, the pure and stainless One, Divine, eternal Man, primal Divinity, Unborn and all-pervading." *Verse 12*

All this was known before as abstract truth, testified to by all the Seers of the past, but "now Thou Thyself sayest it to me." A new and rapturous warmth whose source is in the *buddhi* pervades the mind which soars beyond itself. New vistas, like a landscape half-perceived, open before the mental gaze and the old words and thoughts, words formerly believed, known intellectually to be the truth, now shine transformed within a magic light never before perceived. Useless to try to state in words this new perception with its luminosity. It shows in the note of ecstasy that sounds through Arjuna's words. It is as if one strumming idly on a windless organ should suddenly hear the notes sounding forth in answer to the keys. The thoughts that were but thoughts, bare intellectual concepts, greyly self-sufficient, now waken coloured harmonies that echo through the arches of what seemed a void before. No longer are things seen as separate units but as the interlinked and shining web of a vast splendid pattern still but half-perceived. *Verse 13*

To change this twilit half-perception into the sunshine of true knowledge further advance is needed. It is by the *Atman* itself that the *Atman* is gained,[1] or, as the Gita puts it, "Thou thyself knowest Thyself by Thyself, O Highest Purusha, Sender forth of beings, Light of the Shining Ones, Ruler of the World!" *Verse 15*

Even the *buddhi* shines not by its own light. Beyond it is the Light of the *Great Atman*, the Cosmic Ideation in which the Divine archetypes of past, present and future exist in one vast interpenetrative whole.[2] Here is

---

[1] Compare *Kathopanishad*, ii, 23, the famous words *yamevaisha vrinute tena labhyah*, which may be rendered "that very (*Atman*) which the disciple chooses (*i.e.* clings to), by means of that (*Atman*) is it attained."

[2] Compare Plotinus vi, 9: "Thus we come to the *Nous* (Divine Mind) almost as an object of sense: the Intellectual Kosmos is perceptible as standing above soul, father to soul ... a multiple but at once indivisible and comporting difference."

the splendid pattern of the Cosmos radiant with Divine Light, a wondrous unity of spiritual Beings.

" For There everything is transparent, nothing dark, nothing resistant; every being is lucid to every other, in breadth and depth; light runs through light. And each of them contains all within itself, and at the same time sees all in every other, so that everywhere there is all, all is all, and each all, and infinite the glory. Each of them is great; the small is great: the sun, There, is all the stars, and every star again is all the stars and sun. While some one manner of being is dominant in each, all are mirrored in every other." [1]

All that is in the world is what it is because of the reflection of some portion of that glorious Being. In it the unity of all the manifold is found. It is, as has been said before, the topmost edge of manifested being, what lies beyond is all unmanifest. The soul, united to the *buddhi* (*buddhi-yukta*), must now ascend this snowy peak of being, must see, first by the mental eye, and at last by direct spiritual vision, those Divine Glories by which the Supreme *stands* pervading all the worlds. These are the Divine Ideas spoken of by Plato, the pervading Powers (*vibhuti*) that are the subject of this chapter.

Verse 16 (marginal note: Verse 16)

The phrase "Divine Ideas" should not mislead the reader (as it has misled many intellectuals) into thinking that they are pale abstractions, the conceptual "universals" of academic philosophy.[2] These "Ideas" are not conceptual abstractions at all, but living Spiritual Powers which, as the Gita says, "stand" in their own nature eternally and are reflected in the flux of beings, giving to each its form and its essential nature, not abstracted from beings but formative of beings, the perfect types and patterns of all things here below:

> "Out of the dark it wrought the heart of man,
> Out of dull shells the pheasant's pencilled neck:
> Ever at toil, it brings to loveliness
> All ancient wrath and wreck."

To reach this Divine world is now the task of the disciple and therefore Arjuna asks:

Verse 17 (marginal note: Verse 17)

"O Yogi,[3] how may I know Thee by constant meditation? In what aspects art Thou to be thought of by me, O Glorious One?"

The Divine Realities cannot be seen by eyes of flesh; nor by, it may be added, the so-called clairvoyant eye of pseudo-occultism, an eye whose

---

[1] Plotinus, *Enneads*, v, tractate 8.

[2] The latter are only diagrams constructed by the mind, and while they may refer to, can never be the true "Divine Ideas."

[3] Note that Krishna is here addressed as " *Yogi*" because it is on this plane that the *Wondrous Yoga*, the *Yogamaishwaram*, takes place. It is here that the one unmanifested Self (*Shanta Atman*) unites with the one unmanifested Nature (*Mula-prakriti*). See previous chapter.

realm at best is that of psychic forms. The eye by which they must be seen is that of *buddhi*, the eye of spiritual vision.[1]

But though that eye is now available for the disciple he must first learn to open it and to habituate himself to its use. Just as a man, though having as his birthright mind with all its powers of thinking, yet has to learn by slow and arduous steps how to unfold those powers, so the disciple who has now united mind with *buddhi* must slowly and with effort open up its powers of vision. The mental life in which he still is, for the most part, rooted must be transmuted by the higher vision. A man born blind, but who has gained his sight, finds for some time the new sense unfamiliar and rather trusts his highly cultivated sense of touch with all its limitations than this strange power of sight which now has opened.

Therefore the Teacher now sets forth a method, a discipline by which the soul may learn to use the eye of *buddhi* and to trust its baffling, unfamiliar vision more than the familiar seeing of the mind.[2]

The verses which follow (20-42) are not to be considered as that mere empty hymning of a personal God so dear to theists. Again it must be said, the "I" who speaks is not the personal Krishna[3] but the *Great Atman*, One and manifold, pervading by Its Powers all things that are. These verses contain the practical method by which the soul may learn to use and trust its eye.

The disciple is instructed to try to see in all things, not their separate being, but the *Great Atman*, by whose Powers all have their form and nature. Each type of being on earth is what it is because of the "reflection" [4] of some aspect of that *Atman*. This "reflection" is best seen in those objects which are pre-eminent within their class, for it is in them that the Divine Archetype has best found expression. This is the meaning of the list that Krishna gives.[5] In all things, gods or men or sages, so-called "inanimate" objects or in mental qualities, "He" is to be sought out and contemplated Verse 20

---

[1] *Cf.* Hermes, vi, 4: "For all the things that fall beneath the eye are image things and pictures as it were, while these that do not meet the eyes are the realities."

[2] The mind sees by analysis and separation, splitting the unity of life into the separate aspects named and pinned like insects on the board it calls science. The *buddhi* sees the unity in all and therefore Krishna teaches Arjuna how the Divine Pervading Powers are to be looked for in the things below.

[3] This is made quite clear in verse 37, in which the personal Krishna, son of Vasudeva, is treated as quite separate from the " I " who is speaking. There are various ingenious sectarian ways of getting over this but still the plain statement remains.

[4] "We do not mean that the Idea, locally separate, shows itself in Matter like a reflection in water; the Matter touches the Idea at every point, though not by physical contact, and by dint of neighbour-hood—nothing to keep them apart—is able to absorb thence all that lies within its capacity, the Idea itself not penetrating, not approaching, the Matter, but remaining self-locked" (Plotinus, VI, v, 8).

[5] The various mythological beings and symbols that occur in this list, some of which have now ceased to play a very vivid part in even a Hindu mind, were all quite living to the man for whom the Gita was composed two or three thousand years ago. *Vittesha*, for instance, King of *Yakshas* (gnomes) is at best for us a hieroglyph which must be carefully translated; at worst, he is a charming old-world fancy. But long ago he was, for the many, an actual being as real as, say, the Eskimos to us, or, for the few, a living symbol needing no painful learning to decipher.

in the chief of every class.[1] For He indeed is verily the *Atman* in all beings, their very Self, the base on which they stand.

Verses 21-38

What makes the gods shining and powerful? It is the Light and Power of the One. What makes the *Vedas* holy, worthy of our reverence? It is the ancient Archetypal Wisdom. What is it that calls forth our aspirations in the sight of mountain peaks, calms us in sheets of water, whispers to us in trees, disturbs our hearts in animals[2] or thrills in gleaming weapons? What is it but Him shining through all these beings in spiritual Powers to which, if we give names, they are but poor translation for our weakness?

Verse 36

Even in the greatly wicked, in him who says to evil "Be thou my good," in the fierce pride of *Duryodhana*, in such a type of monstrous wickedness as Shakespeare's Richard the Third, we feel His presence compelling wonder, even admiration, in spite of all the protests of our moral nature.

We must not turn from these perceptions as mere poetic fancies, saying, as many do, that, after all, in fact an animal is but an animal; a sword, a strip of steel. What is thus felt in beings is not a fancy but something truly, if but vaguely, seen within. The disciple must cling to these intuitive perceptions and by constant meditation sharpen them to clearness until the outer forms seem unreal things through whose translucid shells the wondrous Powers shine in their gleaming splendours.

As he proceeds a change will overtake his vision. Not only will he see the spiritual Power in each form, but since these Powers are united in a living Whole, he will begin to *see*, what before he could but think, the vast interconnectedness of all things.[3]

"In our realm all is part arising from part and nothing can be more than partial; but There each being is an eternal product of a whole and is at once a whole and an individual manifestation as part but, to the keen vision There, known for the whole it is." [4]

Thus to the seeing eye all things are linked to all in a great Cosmic Harmony. Flowers in the green are seen as one with the far-distant stars gleaming for ever in the blue abyss of space. Within this six-foot frame blow all the winds of heaven and in the heart of man lie still the glittering pomp, the sometimes cruel beauty, and all the hidden secrets of long-vanished empires buried now beneath the desert sands or ocean waves.

---

[1] Compare Plotinus, vi, 9: "Things here are signs; they show therefore to the wiser teachers how the supreme God is known; the instructed priest reading the sign may enter the holy place and make real the vision of the inaccessible."

[2] In spite of man's ill-treatment of and contempt for the "lower animals" he has always felt a disturbing sense of something strange and archetypal in their being. This is the underlying cause of the "totemism" of so-called primitive peoples, of the animal-gods of the Egyptians (so distasteful to both pagan Greek and Christian) and of the animal signs in the Zodiac.

[3] These connections, vaguely intuited, give life to poetry and art. What the poet dimly senses and dares not take for more than metaphor is clearly seen by the awakened seer. It may also be added that the use of these affinities is an essential part of Kabalistic and other forms of magic, white or black.

[4] Plotinus, v, 8.

There is a story current that on certain days, if one go out to sea from the town known as *Dwarka*, beneath the waves can dimly be descried the towers and pinnacles of Krishna's island city. Legend, no doubt, for *Dwarka* was not there. Nevertheless beneath the storm-tossed surface of our hearts the vanished past still lives. Unseen within these depths the ancient wars are fought, Atlantis shines in glory, darkens with pride and falls; Sri Krishna walks the earth and Buddha leaves his home for love of men.

Nothing is lost, for ever all remains, deep in the waters of eternal Mind. He who can plunge within lives in the Cosmic Heart and sees Its mighty throbs send forth the cycling years to run their changing courses through the worlds back to the blue depths of Eternity.

It is said that in a lotus-seed exists in miniature a perfect lotus. So in that Mighty Being is the seed of all that is,[1] subtle beyond all images of sense, the shining spiritual Cosmos; Infinite seeds and yet one wondrous Seed, beyond the reach of mind, yet to be seen by Mind. Verse 39

All that is glorious, beautiful, or mighty shines by reflection of a portion of that Being. Vainly we seek on earth a symbol grand enough to adumbrate Its glories. In ancient Egypt and Chaldea the starry heaven was Its only symbol; the heaven with its interlinked and patterned stars whirling in gleaming harmonies around the pole. But all the splendours of the cosmic depths, their mind-annihilating magnitudes of time and space, symbol to all men of eternal Law and Beauty, are but a moment of the *Mighty Atman*; infinities ranged on the shoulders of infinities; a wondrous hierarchy of living spiritual Powers where each is each and each is All and all dance forth in ecstasy the Cosmic Harmony.[2] Verse 40

Vast beyond thought as is this spiritual realm, this flaming Cosmos of Divine Ideas, yet still beyond lies That, the One Eternal, the *Parabrahman*, Rootless Root of all.[3] Beyond all Gods, beyond all time and space, beyond all being even, flames Its dark transcendent Light. Verse 42

From that *Eternal Brahman*[4] issue forth the *Mighty Atman*, great beyond all thought, and all the countless starry worlds that fill the wide

---

[1] Gita, x, verses 39-42. Compare this with the so-called Naassene document. "Accordingly they (the Egyptians) declare concerning the Essence of the Seed which is the cause of all things in the world of generation, that it is none of these things, but that it begets and makes all generated things saying, ' I become what I will and am what I am.' Therefore that which moves all is unmoved; for It remains what it is, making all things, and becoming no one of the things produced" (Mead's translation).

Also compare the seed principles (*logoi spermatikoi*) of the Stoic philosophers.

[2] This Cosmic Harmony, known to Pythagoreans as the music of the spheres, was in the Vedic tradition termed rita, the cosmic order in which all the gods exist. Those who find in the *Vedas* mere chaotic polytheism and those who find incipient monotheism are alike mistaken. Unity indeed there was, but it was not the unity of a personal being but of Divine impersonal Cosmic Order within which *Indra*, *Varuna* and *Agni*, the whole pantheon of Gods, all shone and had their being.

[3] Strictly speaking, between the *Great Atman* and the *Parabrahman* are the unmanifested Two. For convenience they are here included in the Supreme Unmanifested One.

[4] Out of this unthinkable abyss which is the *Parabrahman* some have tried to make a personal God!

immensities of space. Yet so vast is Its spaceless, timeless grandeur that all these wondrous emanated worlds are as a drop taken from out the ocean, leaving Its shoreless being ever full. Therefore Sri Krishna, speaking for That *Brahman*, says, "having established this entire universe with one fragment of Myself, I remain."

> "That is the Full; this is the full;
> From that Full has this full come forth.
> Having taken the full from the Full
> Verily the Full Itself remains."[1]

---

[1] *Shanti* to *Ishopanishad.*

CHAPTER XI
THE YOGA OF THE VISION OF THE COSMIC FORM

WITH the opening of the eleventh chapter we find the disciple on the brink of a tremendous experience, one so great that many have thought it to be the final Goal beyond which naught remains. If that were so the Gita would have ended with this chapter; nevertheless, he who has seen this Vision has attained to the third stage, called by the Buddhists *Anagamin*,[1] whence but one last stage remains to tread.

The three great Secrets have been learnt so far, at least as far as *buddhi*-aided mind can grasp them. First the great Secret of the transcendental *Atman*, the source of all that is and yet Itself unmoved for ever. Under the gaze of that unchanging One streams forth the universe of finite beings, coming and going in never-ending change; while between both, the link between the two, stands the Imperishable Greatness,[2] the Spiritual Cosmos, changeless in change, changing in changelessness. _{Verses 1, 2}

The dawn has come, the shades of night have vanished; in a short while the Sun will rise. Eager for yet more Light, the disciple stands straining his eyes towards the East, aspiring to that Teacher in his heart who is, Himself, the Soul of all the world. Not knowing of the terror that the Vision holds for all that yet remains of self in him, he longs to look upon that Face which nothing that is mortal may behold.

"If Thou thinkest that by me it can be seen, Lord of the Cosmic *Yoga*, then show me Thine imperishable Self." _{Verse 4}

No fleshly eye can see that Sovereign Form. Only the *Atman*'s never-closing Eye can see the *Atman*'s self. But, for the disciple "who has made the thought in him a stranger to the world-illusion,"[3] who can pass through himself into the Life beyond, that Divine Eye is now available and flashes _{Verse 8}

---

[1] *Anagamin* literally means one who does not come again (to birth). The common view is that the *Anagamin* attains *Nirvana* direct from some higher world after death. Actually the meaning is that having attained to the *Alaya Vijnana* (the *Mahat Atman*) he is one with all and thinks no more "I die or I am born."

[2] The *Mahat Atman*.

[3] Hermes, xiii, I.

95

into dazzling, all-revealing vision.

Verse 12   A splendour bursts upon his gaze "as though ten thousand suns were blazing in the sky," and in that spiritual Light, which, though so brilliant, dazzles not the Eye, he sees the myriad Powers of the *Great Atman*. There Verse 13 in the body of that boundless Being are all the living Powers that men have symbolised as Gods, not as if standing side by side in space, but each a facet mirroring the Whole, so interfused in being, each with each, that he who sees knows not indeed whether it is one Being that he sees or many Powers.[1]

All who have seen the Vision, for to this day, as in times past, it dawns upon the gaze of all who tread the Path, know the astonishment, the rapture mixed with terror, that fills the soul as the *Great Atman* flashes into view.

Dead to all worldly things, standing outside himself, the disciple sees the great Expanse all blue with quivering supernal Light like lightnings massed in some world-ending cataclysm, the storm-tossed Ocean, glittering with souls, dizzily spinning in the dread Vortex Whirl, the terror of the Sound, throbbing in awful power through the vast Space like some great engine pulsing forth the Cosmic tides to ebb and flow throughout the Universe, and yet beyond the storm the changeless Peace, massively shining in a bliss beyond all words.

All this he sees and more that none can tell, sees with a vividness past all mere human seeing; yet all are symbols cast on the background of the Fathomless, wherein is neither Sound, nor Space, nor Sea, nor Vortex Whirl, nor any form at all.[2]

Filled with great wonder the disciple sees, and in his soul wells up the mystic Knowledge which bursts forth from his lips in an ecstatic hymn.

Verse 15   Within that boundless Form he sees the Gods, Brahma, the great creative Power, and archetypes of all things here on earth. He sees the upward Path, the contemplative *Rishis*, also the Serpent's Way spiralling downwards in divinely urged desire.[3] Mouths, all-consuming, eyes of the infinite, all-seeing vision, arms wielding all things, bellies containing Verses all; the Mace of Time's all-dominating power, the shining Discus of its 16, 17 evercircling flight, the Crown of sovereignty, all these are seen in a great blaze of boundless, world-consuming Light.

Perishing not throughout creation's ages, this Being stands for ever as the Treasure-House in which are stored the jewels of the Cosmos. As Verse 18 Cosmic Order, It maintains eternal *Dharma*, the Principle by which all things are linked to all in faultless harmony:

---

[1] Compare Plotinus, v, 8: "He who is the one God and all the gods, where each is all, blending into a unity, distinct in powers but all one god in virtue of that one divine power of many facets."
[2] This is true not only of these visions but of our ordinary experience as well. All perception is symbolic through and through. When we see a wooden door we see a symbol of a moment of the *Brahman*.
[3] See verse 5 in the Vedic Creation Hymn given in Appendix F.

> It seeth everywhere and marketh all:
> Do right—it recompenseth! Do one wrong—
> The equal retribution must be made,
> Though *Dharma* tarry long.[1]

This is the immemorial Heavenly Man, the *Adam Kadmon* of the Kabalistic wisdom; His eyes, the Sun and Moon, are life and form[2]; His mouth, a burning Fire, consumes the worlds, fife feeding on itself in ceaseless sacrifice. *Verse 19*

The consciousness that streams through three great Halls, the waking, "dreaming" and the "deep-sleep" states,[3] is agitated in its ceaseless ebb and flow by the immortal " Fourth," the Flame which all may see but none can touch. *Verse 20*

The *Maharshis* and the *Siddhas*, mighty Teachers of the past, exist inscrutably within that radiant Being. Christ, Krishna, Buddha, all are there, and he who worships one draws near to them all. *Verse 21*

Spanning the Void, leaping from earth to heaven, gleams the great Rainbow Bridge whose substance is composed of all the Gods. Upwards and downwards flash the waves of Light, weaving the many-coloured garment of the One. Here are the calm *Adityas*,[4] shining in their golden Light, and there the stormy *Maruts*,[4] thrusting downwards with their flame-tipped spears. *Verse 24*

But there is terror in the Vision too, for in that Light all forms are seen to pass. Only the Divine can live in the Divine: all that is human dies upon the threshold. All that in us which fears the so-called cruelty of nature, which trembles at the ruthless ocean waves, all that which clings to form and personality, sees Doom approaching it on flaming wings. *Verse 25*

As in an earthquake men are filled with panic terror, not so much by the actual physical dangers as by the feeling that the solid earth, unconscious symbol of stability, is rocking shudder- ingly beneath their feet, so in this Vision, self is seized by terror, seeing its old familiar landmarks vanish in the Void. Nowhere can self find any standing-place; all is dissolved into an ever-changing fiery flux.

The hundred sons of *Dhritarashtra* who are the facets of the lower self, *Bhishma* and *Drona*, faith and old tradition, *Karna*, the mighty warrior, nobly clinging to ideals but finding them in matter, all these are swallowed up in the great teeth of never-resting Time. These selves of ours, to which we cling so fiercely, are streams of psychic states linked each to each by changeless causal law; and all these streams wind through the fields of *Verse 26* *Verse 28*

1 *Light of Asia.*
2 See *Prashna Upanishad*, i, 5.
3 See Appendix C.
4 See Glossary.

Time like rivers flowing swiftly to the sea.[1]

Verse 29   No forms are permanent; all come and go according to their *karma*. Even the worlds, circling around the sun, are but as moths which flutter round the lamp; their age-old rocks and "everlasting hills" melt into nothing like the down on the moth's wings. Nothing remains but *karma*'s subtle streams, flowing invisible to men, yet stronger than fine steel, linking each pattern of the universe to all that went before.

Terror unutterable fills all self in man as he beholds this world-devouring Fire. The image of a man-like, extra-cosmic God, Creator of the worlds, is seen to be a dream of men's weak hearts, a dream that serves to hide from human eyes the awful depths of Being's shoreless sea. "This world order, the same for all beings, neither any of the Gods hath made, nor any man; but it was always, is and shall be ever-living Fire, kindled in measure and quenched in measure." [2]

Verse 31   If one of unfirm heart should see this Vision he would recoil within the self of use and wont, not daring further question of the Infinite; but the strong soul of the well-tried disciple, not rooted in the self but in the *buddhi*, goes out in aspiration for yet deeper knowledge, seeking the One beyond these flaming ramparts. What is this ever-flowing Emanation, this Cosmic Fire that beats in flaming waves upon his heart?

And with the aspiration comes the answer; a Voice is heard where Verse 32 there is none to speak; letters of Light float on the waves of Fire. A sudden insight comes and the disciple knows that what he sees is the great fluc of Time,[3] Time that is death to all things save the Soul. "Thus at the roaring loom of Time I ply, and weave for God the garment thou seest Him by."[4] All forms are seen to come and go, over-mastered by the cyclic waves of Time, but this insight brings no tragic sense of loss such as inspired Villon's *Where are the Snows of Yester Year?* Rather, there comes a sense of great deliverance, a sense of standing on the Eternal Rock round which the surging waves for ever beat in vain. As from a mountain height the traveller sees the road winding on towards his destination, so, from this vantage-point of insight, the disciple sees his Path and knows for certain

---

[1] Compare the experience of the Buddha on the night of attaining the *Sambodhi*: "With the Divine eye which far surpasses human vision I saw beings in the act of passing hence and of reappearing elsewhere—beings high and low, fair or foul to view, in bliss or woe; I saw them all faring according to their pasts" (*Majjhima Nikaya*, sutta iv).
Compare also the Buddhist term for the individual self, santana, meaning "continuous flow."
[2] Heracleitus, Fragment D 30.
[3] The Time here spoken of is not the same as the abstract times of mathematical physics. The latter is a mere mode of measurement of certain relations between phenomena, and no very clear reason seems to be given for the fundamental character of real time - namely, its irreversibility. The Time here referred to is the great prime mover of the universe. It has its root in Consciousness, of which, indeed, it is the active aspect. The mental construct of four-dimensional Space-Time continuum seens to have little relevance here. To gain an understanding of real Time the best starting-point is the power of selective attention found in consciousness.
[4] Goethe.

that the obstacles will pass.

From the Goal issues forth the Path; to It the Path returns; both are within the Soul. Coming and going, bondage and liberation, all are illusions which the light of jnana dispels. For ever shines the Goal, shining in golden glory; seen from another angle It itself becomes the Path. The Goal, the Path and he who treads that Path are all the same; naught is there anywhere save the One Being which, breathless, breathes eternally within Itself.

It is impossible to state in words this wondrous insight. All things remain the same yet all are changed. Time flashes bodily into Eternity; the streaming Flux itself is the Eternal, which, though It moves unceasingly, moves not at all.

This is the insight which makes the disciple what the Buddhists termed an *Anagamin*, one who comes to birth no more. Life and death have vanished in the Light of the Eternal, and though yet a portion of the Path remains to tread, it will be trodden with the knowledge that by Krishna Himself "already are the foes all overcome" and that no separate treader of the Path remains. Verse 33

Crowned with the diadem of insight,[1] the initiated disciple gazes into the awful Mystery of Light in rapt adoration of the Eternal, clothed in Its flaming Robes, and the mystic Knowledge that now floods his soul pours forth in yet a further hymn of ecstasy.

These Hymns, parallels to which may be seen in the *Poemandres and Secret Sermon on the Mount* of the Hermetic books, are not to be confused with those of ordinary exoteric religion. They are the natural outflow of the mind seeking to give expression in mental terms to the great Knowledge that now streams upon it, the ferment that takes place as all the lower undergoes alchemical transmutation at the touch of the Higher. The difference between the two Hymns should be carefully noted. The first expresses chiefly awestruck terror as the disciple sees his universe dissolve into the Cosmic Fire; the second gives expression to the rapture with which he sees, within the waves of flame, the shining spiritual Cosmos.

Gazing within, he sees that all is ruled by living spiritual Law. Two mighty tidal urges rule the worlds and both of them are living spiritual Powers. One is the movement of the *Rakshasas*, fleeing as in fear to all the quarters of the Universe. This is the great outgoing Creative Breath by which not only is the universe spread forth in space, but all the inner life of thought and feeling flows outwards seeking whom it may devour.[1] This Verse 36

---

[1] Note that the disciple is now (verse 35) referred to as "the Crowned one." This is a reference to the Crown of Knowledge given to the Initiate. A parallel is to be seen in the *Atef* crown worn by *Osiris* in the Egyptian Mystic Ritual and, according to Marsham Adams, placed on the head of the Initiate after he has passed through the pylons and stands before the Throne.

[2] Compare the *Pauranik* accounts of creation in which *Brahma* first created *Rakshasas* who promptly attempted to devour him. That is to say, the outgoing forces would, if left to themselves, dissipate the universe at once. The technical term for this outgoing is *Pravritti*.

is the urge of self-assertion, self-expansion, survival of the fittest, "nature red in tooth and claw." Here is the inner cause of war and all the selfish life of competition, each for himself and devil take the hindmost, but here, as well, the force behind man's mind, wheeling in ever-widening circles to receding frontiers.

The second movement, symbolised by hosts of *Siddhas*, is the *nivritti*, Homeward-flowing Tide. By this all the rich treasures of experience, the Fruits of the World Tree, are gathered in once more to the One Life like mighty rivers flowing homewards to the sea.[1]

He sees the *Mighty Atman*, source of both these Tides, the Primal Man of all the ancient Mysteries, the Cosmic Treasure-House, the Realm of shining Light, Knower and Known both fused in unity. Glimpsed through the robes of Cosmic Ideation stands the unmoved Eternal, poised aloof, Being, Non-being, *That* beyond them both, the Nameless One, worshipped alone by silence of the mind.

Verses 37, 38

Verse 39 The seven great Cosmic planes, here symbolised as Gods, are all within that One, and though the disciple seeks to pour forth all his soul in utter reverence, he knows not where to turn, for now he sees that even *Verse 40* the very earth on which he stands is holy, and that around, above, below, within, without, everywhere is the One and only One, containing all, from lowest earthy clod to that unmanifest, transcendent Self whose Light for ever shines beyond the worlds.[2]

No longer can he think that He whom he has worshipped, the Teacher in his heart, Friend of his nights and days, is any Verses personal being, man or superman or God. Rather he sees that, be the Form what it may, it was the Light of the Eternal which, shining through loved but yet symbolic eyes, has led him on the Path and is both Path and Goal.

Verses 41-43

But yet, while he is human, there must still be Forms for him. He *Verse 44* cannot bear for long the blaze of Light that floods upon him, shattering all his being. No human mind and body can for long endure upon the summits of eternal snow-clad peaks. He must return once more to lower levels, the dazzling Light be veiled in the familiar forms of Father, Lover, Friend; for still the fourth stage of the Path remains to tread and, while he needs a body, he must see the Light in human form.[3]

---

[1] For further discussion of these two movements see Chapter XVI.

[2] Compare the magnificent hymn of Hermes Trismegistus:

"Whither, again, am I to turn my eyes to sing Thy praise: above, below, within, without?

There is no way, no place is there about Thee, nor any other thing of things that are.

All are in Thee; all are from Thee, O Thou who givest all and takest naught,

For Thou ... art all and there is nothing else which Thou art not." Hermetic Corpus, v, 10.

[3] The *chaturbhuja* form of verse 46 should be translated "*four-limbed*" (*i.e.* two arms and two legs) and not, as usually done, "*four-armed.*" The word *bhuja* means limb as well as arm, and verses 49 and 51 clearly show that the form in question was a *human* one, four-limbed in contrast to the thousand arms and legs of the symbolic vision. The *Vishnu* form, no doubt, has four arms; but in the earliest texts, such as the *Mahabharata*, Krishna has always the normal human two.

For this interpretation I am indebted to my friend Pandit Jagadish Chandra Chatterji, Vidya Varidhi.

Therefore he sees once more the Form of his loved Teacher in his own heart and in the hearts of all, though, as reminder of the glorious Vision, the Form is Crowned and bears the Mace and Discus, symbols of the Lord Verse 46 of Time. He knows that He who sits within his heart is throned beyond all Time and that, however thick the fight may press upon him, his final victory is sure, since He who rules his heart rules all the worlds.

Thus ends the Vision seen by union with the Self (*atma yogat*), ends Verse 47 as a vision though its Knowledge will remain for ever in the heart of the disciple. Henceforth that inner Knowledge must be the master-light of all his seeing, must make "the noisy years seem moments in the being of the eternal Silence." Never may he forget what he has seen; always must he realise "the voidness of the seeming full, the fullness of the seeming void."[1] For him, not as a poet's intuition, but in sheer fact, will it be true that

> " ... in a season of calm weather
> Though inland far we be,
> Our souls have sight of that immortal sea
> Which brought us hither;
> Can in a moment travel thither—
> And see the children sport upon the shore,
> And hear its mighty waters rolling evermore." [2]

Not Gods, the great impersonal waves of Light, nor men, the separate Verses selves of mind and body, "none but thyself," the immortal soul of man, 47-54 has ever or will ever see this Cosmic Form. No mystic rites, no study of philosophy, no harsh austerities, no alms or offerings, can show It, for all these are of the mind alone. Only the power of love, the Soul's own power, love that for ever seeks to give itself, straining towards Eternity, can bring about the union of the self with the One Self by which alone the Cosmic Form is seen and ultimately entered.

Therefore the chapter ends with a reiteration of the Path, a purely spiritual Path, one quite distinct from all the mystic rites and outer pieties that most men term religion:

"Giving the self in love to Me, with Me as Goal, doing all actions for Me (the One Life in all), devoid of all attachment to the forms, free from hostility to any being, man comes to Me, O Arjuna." [3]

---

[1] *The Voice of the Silence.*
[2] Wordsworth's *Ode on the Intimations of Immortality.*
[3] This verse has been described by *Shankaracharya* as giving the quintessence of the whole Gita.

CHAPTER XII
THE YOGA OF DEVOTION

IT has already been pointed out that the Vision of the Cosmic Form is not the same as the attainment of the final Goal. To interpret this or the Beatific Vision of Western mysticism as the Goal would be to ignore the whole structure of the Gita. The Vision is, what it purports to be, a vision, not the attainment, and we have seen that at its end the disciple returns to the lower level, the level of form, once more. Before the Goal is reached he will have to learn to live entirely in the Reality, so to transmute his whole nature that not an atom of the lower shall remain unredeemed. This subject, however, will be referred to again later. In the meanwhile we have to deal with a certain problem that has arisen out of the experience of this Vision.

The disciple has seen the great Cosmic Form, the *Mighty Atman*, the One Life manifesting in the world of beings, and he has been told (xi, 54) that by devotion alone can that Form be seen and entered. At the same time, he has also caught a glimpse (xi, 37) of the unchanging Unmanifest behind the Cosmic process and the doubt occurs to him whether this devotion to the manifested Form, this acting for the One Life in the hearts of all, can ever lead him beyond the manifest. Doubtless, devotion to the Life of all will take him to that Life; but will it take him further? Will it not leave him there, just as devotion to the Gods strands men in the enjoyment Verse 1 of heavenly bliss? Knowing that beyond even that *Mighty Atman* lies the indestructible Unmanifest, should not he rather resolutely turn his back on all manifestation, abstract himself from every trace of form and bend all his energies on one supreme attempt to bring about the flight of the alone to the Alone? Are these two separate Paths and, if so, which is better?

Verse 2 To this question Krishna replies that both he who is devoted to Himself as the One Life in all, and he who worships the Ineffable, Unthinkable, Verse 5 Eternal attain to Him, but that the latter is a Path of surpassing difficulty for those who are embodied—that is to say, for those who have the slightest trace of self-identification with their bodies.

To understand this answer we must remember that in chapter three, verse 4 *et seq.*, the attempt to win through to the Unmanifested Goal by a process of pure abstraction and inactivity, the method of some *Sankhyas*, has been condemned as utterly impracticable. Certainly it is not by turning one's back on all activity and refusing any commerce with form of any kind that the Unmanifest is reached, for such a process is impossible. It may be possible to toy in thought with such a path but in reality it is scarcely a path at all. The Homeward Path must be a gathering-up of all the cosmic Fruits, not a retreat, negating all experience, as if the cosmic process were a cosmic blunder which never should have been.

There is, in fact, but one Path, and if we compare verse 4 of the present chapter, which defines the character of him who worships the Unmanifest, with verses 13-19, which give the character of him who is devoted to the Life in all, we see that they are, in effect, the same.

Not by attempting an impossible rejection of the world of sense-experience but by "restraining and subduing the senses," not by trying to turn his back on all forms but by "regarding all forms with an equal vision," not by achieving a stony indifference to the joys and sorrows of the world but by being "devoted to the welfare of all beings," does the true worshipper of the Unmanifest Eternal attain his Goal. *Verse 4*

If, then, both Paths are essentially the same, wherein lies the special difficulty of the Path of the Unmanifested? It lies in the fact that the worshipper of the Unmanifested has nothing to which he can fasten his mind, for that One is beyond all objects of sense, beyond even all concepts of the mind. The point has been excellently stated by Plotinus: "The main difficulty is that awareness of this Principle [*i.e.* the One] comes neither by knowing nor by the pure Intellection [*noesis*] that discovers the Intellectual Beings [the Spiritual Powers seen in the Vision], but by a presence overpassing all knowledge . . . . Our way takes us beyond all knowing; there may be no wandering from Unity; knowing and knowable must all be left aside; every object of thought, even the highest, we must pass by, for all that is good is later than This and derives from This as from the sun all the light of day." [1] *Verse 5*

Even if the disciple thinks of It as God or as the Eternal Mind he still, as Plotinus says, "thinks of It too meanly," for "God" connotes ideas of personality and the Eternal Mind is "lower" than the One, being the level of the Cosmic Ideation. Into that Silence how shall the disciple soar, what steps are there to help him on his way? Not only is the One beyond all thought but also the great wings which bear the soul upon its upward flight, the wings of love, beat vainly in that Void and the bruised soul falls back in desolation, losing the forms but finding not the One beyond all form.

---

[1] Plotinus, vi, 9, 3; the parts in brackets are for clearness.

Fatally easy is it for the soul to sink back on the earth, loveless and sterile. Appearances may be preserved but yet the heart within is eaten all away and the disciple treads the *false* unmanifested Path, rejecting forms as *maya*, fearing even to do an act of mercy lest some bondage for his soul be the result. "To perish doomed is he, who out of fear of Mara refrains from helping man lest he should act for Self." [1]

Therefore Sri Krishna recommends the other Path, the manifested Path through the One Life. The One is the same One, the Goal the same, but on this Path that One is manifest within the hearts of all. This is the way that Plato, too, has mentioned, rising from love of one to love of many, from love of form to love of spiritual beauty, and so by steps to That which is beyond. This also is the Path the *Gopis* trod, first loving Krishna in His sensuous beauty, then feeling in their own hearts and, lastly, with all selfhood gone, rising to union with the One Eternal. [2]

Verses 6, 7

On this Path the disciple does all actions not for himself but for the one loved Figure. For love he acts, for love he speaks and thinks, and so by love he rises swiftly to the Goal. Where there is love no sacrifice can be too great to be performed with joy. Even animals will give their lives for love and countless men have gladly gone to hideous deaths, counting their pains a privilege that so the loved one, country, man, or God, be served thereby.

> " In this is seen why there is hope for man
> And where we hold the wheel of life at will." [3]

Here is the power lying in all men's hearts by which to scale the peaks of the Eternal. But, as its place within the Gita shows, there must first be some knowledge, some desire to tread the inward Path and reach the Goal. Without this knowledge, faith, or aspiration there is no urge to soar beyond the body, and love itself, dragged in the dust by self, turns to desire and works a hideous ruin.

Nevertheless, if guided by knowledge and aspiration, there is no force which will so powerfully bear the soul upwards as that of love. This can be seen by its power to transmute and render beautiful, if only temporarily, the lives of even quite ordinary men. A selflessness which may take the yogi many years of effort to attain along the path of conscious mind-control and which, even then, may be a hothouse plant, constantly menaced by the cold wind which comes from fancying oneself a being apart from other men, may grow quite healthily like a great forest tree in the rich soil of

---

[1] *Voice of the Silence.*

[2] For substantiation of this view, one which runs counter to some accepted ideas, read *Srimad Bhaga-wata*, x, 29, v. 12; x, 47, v. 9 (and many others); x, 82, v. 48, which clearly set forth these three stages. For the middle stage many references might be given.

[3] *Light of Asia.* The original reads "thee," not "this."

love.

It is just the absence of knowledge and aspiration that makes the transmuting power of love so short-lived as a rule. Love which has power, when guided by true knowledge, to carry even the body upwards with it in its soaring flight, is blinded and its wings are clipped by the dark ignorance that sees no reality but that of outward things. Thus it falls down upon the earth, only to share the fate of all things earthly:

> "And or ever the garden's last petals are shed,
> In the lips that had whispered,
> the hearts that had lightened,
> Love lies dead."

Therefore Sri Krishna urges the disciple to place his mind, united with the *buddhi*, in Him and thus to live in the immortal Life that is in all.[1] This "Him" will be at first the human form that draws in love the heart of the disciple. That Form, idealised by love and worship, will be a symbol of the Eternal Mind and will transform into Itself the human soul. Once more to quote Plotinus: "We shape ourselves into the Nous (Eternal Mind); we make over our soul in trust to Nous and set it firmly in That; then what That sees, the soul will waken to see; it is through Nous that we have vision of the Unity." Thus, *if the eye of knowledge has been opened*, the Form will seat itself within the heart and be a window through which the soul takes flight into the blue. *Verse 8*

The power to centre all the being in the Eternal Mind will not, however, be attained at once. *Abhyasa*, or constant practice, is required. The process is described in *Shwetashwatara Upanishad* with the aid of a metaphor taken from the production of fire by the friction of two sticks: "Having made one's body (the lower self) the lower fire-stick and the *Pranava* (the symbol of the Light of consciousness) the upper, by the friction of continued practice (*abhyasa*) of meditation, one should see the God hidden within." *Verse 9*

In plain words, the practice is one of constant withdrawal from the desire-nature and constant self-identification with the higher levels. This effort is twofold. In the first place there must be the effort to churn out the fire, as it were, the attempt to isolate by analytic meditation on experience the watching Self from the participating self. In the second place there must be the effort of the will to identify one's being with the former and from there to rule the latter. If this twofold practice is persisted in it will inevitably culminate in the ability to centre oneself permanently in the Eternal Mind.

If, however, the disciple finds himself as yet unable to perform this *Verse 10*

---

[1] It must be remembered that love is rooted in the *buddhi*. See footnote to Chapter VIII, p. 74.

meditative practice, he should devote himself to Krishna's service. All life, whether in men, in animals, or plants, is a manifestation of the One Eternal Life which in a thousand forms seeks to express Itself in mastery of matter. Behind the struggling forms, behind the petty personalities of men, surge the great tides of Life, beating in tireless power against the narrow confines of the forms. Let the disciple live in such a way that all his acts will help that Life to manifest. Let him "help Nature and work on with her," striving incessantly with all the obstacles that thwart the beauty, bliss and power that are, even now, within the hearts of all. And thus, forgetful of himself, a time will come when he will find himself one with that Life to which his heart is given; performing all his deeds for Krishna's sake, he will attain the Goal.

Verse 11   If even selfless, love-inspired action is out of reach yet one way still remains: he may perform his actions for himself but yet renounce the fruits. Unable to attain the level of action for the welfare of all beings, let him act for himself but from a sense of duty. Let him do what is right, resigning all the fruits into the hands of that disposing Power which some call God, others, Eternal Law.[1] In order to achieve this duty- prompted action he must take refuge in the *Yoga* of Krishna, the *Sovereign Yoga* in which the Eternal Light unites with forms and yet is ever separate. In practice this means that he must be refuged in the *buddhi*, the faculty which gives decisive knowledge. In still earlier stages, when the *buddhi* is as yet out of reach, it means that he must unite his lower mind with " Sanjaya," the voice of the higher speaking as conscience, and make that voice the guide and ruler of all his acts. The voice of conscience is, as we have seen before, in some sense a "reflection" of the *buddhi*, the chief difference being that, while the *buddhi* sees the truth as an all-embracing whole, the con-science, as befits a principle on the hither side of individuation, sees but a single point, the point needed at the moment, and speaks with certainty concerning that alone.

The *buddhi* is a faculty that all possess though few make use of it. It is the Light that shines between the eyes, the Voice that speaks in silence in the heart. To see that Light the fleshly eyes must close, to hear that Voice the fleshly ears be deaf. Only when, for the time at least, the clamour of desire is stilled can that internal monitor be heard which is the Voice of Krishna. Guided by that Voice the disciple will see before him the clear path of duty and, if he treads it, find himself beyond the conflict of his heart's desires.

Verse 12   This is the easiest path. To clamour for an easier one than this is to cry, child-like, for the moon, to flutter feeble wings against the iron ramparts

---

[1] The difference between the former type of action and this is that, while the former disciple acts with the thought of service of the Life in all, the latter acts without any such definite thought but does what seems to be right for him himself. The former feeds the hungry out of love, the latter because he knows that it is right to be charitable.

of Eternity, to ask for what has never been nor, indeed, ever shall be. Renunciation of the fruits of action to follow duty's path has thus been praised as best because it is the easiest of all paths, and from its practice all the rest will follow. Renouncing fruits, the heart will fill with peace and in that peace the *yoga* of practice will be possible. From practice follows knowledge of the Truth and that unchanging state of meditation in which, waking or sleeping, in action or repose, the inner Self will live in the Eternal.

But some will ask why, at this stage, is all this talk of inability, why this insistence on the easier path? Surely the earlier stages have been long ago accomplished; has not the glorious Cosmic Form been seen? Such a question shows a lack of knowledge about the way of climbing on this Path. Great heights, indeed, have been attained, but not by the whole being. A climber on a mountain face first reaches for a hand-hold on the rock above him and, that having been securely grasped, pulls with great effort his whole body upwards. Just so the climber of the Path aspires with all that which is best in him, attains a hand-hold on the heights of vision, but then must pull his lower nature upwards till his whole being stands firmly on the summit.

Plotinus too asks the question how it is that the soul cannot keep the level it has achieved, and answers that it is " because it has not yet escaped wholly: but there will be the time of vision unbroken, the self hindered no longer by any hindrance of body. Not that those hindrances beset that in us which has veritably seen; it is the other phase of the soul that suffers, and that only when we withdraw from vision and take to knowing by proof, by evidence, by the reasoning processes of the mental habit."

Hence all the recapitulation in the teaching. That which was done for part must now be done again for the whole being that all may be regenerate, so that the flashing light of vision may change into the steady blazing of the sun shining beyond the darkness.

Sri Krishna now goes on to set forth, in verse thirteen to the end, the characteristics of the follower of the path of *bhakti*. It has already been stated that these characteristics are the same in substance as those of the follower of the true path of the Unmanifested. Too often is the path of bhakti mistaken for an abandonment to a frothy, uncontrolled emotionalism. What the real path of *bhakti* is may be seen from a study of these verses. The qualities enumerated must be built into his character by the disciple.

Bearing ill-will to none, he looks on all with love and great compassion, Verse 13 for he knows that He who smiles as friend and He who frowns as foe are One, the One great Life, struggling to manifest through countless passing forms.

Knowing that all that comes to him of joy or grief is but the fruit of Verse 14 his own actions in the past, he is content and strives for nothing finite but, with the mind clinging through *buddhi* to the One Eternal, stands like a

107

Verse 15 rock amidst the surge of Time. To none is he a source of grief nor does he let himself feel grief at other's words or deeds, for he knows well that pain inevitably returns to him who caused it and he cares not to be the cause of pain, even the unwitting cause, to those who are in fact his own true Self. He who feels grief at others' words is like a wall reflecting back that grief upon the causer, but he who puts aside all fear, elation, or impatient anger makes himself like the sea, which buries all in peace. By this means the sum of pain and hatred in the world is actually decreased, and thus we understand the meaning of the Buddha's words: "Not by hatred but by love does hatred end; this the eternal Law."

Verse 16   Seeking nothing for himself, he renounces every undertaking, that is to say, he renounces the fruits of all his actions, for, as will be shown later,[1] the renunciation of action itself is neither fitting nor even possible for one who is embodied. Acting solely for the One who is in all, his acts are expert, passionless and pure. Note the word expert (*daksha*). There are some who in the name of devotion give up their grip on life and muddle through all things, making spirituality an excuse for unpracticalness. The true disciple is no mere ecstatic dreamer, one so dazzled by the white eternal Light that he sees not his way among the shadows here. Rather, since "yoga is skill in action," he shows by the fact that he performs all actions better than other men, that this Path leads to mastery of the world, not to a weak withdrawal.

Verses
17, 18   If skill in action is one of the definitions of yoga, balance of mind (*samatwa*) is the other.[2] The ordinary man is ruled by the pairs of opposites, cold and heat, pleasure and pain, friendship and enmity, attraction and repulsion. His life is one perpetual oscillation between these pairs, but the yogi is one whose mind is balanced beyond their sway and whose life is guided, not by the blind forces of attraction and repulsion, but by one deep-seated urge to give himself in service of the one great Life of all.

Even ideas of good and evil, as those words are understood by men, no longer sway his acts. Those two great words, which all invoke so freely to justify their acts or to condemn their enemies, are, at the best, constructions of the mind, and he now lives rooted in realms beyond. He thus transcends them both and knows but one great Law, to help the play of the Eternal Life as It shines forth or hides Itself in forms.

Verse 19   Whether his actions bring him praise or blame, whether they harmonise with men's ideas of moral law or, as may sometimes happen, they depart entirely from what most men, even most good men, think right, is a matter of indifference to him. This may seem dangerous doctrine but it is the truth. What most men call ethics is an affair of actions and their consequences and, as we have seen, the disciple is one who has renounced

---

[1] See Gita, xviii, verses 2 and 11, where the subject is treated in full.
[2] Gita, ii, verse 48.

all concern with personal consequences. He is not lawless for he knows one all-transcending Law—obedience to the voice of the Great Teacher in his heart.[1] That Soundless Voice, speaking within his heart, drowns for him all the clamorous judgments of the world. Listening ever to the Voice of that inner Lord, he pursues his way "unperturbed as the earth is unperturbed, firm as a pillar, clear as a waveless lake."[2]

Like the pure mountain air that blows among the pines, fertilising all *Verse 19* and yet attached to none, the disciple moves about amidst the throng of men. Whether he lives in crowded cities or on lonely mountain peaks he is a Homeless One, for though he may fulfil all social duties, yet neither family, nor caste, nor race holds him in bondage. In the words of Hermes, he is "one who has struck his tent," and though he may not wear the outer garb of a *sanyasi*, yet of no place in all the world does he feel "this is mine; here I belong."

Such is the path of *bhakti*. Those who follow it, not for the sake of their *Verse 20* own soul's salvation, but as the service[3] of that one Eternal Wisdom which gives true Life to all who drink its waters, they, the beloved disciples, shine like lights amidst the darkness, servants of the Eternal, crest-jewels of the world.

---

[1] This should not be taken as supporting ordinary amorality: these words apply *solely* to the disciple who is selfless enough always to hear the Voice of the Teacher, balanced enough always to discriminate it from other voices, and devoted enough always to obey its commands. Till then, no merely intellectual insight into their limitations should justify a man in disregarding the accepted moral laws. The fate that overtook Nietzsche stands as a solemn warning.

[2] *Dhammapada*, 95.

[3] The word *paryupasana* has the primary meaning of "to attend upon, to serve." The usual rendering as "worship" is a secondary one, and obscures the meaning here.

CHAPTER XIII
THE YOGA OF DISTINCTION BETWEEN THE FIELD AND THE KNOWER OF THE FIELD

WE have now reached the beginning of the third section of the Gita, and before commencing the study of the actual chapter it is necessary to say a few words of a general nature. In this last block of six chapters are contained detailed teachings of a philosophic nature. Many of them have been outlined before, but to have set them forth in full in the earlier chapters would have interrupted the flow of the exposition. Moreover, too much emphasis on systematic explanation during the earlier stages of the Path is apt to develop intellectual grasp at the cost of intuitive perception. But, as cannot be too strongly emphasised, the Path is the path to mastery of the world, and now that the disciple has a firm hand-hold on the heights of vision, it is necessary that his intellect, suffused by the Spiritual Light, should have a clear grasp of the principles of the cosmos in which he is to work. Hence the effect of slight anticlimax that some readers of the Gita find in these chapters.

The first thing that has to be understood is the division between consciousness and the objects which that consciousness observes. If we examine our experience we find that it is composed of a number of concrete forms all lit up by the light of consciousness.[1] This is the distinction between the Field—that is, the field of consciousness—and the Knower of the Field, the clear light of awareness itself. Reflection will show that the physical body which the ignorant foolishly suppose to be the self is but the focus in which the forms or data of our sense-experience are, as it were, collected. The materialist's idea of the body as standing in its own right, as a collection of flesh, bones, nerves and so forth, is an artificial mental construction obtained by abstraction from conscious experience, useful, like many other abstractions, for purposes of scientific understanding but an irrelevance in the realm of metaphysics.

But the analysis of experience does not stop here. If the disciple

---

[1] See Appendix A.

abstracts the light of the witnessing consciousness from all the witnessed forms, the forms of sense, of feeling, or of thought, he will perceive at once that the light is not something which is different in different beings, but something like the sunshine which is the same whether illuminating the blue sea or the red earth. That light of consciousness, though associated with an individual point of view, is something which can only be described as all-pervading, something which, however different may be the Fields which are illumined, is the same in an ant as in a man, the same even, though science may not yet be ready to admit it, in a piece of rock as in a living being.

The disciple is now in a position to understand why Sri Krishna says *Verse 2* that He, the *Atman*, the all-seeing Consciousness, is the Knower of the Field in all Fields. If he will follow up this distinction between the Field and its Knower in his own heart, the disciple will find himself on the highroad to an understanding of the Cosmos; he will have a clue to guide him through the mazes of this world.

The beginning lies here in the midst of our sense-experience, for it must be emphasised that the Gita's teaching is not concerned with wondrous far-off things but with what lies right here to hand, would we but open our eyes and see. Again it must be said: "What is There is here; what is not here is nowhere." So clearly shines this truth that he who has seen it once cannot understand why he was blind so long. He has lit his lamp and truly the effect is like a sudden shining of a light in a dark place. "Within you is the Light of all the world": so all the ancient Seers have always said and now their words blaze with a vivid light in which all false belief and superstitions die like candles in the sun. "Knowledge as to the Field and the Knower of the Field, that in my opinion is Wisdom."

The Field, or content of experience, has been analysed by the ancient *Verse 5* Teachers into twenty-four *tattvas*, or principles. First come the five great elements, known symbolically as earth, water, fire, air and space.[1] Connected with these are the five contents of our sense-experience, smell, taste, visual form, touch and sound. Next come the eleven senses, five the faculties by which we gain knowledge of the external world, five those by which we react upon that world, and the eleventh the (lower) mind, the mind which functions as the common inner sense. Then comes the ego centre (*ahan-kara*), elsewhere called higher *manas*, the *buddhi* (here, as often taken with *mahat*, being the intuition which gives knowledge of that Cosmic Ideation), and lastly *Mula-prakriti* itself, the great unmanifested matrix of all forms.[2]

These principles constitute the frame or skeleton on which the universe of forms is built. It should be noted that only the lowest of them

[1] See Appendix H.
[2] Space forbids more than the merest enumeration of these *tattvas*. For a detailed study of them the reader is referred to any book on the *Samkhya*, and especially to the excellent account given in J. C. Chatterji's *India's Outlook on Life* (Kailash Press, New York).

Verse 6   are what we call material and that the other levels are what we should class as mental. Their modifications are known to us in the form of desire, aversion, pleasure, pain, thought, feeling and so forth, but nevertheless all of them are objective to the light of consciousness and make up in totality the content of experience, for it is to be observed that the feelings and thoughts, no less than the sensations, are analysable into a content-form and the awareness of it.

Verses 7-10   There follows a list of qualities which are said to constitute Wisdom in the sense, that is, that they are the qualities which lead up to Wisdom. They are all calculated to cause a perception of the fact that all these objective forms are not the Self, or, in the Buddha's words, "this is not mine, I am not this, this is not my Self." [1] Thus is brought about a cessation of that process of projection by which the Light is bound Verse n. within the

Verse 11   passing forms and the Eternal Wisdom is attained, the knowledge of the ever-changeless Self, witnessing all and yet attached to none.

Verse 12   For that Eternal Self is what is to be known, "which being known immortality is enjoyed." It is the great transcendental *Atman*[2] which, being unmanifest, is neither being nor non- being. It is the one Subject of all objectivity whatever, everywhere having hands and feet, everywhere ears and eyes. When it is said that "It standeth enveloping all" it is no piece of

Verse 13   meaningless religious rhetoric but a plain description of that wondrous *seeing* Light, that great "awaring" holding in Its bosom each grain of dust in all the countless worlds.

One of the greatest difficulties in understanding such books as the Gita lies in the fact that we have got used to reading them in a special "holy" mood in which, even if we "believe" the facts described, we surround them with a supernatural aura, thus placing them out of relation with the actual world of life. But this is fatal; we must learn to see that what is being described is what is here around us and can be seen just now even though long ages may elapse before we plumb the shoreless Sea of Light.

The Ancient Wisdom is inscribed in glowing letters in the *akasha* of the heart: let the disciple plunge within and read its message for himself. He will find that the deathless Consciousness within, though separate from all the organs of sense, yet shines with their powers. In fact the apparent

Verse 14   power of the eye to see depends entirely on the power of vision inherent in that Light which sees through the eye but which the eye does not see; which hears through the ear but which the ear does not hear; which thinks through the mind but which the mind does not think.

"It is the unseen Seer, the unheard Hearer, the unthought Thinker.

---

[1] *Majjhima Nikaya*, i, 135.

[2] The Gita here uses the term *param Brahma* but what is meant is the Unmanifested Self (see the chapter on Gita viii), what the *Kathopanishad* terms the *Shanta Atman*, for the *parabrahman* itself is not strictly speaking an object of knowledge at all. For most purposes, however, the two may be taken as one and, indeed, are often so considered. See Appendix E.

Other than It there is no Seer, no hearer, no thinker. It is the Self, the Inner Ruler, the Deathless." [1]

It supports everything in the sense that It holds all forms within Its embrace, and were Its support withdrawn, even for a moment, all things would collapse at once. Witnessing all, It is attached to naught, so that experiences of pleasure and pain are as one to Its impartial gaze. Although It is the enjoyer of all qualities yet It itself is free from quality (*nirguna*). In fact, this qualitylessness or "neutrality" is, notwithstanding the views of certain theologians, one of the first aspects to be noticed.

Though the Light shines within the hearts of men and it is in the heart that It is first perceived, it would be a mistake to suppose that It is only there and not in the outer world as well.[2] The heart is a focus through which It shines but It is equally "outside" us, for the entire content of experience floats in Its all-supporting waves: Verse 15

> "As a cloud that hides the moon, so matter veils
> The Face of Thought." [3]

So subtle is It that, though all-pervading, It is unperceived by men and, though "nearer to us than breathing," yet there is no cosmic depth so far away but It is farther still. From Its profound abyss this universe in which we live and all the island universes in the Cosmos are seen to shrink into a starry cluster no bigger than a man's hand.

Its firm immovability supports the universal "changeless" laws of science and yet that firmness is a living one, and gleams with inner motion whence arises all the movement in the Cosmos.

Just as the sun, or, better still, the daylight, is one and yet is, as it were, distributed in all reflecting objects, so is the Light a perfect unbroken unity notwithstanding that It appears divided by self-identification with the separate forms. In speaking of It we cannot avoid the language of paradox. It has already been said that a certain "neutrality" is one of Its most characteristic features, and yet it would be entirely wrong to think of that neutrality as something dull and featureless; rather, it is a calm and shining bliss. Verse 16

Similarly, it is only too easy to misunderstand Its actionless-ness which, together with the neutrality, is one of the first characteristics to become clear to the disciple. In spite of this fact, and that it is a fact no one who has experience will deny, and notwithstanding the categorical

---

[1] *Brihadaranyaka Upanishad,* iii, 7, 23. See also *Kenopanishad,* where the Gods (sense-powers) find themselves unable to perform their functions without the help of the *Brahman* (the Light).

[2] Compare *The Secret of the Golden Flower*: "The Light is not in the body alone, neither is it only outside the body. Mountains and rivers and the great Earth are lit by sun and moon; all that is this Light. Therefore it is not only within the body."

[3] *Nō Plays.* Trans, by Arthur Waley.

Verse 16 statement in verse 29 that all actions spring from the *Mula-prakriti*, yet it remains true that the creation, preservation and destruction of the forms are rooted in the nature of the Light.

Words fail us here: we must plunge deeper yet within the heart and see that in that mystic inactivity, within its very being, lurks Divine creative power. It gazes and the forms spring into being; gazing, It holds them fast; ceasing Its gaze, they fall back in the matrix once again. Here lies the mystery of the Will both in the macrocosm and the microcosm. The Will, even the individual will, is not the creature of mere outward forms. A Divine freedom is its very essence: the Light has an inherent power to gaze or not to gaze, also to change the level of Its gazing.[1] This cannot be described; it must be seen and known within the heart. Failure to understand this mysterious actionless activity has disastrous consequences, for it transforms the central Fount of joyful, radiant Light into a static Absolute, an eternal Futility, throned in the heart of being.

No worship of the Gods, no outer ritual, no mantras, prayerful pieties, or magic touch of saints can be a substitute for the heart's Knowledge by which alone that Wisdom can be reached. Only the clear, far-shining light of Mind can mingle with that Light, the Light of lights, and pierce beyond the Darkness to the Goal. "By the Mind is It to be gained," say the Upanishadic seers and Hermes, too: "this Mind in men is God and for this cause some of mankind are Gods and their humanity is nigh unto Divinity."

So far we have been studying the Field and its Knower chiefly with a view to their separation[2]; we have now to glance at the mode of their Verse 19 interaction. In the first place it is to be noted that, if not the Field itself, its source the *Mula-prakriti* is, like the Knower, the *Purusha*, or *Shanta Atman*, beginningless. These two are, as we saw in chapter eight, the two unmanifested moments of the *Parabrahman*.

On account of the mysterious selective gazing of the Self the *Mula-prakriti* manifests in a graded universe of forms and qualities. The following quotation will perhaps be of interest as showing that modern physics is feeling its way to a substantially similar view:

"The physicist's world is a spatio-temporal flux of events whose characteristics are limited to severely mathematical (i.e. *abstract, ideal, non-sensory*) properties. Upon them the mind imposes, or from them it selects (accounts differ) certain patterns which appear to possess the quality of comparative permanence. These patterns are worked up by the mind into continuing objects and become the tables and chairs of daily life. . . . Different minds with different interests, selecting different patterns,

---

[1] See *ante*, the end of Chapter III.
[2] Compare this with the *Manichcean* doctrine that it is the duty of the faithful to separate out all the particles of Light that are entangled in the darkness of matter. In Mani's hands, however, the doctrine seems to have stopped at a dualism.

would 'perceive' different worlds."[1]

The last sentence is of particular interest as throwing light on the nature of the different levels or *lokas*, for the hypothetical different minds of the writer have real existence as the different levels of consciousness.

The *Mula-prakriti*, then, is the root of the causally interlinked series of spatio-temporal events, but that that series should manifest as living sequences of sensation, feeling and thought, pleasant or painful, is due to the Light of Purusha, the witnessing consciousness. The latter, gazing on the flux, draws out from it the patterns which on any given level are to achieve significance as objects and in so doing identifies itself with them.
Verse 20

Just as a spectator at a cinema, seated in self-contained comfort, experiences joy and sorrow through self-identification with the patches of light and shade that make up the pictures on the screen, so the free, blissful nature of the Self is or appears to be stained by joy and sorrow arising from the purely neutral flux. Birthless and deathless, It is born and dies with forms Itself evoked and gazed Itself into.
Verse 21

This union of the seeing Self with forms takes place not all at once but on five levels[2] which are enumerated here from below upwards, but which it will be more convenient to consider in their order of evolution. Beyond all levels is the *Parabrahman*, here styled the highest *Purusha*, in which seer, seen and seeing are all merged in one. In that inconceivable Abyss a movement of limitation takes place as a result of which, abstract, unmanifested Selfhood, here termed the *One Enjoyer*, the *Great Lord*, the *Transcendental Atman*, as it were settles out and contemplates with calm aloofness the other moment of the *Parabrahman* appearing as the unmanifested Matrix.[3]
Verse 22

Gazing selectively on that Matrix, a process of self-identification with various aspects of it takes place, and thus we have the second level, here termed the *Supporter*, the One Life. Out of the infinite potentialities of the first level a certain number have been selected (in accordance with the sanskaras or karmik tendencies remaining over as seeds from the previous manifestation) to form the basis of a universal manifestation and are hence known as the Cosmic Ideation.

The third level, that of the *buddhi*, is not separately mentioned here. *Buddhi* and *Mahat* are often taken together and in later books they came to be completely identified. The former may be considered as the purely cognitive aspect of the latter. The difference between the two is not easy to explain; attaining the level of the *buddhi*, one is in touch with the *Mahat*.

The fourth level is here termed the *Sanctioner* or Inner Ruler. It is the level of the Higher Mind in which, out of the all-grasping, all-uniting levels of *buddhi-mahat*, the Light selects a given point of view and thus becomes

---

[1] *Return to Philosophy*, by C. E. M. Joad. The italicised portion has been added.
[2] Compare Gita, viii, verse 9. See also diagram in Appendix E.
[3] See Appendix F.

the individual Self. Hence arise the countless separate individuals. The "content" of experience on this level is, though grouped with reference to an individual viewpoint, of a non-sensory nature, what some would, perhaps wrongly, term abstract. It is what the Buddhists term the *rupa loka* as opposed to the *arupa loka* of the *buddhi-mahat* and the *kama loka* of the fifth (and sixth) levels.

The fifth level is that of concrete sensing, feeling and thinking. Out of the "abstract" possibilities of the fourth, the Light (the same Light, it should be noted) selects the concrete patterns which It works up into the objects of sense and feeling which are the content of our ordinary consciousness. This is the level of the sense or desire life and on it the Light is known as the *upadrashta*, Overseer or Watcher.

Strictly speaking this fifth level may be divided into two according to whether the concrete patterns which form its content are these "inner" ones that we term dream images, fantasy images, or merely images, or whether they are these "outer" sense-data from which we infer physical objects. As they are both of similar nature the Gita does not count them as separate levels though sometimes they are so counted. If reckoned separately they would form a sixth level. Similarly the seven of some traditions are accounted for by taking the *buddhi* as separate from the *mahat*.[1]

The so-called physical objects, tables and chairs, as opposed to the coloured and other sensory shapes of perception are but inferred or imagined causes with which we explain to ourselves the observed regularities in the data of sense, the data of the *upadrashta* level. They form a sort of underworld, an eighth world of pure *Maya*, peopled by ghosts with no reality. And yet it is these "ghosts" that are the basis of the materialism which vaunts itself as rooted in realities!

The importance of this knowledge cannot be overestimated, for it enables the disciple to see that even on the lowest levels the Self is one in all. He will be able to see with perfect clarity what he was taught long ago in chapter two—namely, that the Self cannot be pierced or injured, cannot be born or die. The separate self, that burden on his back for which he felt anxieties, hopes and fears, is seen to be illusion and with calm heart he can address himself to the Great Work with its two aspects; first, of climbing up the Ladder of the Soul by identifying himself with higher and ever-higher levels of consciousness, and second, of transmuting the lower

Verse 23 levels by irradiating them with the Light of the higher. Although it may be several lives before the Heights are scaled yet is he born no more, being the birthless Light.

Verse 24 Several methods exist to reach this Knowledge. Some by the mind's clear vision see the Self within the self, within the body even. They see that even the lower is what it is because drawn forth and upheld by the Light

[1] See Appendix E.

and thus they meditate upon that Light within all forms. Others follow the path of the *Sankhya* and reject the forms as not the Self. Unable to escape from dualism, they analyse away all content of experience as forms of *Prakriti*. Rejecting thus the lower, what remains is Self, or *Purusha*, not in the world but, star-like, far apart.

Others attain the same result by the *Yoga* of Action, transcending self Verse 25 by acting for the one great Self of all. Still others hear the Truth from teachers or, in modern times, read of it in the writings of great Seers and, as they read, some inner feeling wakes telling them of its truth and they adhere with faith to what they hear. These also tread the Path of Life.[1]

Thus it has now been seen that all beings arise from union of the Light with forms. He who allows his mind to sink the Light in the illumined forms, to feel "this form is me, these forms are mine," turning his back on immortality, he slays his own true Self. Let him open the eyes of the heart amidst the surrounding blackness and *see* the mighty Ruling Power, the Verses wondrous Light seated within all beings. Let him *see* that It is unperishing 26-29 within the forms that perish; *see* that It is the same in all and *see* that all the fret and fume of action is but the interplay of form with form and has no power to soil the stainless, all-supporting Light which, actionless, yet draws them forth from the great Matrix.

When he has seen all this (and even here and now it can be seen) a calm liberation will come to his spirit. He will perceive the great diversity Verse 30 of forms standing together in one mighty Being. The best method of trying to understand this unity, which is by no means a blank and featureless one, is to contemplate a constellated system of thoughts in one's own mind, a system in which no thought is anything except in relation to the rest of the system, in which all are one by virtue of their interlinkedness and, above all, by virtue of the fact that all have their being in one beam of consciousness.

Anyone who has served in a regiment knows the sense of being set free from the burden of self that comes from feeling oneself a part of a larger whole. There, however, the absorption is only partial and is often mixed with much that is undesirable. The perception of the great Unity gives such a wonderful liberation just because the self is completely and absolutely absorbed in That of which it is a part and because it is not something alien in which the self is lost but one's own Self.

Without beginning, parts, or limitations, untouched by actions even Verses though seated in the body, the Sun of Consciousness irradiates the Space 31-34 of Thought. He who has seen Its calm, immortal shining feels no more fear in all the triple world. He knows that all the whirling flux of sense has its sole being in that radiant Light: he is himself the Light, the Stainless, the Serene. For him—

[1] This "faith" is not the same as blind belief. Discussion of its nature is postponed to Chapter XVII.

"In the wind of the hill-top, in the valley's song,
In the film of night, in the mist of morning,
Is it proclaimed that Thought alone
Is, Was and Shall be." [1]

[1] From a Japanese Nō play. Translated by Arthur Waley.

CHAPTER XIV
THE YOGA OF THE DIVISION OF THE THREE GUNAS

HAVING set forth the distinction between the Field and its Knower (in *Sankhyan* terms, the *Prakriti* and *Purusha*) the Gita now turns to the further analysis of the Field. The Root or *Mula-prakriti*, termed in verse 3 the *Great Brahman*, is characterised by three moments known as *gunas*. The word *guna* is usually translated as quality but it should be borne in mind that there is here no question of a substance-quality relationship between the *Mula-prakriti* and the *gunas*. The *gunas* are the *Mula-prakriti* and the latter is the *gunas* in a state of equilibrium. For this reason some have preferred to speak of the three Strands the totality of which make up the twisted rope of manifested being.

In order to understand something of the nature of these *gunas* it is necessary to remember that the *Mula-prakriti* is not a substance standing in its own right but a dark matrix full of unlimited potentialities, the appearance of the *Parabrahman* to the abstracted Light of Consciousness. Its potentialities are unlimited because it is the whole objective aspect of the *Parabrahman* and it is "dark" because the Light has been abstracted as the *Atman*. While it would be a mistake to equate it with the collective unconscious of Jung, yet the comparison will give a truer understanding of its nature than any study of those neatly intellectualised diagrams to be found in most books on *Sankhya*.

Under the contemplative gaze of Consciousness, three tendencies manifest themselves within the Matrix. One moment of it reflects the Light and is irradiated by It, itself becoming, like a fluorescent substance, an apparent source of light. This is the moment known as *sattva guna* and it has the characteristic of radiance (*prakasha*).[1]

A second moment as it were transmits the Light, not reflecting it back towards the Source but ever speeding it onwards and outwards. This moment is known as the *guna* of *rajas*, having as its characteristic

[1] Verses 6, 11, 22.

outward-turned movement (*pravritti*).[1]

The third moment neither reflects nor transmits but absorbs the Light that falls upon it. This is the *guna* of *tamas*, characterised by a stagnant inertia, a heedless indifference.[2]

The operation of the *gunas* can be observed in the micro- cosmic matrix of unconsciousness from which we wake each morning. First from the dark background of dreamless sleep arise a set of memories which by reflecting back the consciousness proclaim: "I was, I am." Next *rajas* comes into operation and the contemplative self is swept away along the crests of associated ideas into desire-filled plans of: "I will do." Still later the fluid universe of thought ossifies under the veiling power of *tamas* into the outer world of rigid objects which, though in truth sustained by consciousness alone, yet seem to be hard lifeless things existing in their sheer inert material right and amongst which the planning self of dawn only too often passes from itself under the dull compulsion of the outer.

In the macrocosm we see the same processes at work. First by the operation of the Light on *sattva* arise the calm and light-filled worlds of *mahat-buddhi*, the Cosmic Memory which is the Cosmic Ideation. The radiance and harmony of those worlds arise from their *sattvik* nature, and Krishna's direction to stand firmly in *sattva* (*nitya sattvastha*, chapter ii, v. 45) has the same meaning as his constant counsel to be ever united with the *buddhi* (*buddhi-yukta*).

As the Cosmic manifestation proceeds we find the mobility of *rajas* coming into play. Out of the Light-filled unity of the spiritual worlds arise the many points of view which form the mental (*manasik*) level. The movement of the Light as it is transmitted through the Field gives rise to point-like individual selves from which the Light radiates in a network of intersecting lines of experience.[3]

The upper worlds are Spinozistic in their general nature. The attributes and modes shine forth in a majestic and impersonal unity, rising and falling like the ocean swell beneath the Moon of Light. But in the mental world of *rajasik* plurality we pass into a Leibnizian world of monads in which each monad mirrors the universe from a given point of view and thus, though separate from its fellows, is united with them in the ideal unity of all. The main difference is that Leibniz's monads were "windowless" and could perceive nothing but their own inner states, while these monads are not

---

[1] Verses 12, 22.

[2] Verse 13.

[3] There are many interesting references to this symbolic net in ancient mystical literature. In S*hwetashwatara Upanishad* I'shwara is termed the Wielder of the Net and in the Egyptian *Book of the Dead* (chapter cliiiA, Budge), under the vignette of a net occur the following interesting words: "Hail, thou 'god who lookest behind thee' (*manas* united with *buddhi*), thou 'god who hast gained the mastery over thy heart,' I go a-fishing with the cordage of the (net), 'uniter of the earth' and of him that maketh a way through the earth. Hail, ye fishers who have given birth to your own fathers (*manas* in which the Divine birth has taken place)."

thus shut in but are, in truth, each a window through which the One looks out upon Itself.[1]

But the effect of *rajas* does not stop at pure plurality, or, rather, in plurality itself is found the basis of the next tendency. Once the unity has been lost the separate parts strive to complete themselves by a passionate outward-turned seeking. This is the *trishna* (Pali, *tanha*) of the Buddhists, the "constitutional appetition" with which Leibniz endowed his monads, by which they tend to pass from state to state. If not identical, it is yet related to what Jung terms libido and, stripped alike of Sanskrit terms and of the jargon of philosophers, it is that burning thirst which drives the soul out from itself to range throughout the world, seeking its food, devouring all it meets.

From this tendency arises the great natural law that life must feed on life, but metaphysically we should observe that this most terrible of all the laws of nature, by which the tiger rushes on his prey and man himself murders the thing he loves, is also a manifestation of the unity of all. Under the outward-rushing impetus of *rajas* the soul no longer sees the unity within. But since, even though unseen, that unity can never be denied, the soul goes forth in passionate desire to seize and grasp whatever lies outside, subordinating others to its will and even, on the lowest plane of all, devouring their material envelopes that so itself may grow. Thus all the horrors of the world we know arise from ignorance, which turns the soul to seek in vain without what is already there within; desire is based on love and strife on unity.

As soon as the plurality has been established, the sinister power of *tamas* begins to make itself felt. Once the division between self and other has been made, the veiling power of *tamas* drains that "other" of all Light. It is no longer "me," instinct with life and movement, but something dead, inert, passively hostile, a death-hand gripping with a cold inertia the soul of man that struggles to be free. Thus is the outer world of objects formed. Our Self has drawn them forth and given to them "a local habitation and a name," and now they turn upon that Self, denying It reality. The brain, says someone, "secretes thought as the liver secretes bile." In truth it is not the brain that "secretes thought" but thought that has called forth the brain for, as the Buddha said, "of all phenomena mind is the caller-forth; pre-eminent is mind, of mind are all things made." [2]

It is *tamas* that veils the mind's creative power so that it quails before its own creation. Even religion, which should have taught the Path of Light to men, has ended, for the most part, in succumbing to the deadly drag of *tamas*, taking all power from Man to bestow it on imaginary Gods. In most

---

[1] Readers of the *Secret Doctrine* will remember a statement of H.P.B.'s to the effect that the esoteric philosophy involved a reconciliation of the apparently conflicting monadism of Leibniz with the monism of Spinoza (*Secret Doctrine*, i, 628, 1st edition).

[2] *Dhammapada*, I.

religions it is thought a sign of grace to hold that man is essentially a poor creature, one who can do nothing of himself, one who must supplicate on bended knees imaginary Gods who wield the Cosmos.[1]

But, as Hermes says, "if thou lockest up thy soul within thy body and dost debase it, saying: I nothing know; I nothing can; I fear the sea; I cannot scale the sky; I know not who I was, who I shall be; what is there then between thy (inner) God and thee?"

These three *gunas, sattva, rajas* and *tamas*, are, as has already been said, the strands of which the twisted rope of being is woven. All things, from grossest "matter" to subtlest cosmic thought-stuff, are the manifestations of one or more of these three tendencies, and it is one of the tasks of the disciple to analyse all phenomena in terms of these *gunas*. His effort is to be able to stand firm in *sattva* for, as we have seen, it is *sattva* alone that can reflect the Light. He must therefore be able to say of any phenomenon: " this is *sattvik* for it brings increase of Light and harmony and so will lead me upwards; this is *rajasik* for it leads but to motion and is founded on desire; this is *tamasik* for it fills the soul with darkness, taking it captive to an outer Fate."

This division applies to all things in the Cosmos, food (see Chapter XVII), recreations, companionships, or books; all may drag downwards, outwards, or lead upwards. But above all he must watch the *gunas* as they manifest in his own mind, for the mind is the gateway to the Real and the disciple must, in Hermes' words, be one "for ever living at the Inner Door." At that Door he must constitute himself a doorkeeper, letting all *sattvik* tendencies pass through, checking all *rajas*, overcoming *tamas*.[2]

Verse 11   Therefore the Gita gives some indications whereby the movements in the mind may be marked down. "When the light of knowledge is born in all the gates of the body, then it may be known that *sattva* is increasing." In other words, a state of mind that fosters clear, unclouded knowledge, that brings a peace and inner harmony, stilling the lake of mind till it reflects the stars, bringing a sense of calm eternity, that state is *sattvik*, and all outward things, food, friends, or occupations, that help forward such a state also partake of *sattva*.

Verse 12   The *rajasik* state, on the other hand, is characterised by passionate mobility. The mind is restless, occupied by greed, full of desire for things outside itself. Bright dreams may fill it, dreams of great things to be done, yet all those things are for the sake of self though they may sometimes wear the glittering robes of altruism and service of the world.

This *rajasik* restlessness is often confused with the Divine activity. There are many who cannot sit still for a moment, who think that to be

---

[1] Apologetics notwithstanding, it is unfortunately not Christianity alone that has thus bogged itself. With few exceptions, such as Buddhism (for *Vedanta, yoga,* etc., are more philosophies than religious cults), popular Oriental religions are just as *tamasik* and soul-abasing.

[2] Compare the four exercises in recollectedness (*satipatthana*) of the Buddhists.

always up and doing, no matter what, is to be full of life, and they bow down before activity in any form whatever. But this *rajasik* lust for movement is not the same as the Divine action, for it will be found, if analysed, that it is always tainted by some personal desire, always in bondage to some personal gain, while the Divine activity is free, calm and majestic in Its selflessness.

Tamasik states of mind are dark and stagnant, the mind is overcome by Verse 13 lethargy or broods in dull depression. Nothing seems worth doing, nothing can be done; all things oppress the soul, which sinks in sheer inertia. The Path is nothing but an empty dream or else a task beyond our feeble powers, while cynicism lends its venomed dagger to cut the very root of worldly action. "All things are shows, and vain the knowledge of their vanity."

This *tamasik* despondency is the greatest obstacle to one who seeks to tread the Path. The soul "flags wearily through darkness and despair."[1] It is a state which must be fought off at all costs, for not even the fierce, burning winds of *rajasik* passion are so fatal to all progress.

Unfortunately, just as some people mistake the restless urge of *rajas* for Divine activity, so others mistake the dull indifferentism of *tamas* for spirituality. Mealy-mouthed cowardice is called "turning the other cheek," lazy inefficiency is termed indifference to material circumstances, shallow fatalism is confused with wise acceptance of the *karma* of one's past, cold indifference to one's fellows becomes a rising above love and hate, and that dull poverty of spirit that ignores all art and literature becomes transcendence of the lures of sense. All is *Maya*! All is *Shunya*! All is the Play of God! What does anything matter? This is not spirituality but *tamas*. The "Dark Night of the Soul," that phrase coined by St John of the Cross to express certain of his experiences, has in the West been made by many an excuse for yielding to the fits of depression that come upon everyone from time to time.

The disciple must thus keep constant watch upon his mind so that when *tamas* makes itself felt therein, if he cannot at once rise to *sattvik* light, he will at least be able to overcome it with the outward-turned activity of *rajas*. In general it may be said that *sattvik* states will lead him upwards to higher levels of being, for their transparent luminosity allows a reflection Verse 18 of the next higher level to show itself, suffusing the lower with the fight of higher *manas*, or *manas* with the *buddhi*.

Rajasik states will leave him stationary, since, though he fill the world with his activities, he moves but outwards and can never leave the plane whereon he stands. *Tamasik* states will drag him downwards till he loses all he has and sinks into a less than human, mindless state. The phrase "sinks downwards" should not, however, be interpreted, as is sometimes done,

---

[1] These lines of Shelley were written of Coleridge, who, it will be remembered, composed an " Ode to Dejection."

to mean that the ego enters on an animal incarnation. That is impossible, though it may sometimes happen that a process takes place which is best described as the ego's having to watch over one or more animal lives with which it will feel itself bound up. In general, however, the meaning of the phrase is that he sinks gradually into the lowest grades of human existence.

It is interesting to note the extreme manifestations of *rajas* and *tamas* that are to be seen in our asylums. The *rajasik* is seen in what is termed *manic excitement*:

"The patient is in a state of constant activity, commencing a new occupation at every moment and immediately abandoning it in favour of another. He is never still but exhibits a continual *press of activity*. He talks rapidly and without intermission ... his attention is caught by every trivial object, and as soon diverted again. He is generally abnormally cheerful and absurdly pleased with himself . . . though his mood changes to anger at the smallest provocation." [1]

From the same source I take a description of a *tamasik* manifestation, the so-called *emotional dementia*:

"The patient sits in a corner with expressionless face and head hanging down, making no attempt to occupy himself in any way, evincing no interest in anything that goes on around him, and apparently noticing nothing. . . . The patient is completely inert and makes no use of his mental faculties (not because he has none but) because he has no interests or desires. The whole external world for him . . . is an object unworthy of the expenditure of any mental energy. He is without interests, hopes, plans or ambition."

In these descriptions who cannot recognise processes that go on in less extreme forms in his own mind?

Verse 10   Another characteristic of the *gunas* is the constant interplay of action and reaction that goes on between them. The world, "the moving thing" in Sanskrit, is never still. *Sattva* gives place to *rajasik* activity, which, carried to extreme, provokes a *tamasik* rebound.[2] Everyone knows how states of elation pass without apparent cause into a dull depression. This instance, alone, will show how important it is for the disciple to gain an understanding of the operation of the gunas, passing and repassing as they weave the web of life.

Verse 6   Because of its power to reflect the steady poise of the eternal Light, *sattva* alone is relatively stable. Yet even *sattva* has its binding power. Stainless and sorrowless, its light is still reflected light and binds the soul to the happiness and knowledge that are its manifestations. At any time the love of happiness, the sacred thirst for knowledge, may, through the touch of *rajas*, degenerate into lust for pleasure and mere curiosity.

Therefore the disciple must bend his energies upon transcendence of

---

[1] *Psychology of Insanity*, by Bernard Hart.

[2] The extreme illustration of this is to be found in the alternations which characterise the so-called *manic-depressive* type, perhaps with lucid intervals which are (relatively) *sattvik*.

the *gunas* altogether. He must strive to see that all their play is objective to himself: he is the *seeing* Light. Refuged within that Light, the Heavenly Ganga wherein who bathes is rendered pure and sinless, "he drinks the nectar of eternal Life." The movements of the Cosmos, shining with knowledge, passionately active, darkly inert, he sees with steady vision. His is the calm immortal gaze of Spirit, cool as the moonlight on a tropic lake. Nothing that comes can be unwelcome to him; nothing that goes can be a source of grief. He knows that all is needed for a Cosmos, that in the darkest *tamas* shines the Light. And so he stands, rock-like, in *inner* meditation, whether in cities or on lonely mountain peaks, watching the *gunas* weave their web, alike to friend and foe. Sorrow and joy, honour and evil fame, are one to him and, though he acts quite freely, the fatal thought "I am the doer of these actions" can find no entry in his Light-filled heart. *Verses 19, 20* *Verse 22* *Verses 23-25*

Rent is the threefold Web of Fate. The *gunas* have been crossed and the one-time disciple stands on the edge of the *Eternal Brahman*. His light can merge in the transcendent Flame and blaze in bliss beyond the world of men; the Stream is crossed, the great Reward is his. But Krishna tells us of another Path that opens as a possibility before him. He may elect not to withdraw his Light to the Unmanifest Eternal but to stay and serve the one Eternal Life that is in all. His freedom won, he may devote himself to freeing others, silently guiding pilgrims on the Path. His is no shrinking from the final plunge, for Krishna says that he is "worthy of becoming the Eternal," implying that he stays by his own choice to serve the One Great Life that is the manifested basis[1] of the *Parabrahman*. Nor is he man at all, but a great Power which, by Its presence, though unknown, unseen, lightens the bitter sorrows of the world. *Verse 26*

---

[1] *Pratishtha*. Compare the phrase "the Nest of *Brahman*" in *Maitri Upanishad*, vi, 15, which is there identified with the *samvatsara*—i.e. the great Cycle of Time, the *Mahat Atman*, whose discus Krishna carries.

CHAPTER XV
THE YOGA OF THE HIGHEST SPIRIT

JUST as the subject of the last chapter was the analysis of the Field, so that of the present one is the analysis of the Knower, the Consciousness, especially in its threefold aspect as individual Self, Cosmic Self and Supreme Reality.

The chapter commences, however, with an account of the World-Tree. This great symbol, mentioned in the *Rig-Veda* and *Upanishads*,[1] was known to all the ancient peoples. The Scandinavians knew of it as the sacred ash-tree, *Igdrasil*, with its roots in the death-kingdoms and its branches in the sky. In his poem to Hertha, the Norse nature-goddess, Swinburne writes of—

> "The tree many-rooted
> That swells to the sky
> With frondage red-fruited,
> The life-tree am I;
> In the buds of your lives is the sap of my leaves:
> ye shall live and not die."

The Egyptians worshipped the sacred sycamore fig-tree, the Aztecs of America had their sacred agave-plant and the ancient Sumerians of Eridu tell of a wondrous tree with "Its roots of white crystal stretched towards the deep, its seat the central place of the earth, its foliage the couch of the primeval Mother. In its midst was *Tammuz*." [2]

Space forbids any attempt to go into the extremely interesting symbolism connected with this subject. Here it can only be stated briefly that the Tree was a symbol of the great World-Mother, the Goddess of Nature who nourishes all life with the milk of Her breasts. Hence the

---

[1] *Rig-Veda*, I, xxiv, 7, and *Kathopanishad*, vi, I.
[2] D'Alviella, *The Migration of Symbols*, p. 157.

choice by the Egyptians of the sycamore fig with its milky juice, and hence the fact that the three most sacred trees of the ancient Indo-Aryans were the *ashwattha*, the *bat* (banyan) and the *udumbara*, all of them being species of the fig-tree.

The name *ashwattha* is usually derived from *a-shwa-stha*, "not standing till to-morrow," but while this is an appropriate enough description of the world which is ever passing away before our eyes, there is an earlier account which tells how *Agni*, the desire-consciousness, hid in this tree for a year (the cycle of manifestation) in the form of a horse (*ashwa*), the well-known symbol of the desire-mind.[1] This myth is of great significance as it links up with the statement already quoted that *Tammuz* was in the midst of the Sumerian World-Tree and also, perhaps, with the growth of an erica-tree round the coffin of the dead Osiris,[2] for both these "dying Gods" were, from the inner point of view, symbols of the *Atman*, dismembered and imprisoned in the world.

The authors of the ancient Indian tradition introduced, however, one modification into the symbol which is not, so far as I know, found elsewhere. The other World-Trees all have their roots in the underworld and branches in the sky, but the Tree of the Gita, following that of the Veda "whose root is high above," is rooted in the unmanifested *Brahman* and sends down its branches, the various levels of objectivity, the evolutes of the *Mula-prakriti*,[3] to form the worlds of manifested being. The Tree as a whole is termed the *Veda* as it is the content of all knowledge and the leaves, the individual selves, are the separate verses (*chhandansi*) of that cosmic *Veda*. "He who knoweth it is a *Veda*-knower." *Verse 1*

Nourished by the three *gunas* of which all phenomena are made (compare the three roots of *Igdrasil*), the branches spread both upwards and downwards, referring to the Cosmic Tides which flow upwards in the upper worlds and downwards in the lower.[4] The sprouts, peculiarly sticky in this tree, are the ensnaring objects of the senses and the roots, the *karmik* tendencies from the past universe,[5] grow downwards to generate "the bonds of *karma* in the world of men." *Verse 2*

---

[1] *Taittiriya Brahmaya*, III, viii, 12, v. 2. See Tilak's *Gita Rahasya* on this verse. The myth also occurs in *Mahabharata*, *Anusgasana Parva*, s. 85. It may also be noted that one of the meanings of *Ashwa* is "seven" (see Apte's *Dictionary*), that a vignette in the Egyptian *Book of the Dead* represents the sacred sycamore fig-tree with seven branches, that the same is true of some representations of the Assyrian Tree of Life, and, finally, that the trunk of the famous many-breasted statue of Artemis of Ephesus is divided into seven levels, five of which are filled with representations of living creatures. See Mackenzie, *The Migration of Symbols*, pp. 162-169, for drawings of these.

[2] See Plutarch's *Isis and Osiris*. The ramifications of this subject would take us all over the world.

[3] See Gita, vii, 4. There is also a microcosmic correspondence with the cerebral nervous system, rooted in the brain, the seat of consciousness, and ramifying downwards to the sense organs all over the body.

[4] See Chapter XI.

[5] Or, microcosmically, from past lives. It is a peculiarity of the *ashwattha* that its roots, instead of merging into the trunk at ground-level, often maintain a semi-independent existence for several feet above ground till they finally merge into one. Many explanations of this verse are vitiated by confusing the *ashwattha* with the banyan, which sends down aerial roots, whereas the former does not.

While man is in the world, his consciousness absorbed in the forms which he perceives, it is impossible for him to see the Tree as a whole. Still Verse 3 less can he see that fundamental Light which has drawn forth the forms, holds them in being and, in the end, will dissolve them once more in the Matrix.

"Now then the inquiry into *Brahman*" says the author of the *Brahma Sutras*, and then he goes on to define *Brahman* as "That from which the origin, by which the preservation, and in which the end" of the whole world of forms is found. The answer is there, lying close at hand, but the inquiry will lead to nowhere but a maze of intellectual subtleties unless certain preliminary qualifications are present in the inquirer. These qualifications are usually given as four: *viveka*, discrimination between the constant and the transitory; *vairagya*, a turning-away from what is transitory; *shat-sampatti*, a group of six attainments comprising control of mind, control of sense, endurance, a turning-away from the outer (whether in experience or in religion), faith (in the Gita's sense) and mental balance; *mumukshutva*, desire for liberation from the bondage of ignorance.

The Gita, however, mentions only one supreme qualification, which, if truly attained, includes all the rest, the qualification of non-attachment. This is the axe that will cut down the firmly rooted Tree, but non-attachment means a great deal more than mere ascetic refusal of commerce with the world. The latter may strengthen personal will-power but, as the Buddha found, will take the ascetic no nearer to the Goal. In fact, by strengthening his personal will, it may even rivet him more tightly in his bonds. *Non-attachment can never be attained while standing in one's personality*, nor even while standing in the individual ego, the separate *Jiva*. The disciple must see his personality as something separate from himself, like the personalities he sees in dream, and must take refuge in the impersonal Light. Then alone will non-attachment flower in his heart because the Light is ever unattached.

"Destroy all sense of self," said Buddha; "come unto Me," said Christ; "still all the movements of the mind," said Patanjali, that mind which, by attachment to all outward things, produces the false self. These and all other Teachers of the Way were, in their different language, saying but one thing: that man must come from self into the Self, from death to Life, from darkness into Light. Established in that Light, cohesive power will leave the Cosmic Tree and it will fall to pieces like those fabled ships which, on approaching the magnetic mountain, lost all their nails and sank into the sea. "Not by any travelling is the world's end reached. Verily I declare to you that within this fathom-long body with its perceptions and its mind lies the world, its arising and its ceasing and the Way that leads to its cessation."[1]

Verse 4 Detaching himself from the union with the objects of both outer and

[1] Buddha, *Samyutta Nikaya*, ii, 3, 6.

inner senses, detaching himself in fact from all form whatsoever, the disciple must soar upon the trackless Path of Light towards the Primal Consciousness from which in ages past the Cosmic Energies streamed forth.

That Consciousness, however, being Absolute, is far beyond all that *Verse 6* we know as such. Knower and Known exist as one in It as, in another way, they are at one in absolute matter, if any such exist save as abstraction. It is in fact no consciousness for us, being beyond the Fire of manifested life, the Moon of Milla-prakriti, the Sun of the unmanifested *Atman*. It is the Void; It also is the Full. Having gone thither, none return again. That, Krishna says, is His supreme Abode [1]; That is the Goal; That is the final bliss.

But now the Gita turns to lower levels and deals with the mystery of *Verse 7* the incarnation of that One. A constant moment of that partless Whole, the point of view explained in previous chapters, stands in the "matter" of the mental world uniting with its forms. As it turns outwards under the urge of *rajas* it becomes the lower, the desire-infected mind, and the integral power of knowing that is inherent in its light, in the attempt to grasp the various aspects of the world around, manifests as the five organs of sense-knowledge. These are at first the *inner* senses but they exteriorise into the so-called physical organs under the pull of *tamas*, as explained in the previous chapter. Moreover, from our point of view, the physical body belongs, not to the subjective, but to the objective side of experience. It is in fact only a specialised portion of what is actually environment, as it is merely a part of the content of consciousness upon the lowest level.

It should always be remembered that the sense-powers are differentiations of the integral illuminating power of Consciousness and are by no means something belonging to the material manifestation. This explains the fact noted by biologists that the senses are formed by differentiation from one primitive sense and the fact that under certain conditions one sense-organ can be made to do the work of others. The sense of touch can even be made to manifest at a distance of several inches from the surface of the skin.[2]

When the Ego, the inner Lord, takes a body it manifests these senses as *Verse 8* powers of gaining experience of the outer world. Here we must be careful not to confuse the scientific with the metaphysical account. Scientifically, or from the point of view of form, the process of incarnation may be described as the actual entry into a suitably organised vehicle (the embryo) of a subtler but still "material" body, the body of desire.[3] Metaphysically,

---

[1] Note that the word *Dhama* means Light as well as abode.
[2] See *L'Exteriorization de la Motricite*, by de Rochas; also *Eyeless Sight*, by Jules Romains. The interchanging of the sense-functions is also a practice of certain types of *yogi* in India.
[3] The "stuff" of this subtle body may perhaps be identified with what in spiritist circles is termed ectoplasm. But all references to matter or stuff should be taken in the light of what is written in Appendix B.

the process is to be viewed as a hardening-out of the forms with which the consciousness identifies itself, their so-to-speak de-illumination under the veiling power of *tamas*, so that the fluid form of the desire-mind crystallises into the relatively rigid material body.

Once it has come into being, the physical body is a battleground for the opposing forces of *rajas* and *tamas*. There are two sets of processes, known to biologists as *anabolism* and *katabolism* respectively, which go on simultaneously in the body from its first formation till its ultimate decay. One set, under the urge of the *rajas* of the desire-nature, are always building up the organism and repairing any damage, while the other, under the *tamasik* pull of "matter," are as busily engaged in breaking down whatever is built up. During the first half of life the former are in the ascendant, but gradually the destroyers assert themselves more and more, until the body refuses to obey the promptings of the ego and desire-nature and forces them to withdraw and leave it to disintegrate in peace.

The sense-powers, however, as we have seen, are no property of the material body but belong to the Ego itself, and therefore the latter is said Verse 8 to seize them and return with them to its own plane "as the wind takes fragrances from their retreats." As it withdraws it of course leaves behind it, not only the doomed physical body, but also the desire-nature, which is, as we have seen, intermediate between the Ego and the body. The *essence*, therefore, of our sense-experience is taken up by the ascending consciousness to be assimilated in that purely mental form which is built up around the central point throughout the age-long alternations of physical life and death.

There, as the Gita says elsewhere, the Ego on its purely mental plane "enjoys the spacious heavenly realm," reaping, as the Egyptians put it, the heavenly corn in the Fields of *Aahlu* until, when all the fruits have been reaped, a process that may last centuries or even thousands of years, the downward pull of mingled *rajas* and *tamas* asserts itself once more and the Ego seeks a further incarnation.

The deluded do not perceive the Self as it departs nor even as it stands Verse 10 within the body. "How shall that Seer be seen?" asks the *Upanishad*, and those whose vision is engrossed in outer forms, with all their scalpels and their microscopes see naught but forms. Even the would-be yogi, absorbed in outward practices with breath, or even struggling to subdue his mind, Verse 11 unless he makes the inward turn towards the *Atman*, detaching himself from forms, will gain no more than wretched psychic powers. Only the wisdom-eyed, those few who, seeking immortality, turn their gaze inwards, behold the individual Self, seated within the heart.[1]

Nevertheless, that individual Self is but a moment of the Cosmic Self. The Light which shines within the ego (as opposed to the latter's built-up Verse 12 form) is the same Light that shines within the other Selves as well, and

---

[1] *Katha Upanishad*, iv, I.

he who sees It rightly sees the unity of all, founded on that great Unity of *Brahman*, beyond Sun, Moon and Fire.[1]

That *Parabrahman* in the form of Its Light-Energy (*ojas*), entering the "earth" of Its objective aspect (*Mula-prakriti*), supports all beings and then again, having become the desire-natured immortal one (*rasatmaka* soma), It nourishes the "plants" of personal life (*aushadhi*).[2] Lower still, It becomes *Vaishvanara*, the Fire of the desire-life which burns throughout the world. Organised round, though not itself the Ego, its fierce, impersonal but living flames, in union with a living, breathing body, grasp and digest the food of the four elements of matter.[3] Verse 13 / Verse 14

Of all the manifestations of the *Brahman*, the most important in practice is the monad Self, the Ego, the pivot of the universe, poised between Light above and Fire below. That Point it is that goes from life to life and therefore in its mental vehicle are found the memories of all the linked succession of past lives. Backed as it is by the all-comprehending Light of *buddhi*, it is the source of Knowledge which thus lies within ourselves. Moreover, as the centre to which all our experiences are ultimately referred, it is the source of the reasoning faculty (*apohanam*[4]), for the essence of reasoning is the bringing into relationship of the data of experience and thought. Verse 15

That Self is what is to be known in all the *Vedas*, for the Vedic Gods, at least in their *adhyatmik* or spiritual aspect, were symbols of the Consciousness on different levels. In fact, the Vedic Indra,[5] wielding the thunderbolt of resistless will, drinking the Soma of immortality, is but a symbol of that individual Self. That Self is the great Knower of the Veda, for in it is reflected the Great Tree; it is the fount from which the wisdom of *Vedanta* wells up within the heart to give eternal Life.

Thus there are two great Selves (*purushau*) that must be known, that which is mutable or "melts away" and that which is unchanging. The former is the individual Self (*jiva*), which, though it lasts through manifested ages, is but a focus of the one Great Life and melts away at last within that Whole. The latter is the unmanifested *Atman*, gazing unchanged on the *Mula-prakriti*, seated above the mountain peak of being (*kutastha*), the unmoved Witness of the Cosmic whirl.[6] These two Selves are the two birds of the *Upanishad*, fast friends, perched on one tree, the Verse 16

---

[1] See above for explanation of these terms.

[2] The *aushadhi* are plants like corn, etc., which wither after bringing forth their fruits and spring up again from seed the following year. Opposed to them are the *banaspati* which, like trees, remain from year to year. The former symbolise the transient personal selves; the latter the relatively permanent egos or *jivas*.

[3] Itself being the fifth.

[4] *Apohanam* is rendered by Shankara as loss of memory and knowledge, but it has also the sense of removal of doubt and is used of the reasoning faculty (see Apte). The latter meaning seems to be the most appropriate here, but if the former be preferred it will refer to the fact that our inner knowledge must remain obscured until the Ego is able to manifest itself.

[5] In *Pauranik* times the meaning of Indra seems to have been lost or changed.

[6] The *Shanta Atman*.

Cosmic Tree. One, the individual Self, eats the sweet fruits and is bound thereby, the other watches but partakes of naught.[1]

Beyond that Cosmic Self is yet the Highest Being, termed in the Gita *Purushottama*, Highest Spirit. That is the Supreme Self, the *Parabrahman*, Verse 17 no Self at all but Ground of all that is. "The great Abode! therein is placed whatever breathes and moves. What That is know as Being and Non-being, the Goal of all, most excellent, beyond the intellect of beings." [2]

Beyond alike the finite Selves of men and the great, calm impassive Self of all, no finite thought can plumb Its awful depths. Even to the vision of the Cosmic Self It can appear but as the *Mula-prakriti*, for in Its bosom subject and object can exist no more. From It have all things come: to It will all things go; all we can know of It is that It stands, pervading with Its power the triple world, showing Itself to us as changeless Ruling Power; Eternal Law and yet Eternal Freedom.

He who thus knows the *Atman* as Supreme Spirit is undeluded in Verse 19 the world of men.[3] For him is neither high nor low, subject nor object, consciousness nor form. He, the All-knower, sees all as the One and therefore serves that One, not as do most with what is best in them, but with Verse 20 his wholly integrated being. He who has understood this deepest Mystery may be considered ripe for full Enlightenment. "In him, thus set free, there arises the knowledge of his emancipation and he knows: "Rebirth has been destroyed. The higher life has been fulfilled. What had to be done has been accomplished. After this present life there will be no more!" [4]

---

[1] *Mundaka Upanishad*, iii, I, v. I, also Rig-Veda, I, clxiy, 20. Similarly, on the highest bough of Igdrasil was perched an eagle while other creatures occupied the lower branches.

[2] *Mundaka Upanishad*, ii, 2, v. I.

[3] This does not mean that the *Parabrahman* (or *Purushottama*) can be an object of knowledge. The knowledge referred to in the verse is the knowledge that Krishna, the One Divine Life, is in reality the eternal *Parabrahman*, what Mahayanist Buddhists term the Void (*Sunyata*),. in which, as Nagarjuna said, " there is no arising, no cutting-off, no annihilation, no eternal persistence, no unity, no diversity, no coming in, no going out." Compare also this description of the disciple who has reached the Goal with that of the highest type of *Bodhisattva* in the *Mahayana*, one who knows that all things are the Void, that there are in reality no beings to be served and no sorrows to free them from, and yet, *though knowing this*, does not merge his being in that Void but, perfect in love and compassion, serves on till all can attain *Nirvana*. Without the knowledge that there is in reality neither server nor served, service is apt to degenerate into a sort of egoism.

[4] *Dialogues of the Buddha*, i, 93.

CHAPTER XVI
THE YOGA OF THE DIVISION BETWEEN THE BRIGHT AND DARK POWERS

LITERALLY translated, the title of this chapter would read "the division between the divine and demoniacal endowments," but such a rendering suggests, to Western readers at least, a Miltonic dualism which is far from what is meant by the Gita. The word *deva* and its adjective, *daivi*, come from a root meaning "shining," while *asura*, though originally a title of Indra and other Vedic Gods, came to have the sense of "not-divine," hence "dark."

There are two natures in this world, the Bright and the Dark, and the purport of this chapter is to trace the differences between them. But the differentiation in question is not an arbitrary division into good and bad based on the will of some personal God or Teacher, but one which is rooted in the very nature of the Cosmic manifestation. Verse 6

Mention has already been made of the two great tides or movements of the Cosmos, technically known as *pravritti* and *nivritti*. The former is the great outgoing breath by which the universe comes forth from *Brahman*, the latter is the inflowing counterpart by which all things return towards the One.

We must be on our guard against any introduction of ordinary ethical ideas in giving the names Bright and Dark to these two movements. The former is dark because it is characterised by an ever-increasing absorption of the Light within the forms, while the latter is bright because its tendency is towards the liberation of the Light. Such mental states as aid or manifest the outgoing movement are also called dark, and those that express the movement of return are termed bright.

This is the real basis of the ethical dualism that we find in the world. It is a great mistake, however, to set up an ethical dualism as absolute and then to rack one's brains to account for "the origin of evil." The dualism of the Cosmic Tides is inevitable in *any* universe whatever. It is no more possible to have a universe based on one movement alone than to have a gun that will fire without a recoil. Action and reaction are the conditions of all manifestation and not even the great Machine of the Cosmos can escape the operation of this law.

Most so-called ethical science is an attempt to find some sort of reputable intellectual sanction for the prejudices and customs of the society in which the particular thinker has been born. Certain actions are labelled good, others—for instance the appropriation of "someone else's" property, or certain forms of sexual behaviour—are termed evil. But this labelling not only raises the problem of why there should be evil in the universe but also leads to the discovery that other societies in the world have no cognisance of these particular labels, or even apply them in the opposite sense. Since, moreover, the universe as a whole, apart from supernaturalist assumptions, shows no sign of acting in accordance with the labels, the conclusion is reached that the universe is non-ethical and a further dualism between man and nature is set up, so that the former finds himself in the unenviable position of being concerned with good and evil in a universe that is profoundly indifferent.

Such a conclusion is extremely unsatisfactory, since it leaves man either a worshipper of the image that his own hands have made, one that he knows has no reality behind it, or else drives him into the arms of his own unregulated desires.

Our ethics must in fact be based upon the twofold Cosmic Movement and therefore must be relative. Buddhist philosophy speaks of two types of *kalpa* (period of manifestation), termed respectively *vivarta kalpas*, or periods of "unrolling," and *samvarta kalpas*, or periods of "rolling up," and when, on the eve of Enlightenment, the Buddha saw the whole series of His past lives, He remembered having lived through several of these alternate periods of evolution and involution. The universe is not then to be regarded as a perfectly straight unrolling followed by an equally straight rolling-up but as a cyclic process, spiralling downwards through many alternating ages and then reascending in the same spiral fashion.

From this it follows that, if ethics are to have any foundation in the Cosmos, we must define good and evil in terms of the processes that aid or hinder the cosmic tendencies that are dominant at the time, and these will be different according to whether the age we are living in is one of unrolling or one of rolling-up. The qualities that are of assistance during an outgoing period of further descent into matter and which therefore must at that time be termed "good" are precisely the opposite of those which will be of use during a period of ascent or involution. Thus the virtues of the one period will become the vices of the other.

This ambiguity or relativity can be avoided by the use of the ethically neutral terms Bright and Dark, for they express simply the characteristics of the period in question without passing ethical judgment upon them.

Traces of this alternation of values have been preserved in Hindu mythology. We read in the Puranas how, at certain early periods of the world, certain egos were entrusted with the work of generation of the species and ordered to produce offspring. They, however, refused to do so and became chaste ascetics, a course considered meritorious at other epochs but here evidently considered a "sin," since we read that they were cursed in consequence of their refusal.

The reversal of meaning that came over the word *asura* is perhaps a further indication of the same sort. Originally, as has been said, the word was a title applied to the great Gods, *Varuna, Indra* and *Agni*—a sense which has been preserved in the *Ahura Mazda* of the Iranian tradition—but in later times it came to signify the "dark" enemies of the Gods. The same may be said of the process by which Lucifer, "Son of the Morning," whose very name of Light-bearer shows him to have represented the downward movement of the Light, became in later times the Christian Devil, the enemy of God and righteous men.

When we leave theory and come to practice we find ourselves at once confronted by the question how we are to know whether the period in which we are living is one of evolution or of involution. The answer is primarily to be found in our hearts, which, reflecting as they do the whole of Cosmos, are able to know which tendency is operating at a given time. But that still small voice within us is reinforced by the words of the great spiritual Teachers of the epoch who, being Seers, teach in accordance with the voice of Cosmic Law.

Now it is noticeable that all the great Teachers of the historic epoch have inculcated an ethic of a definitely ascending or *nivritti* type. The ascending character of the ethics of the Gita, of Buddha, Christ and Shankara, is so obvious that we are apt to identify such teachings with ethics pure and simple and to assume that teachings of the opposite sort are evil for all time.

But there are definite indications that such a conclusion is erroneous. If we look back to the earliest cultures of which we have any historical knowledge, the civilisations of the five or six millennia preceding what we call our era, we see that the religions of those civilisations were of a fundamentally different type. I have written religions but perhaps the singular would have been more appropriate, for, just as there is a certain uniformity about all modern religion, so there was a similarity between all the ancient religions.[1] Comparison of Babylonian, ancient Egyptian, or Cretan religion with the religions founded by "historical" Teachers shows that a fundamental difference of attitude prevailed in the ancient cults.[2]

---

[1] I am not referring to the thin stream of "mystery" tradition reserved for the few who, at all times, have been treading the upward Path, but to the great exoteric cults designed for the masses of men.

[2] It would be easy to controvert this by the selection of appropriate instances, but a sensitive study of the popular ancient religions will, I think, reveal profound *qualitative* differences of values and of general "atmosphere." Notice how D. H. Lawrence, for example, in revolt against accepted spiritual values, was attracted to old-world cults such as that of Etruscans, and notice also his worship of "dark Gods." Writing about Saturnalia and kindred festivals, Sir James Frazer says in his *Golden Bough*: " All these things appear to hang together; all of them may, perhaps, be regarded as the shattered remnants of a uniform zone of religion and society which at a remote era belted the Old World from the Mediterranean to the Pacific."

There is in all of them an emphasis on *pravritti*, especially as manifested in the great forces of sex, and an inculcation of practices that seem to us of very dubious morality. The Great Mother was then the chief object of worship. To the type of religion represented by the Gita she has become the great World-Tree that is to be cut down with the axe of non-attachment. It is easy to gloss over such a difference with talk of the evolution of man's religious sense, but such a phrase only masks a real change in the values appropriate in the two epochs.

Orphic and kindred movements in Greece, " Hermeticism " in Egypt, Buddhism in India and Christianity in the Near East and Europe were not simply religion *par excellence* coming into an irreligious world, but movements which came to initiate a new age, and, by reversing many previous values, directed the hearts of men along the path of *nivritti*, which is the tendency at present ruling, not, indeed, in the sense that it yet dominates humanity but in the sense that the values for the present epoch are the spiritualising ones of the ascent.

But it is time to return more directly to the Gita. The teaching about the bright and dark tendencies which, like the *anabolic* and *katabolic* processes in the body, go on simultaneously in all ages, has been deferred till the disciple was at such an advanced stage of the Path because the effect of such teaching upon immature souls is always to make them identify their own party with the bright and their opponents with the dark forces. They are themselves the "chosen people of God," while their opponents are the people of the Devil! Each of the nations fighting in the last war was, in its own opinion, fighting for Justice and the Right.

In studying the lists of bright and dark qualities enumerated in the Gita we should be careful to disinfect them somewhat of the atmosphere of "holiness" and "sinfulness" that centuries of popular ethical thinking has surrounded them with. *Dana*, for instance, must be divested of its associations with almsgiving, charitable institutions and sanctimonious merit-mongering, while "study of the scriptures" (*swadhyaya*) has little connection with the Bible classes of the West or with the futile mechanical intoning of the Gita that is so popular in orthodox circles in India. *Dana* is the process whereby the good things of the universe are made to circulate and penetrate the whole instead of being locked up in stagnant individual centres, and is thus obviously a means of breaking down the barriers of egoism, while *swadhyaya* signifies the pursuit of knowledge by study, not necessarily the study of "holy" books.

It is not necessary to go in detail into all the other qualities enumerated; all that is needed is to sound a warning against taking them in their conventional senses, for, in those senses, they often become vices, accorded lip-service by the great majority of men but instinctively rebelled against in the heart. It is not without significance that the conventional virtues of the conventional saint are objects of dislike to healthy-minded men. The task of thinking out the real meanings of these qualities and of divesting them of the accumulated holiness of centuries is a useful and important exercise for the disciple of this Path. Only he who has made the attempt knows what valuable results it yields and what a profound ethical enlightenment comes from the discarding of the copy-book conceptions. Above all, the disciple will be cured of the almost universal habit of judging by appearances, for he will learn that apparently identical actions performed by two different men have very different values from the inner point of view.

It will be noticed that all the qualities which are described as bright are ones which help the liberation of the Light. In themselves, of course, they are qualities, not of the Light itself, but of the psycho-physical vehicles in which it is entangled, but, just as it is easier to extract water from a sponge than from a brick, they are such as make it easier for the Light to detach itself and dominate those vehicles.

Thus, *ahinsa* (harmlessness) involves a checking of the outgoing forces of *rajas*, which, as we saw in connection with chapter fourteen, are what lead to the transformation of the unity-based love into a Nature "red in tooth and claw," and worse, into man red with sword and bayonet. Similarly, *teja* (vigour) is the means of overcoming the *tamasik* drag which sinks the Light in the stagnant inertia of matter. *Verse 3*

In dealing with the dark qualities one difficulty appears at first sight. Contrary to what we should expect from the foregoing conclusions, a certain moral odium appears in the phrases which are used to describe them. "Dark" men are not even allowed to have a proper knowledge of *Verse 7* *pravritti*, which one might have thought was their special province. They are "ruined selves" (*nashtatmanah*), that is to say, those whose Light is *Verse 9* sunk in matter, and they "come forth for the harming of the world."

But this condemnation is explicable when we reflect that the Gita is written for an epoch of *nivritti*[1] and that therefore the dark qualities described are not the outgoing (*pravritti*) tendencies in their own proper forms but, as it were, the aftermath of those qualities, the distorted and ugly forms in which they manifest themselves when prolonged beyond their proper time into an epoch of *nivritti*. They have the same relation to the qualities of pure *pravritti* that the sexuality of an old man has to the normal passion of youth.

The *pravritti* of a *nivritti* age is not the healthy and vigorous outgoing that it is in periods when it has the backing of the Cosmic Law but a sporadic, disruptive and harmful manifestation comparable to that unwanted cell-activity which produces the growth of tumours in an organism. That is *Verse 7* why it is said that "dark" men (in an age of *nivritti*) "know neither right *pravritti* nor right *nivritti*."

Verse 2 appears beside the *ahinsa* paragraph.

---

[1] This is implied by Sri Krishna's assurance to Arjuna, the individual Soul, that he is born with the bright endowment (verse 5).

It is in that sense too that we must understand verse eight. "The universe, they say, is without truth, without basis, without any Ruling Power, brought about by mutual union,[1] caused by lust and nothing else." Conscious as they are that their own activities are without any underlying harmony or truth, and that they are motivated by sheer desire and have no sanction in the Cosmic Law, they naturally erect philosophies which deny the presence of those attributes in the Cosmos as a whole. We can see nothing in the universe which we have not first perceived in our own hearts, and if a man's heart is given over to "insatiable desires" he will be able to see nothing in the Cosmos but the wild strife of untamed forces. Verse 11 Thus his lack of vision will seem to justify his self-indulgence and he will abandon himself to the gratification of his desires, "feeling sure that this is all."[2]

One particular consequence of this yielding to desires must be noted. We have seen that the forces of desire are not really personal forces seated in the Ego but great impersonal Verses tides that sweep a man away. Just Verses as a man experiences a rather fatuous sense of gratification and power 13, 14 when travelling at high speed in a motor-car, even though that power and speed are no attributes of his, for he may be the merest weakling, so we experience an exhilaration in yielding ourselves to powerful currents of desire quite oblivious of the fact that they are neither us nor ours, but swirling tides that bear us to destruction.

A man need only examine himself when carried away by violent anger, passion, or grief to realise how much he is enjoying the swift rush and how reluctant he is to allow its luxurious ecstasy to come to an end. Although most (though apparently not all!) modern societies will not allow us to exult in the naif fashion of verse fourteen over the enemies we have slain and are about to slay yet we can all recognise the desire-born thrill of the next verse: "I am wealthy, well-born; who is there that is like unto Verse 15 me? I will sacrifice, I will give alms, I will make merry. Thus, deluded by ignorance."

The ignorance in question is ignorance of the fact that the current of desire is something quite outside the Self, its exhilaration being that of the Gadarene swine as they "rushed down a steep place into the sea." For, Verse 16 truly, the end of such wild careering is, as the Gita puts it, "in a foul hell." The fire and brimstone of the mediaeval Christians and the ingenious tortures of sadistic hell-makers in India are mere superstitions, but for all that, there are hells enough, both in this world and after death, the hells of unsatisfied desire which are entered by "the triple gate of lust, anger and

[1] In using the words "mutual union" the author was probably thinking of sexual union, but the words would apply equally to the theory that the world arose, in the last resort, from a "fortuitous concourse of atoms."

[2] It is not proposed to point a moral by applying these verses to current societies, East or West. Readers must judge for themselves whether or not they constitute an indictment of their particular society and whether the ways of their civilisation are "bright" or "dark."

greed." Equally true is it that these hells are "destructive of the Self," for Verse 21 the Light of the Self is dissipated among the objects of desire.

In chapter eleven, verse thirty-six, we read of the Rakshasas fleeing in fear to the uttermost boundaries of the universe. That was the cosmic aspect of the process and here we are told how the "dark" ones who are its actual embodiments turn from the Light within and are carried by the Verses 19, 20 fierce currents of desire through birth after birth into the furthest abysses of materiality and Self-loss. For, once a Soul has attached itself to these currents, it is not easy for it to stop and reverse its course. "Easy is the descent into hell," as Virgil wrote; it is the return that is difficult and laborious.

Yet it must always be remembered that underlying all the moral indignation of the text is the knowledge that those who follow the path of Darkness do so because they are those who have not yet plumbed the depths of matter, depths that those who love the Light have also plumbed before. The Soul Itself perishes never; all movements, Dark and Bright, take place within the One, and so from every depth there is return. As Plotinus expresses it: "It is not in the soul's Nature to touch utter nothingness; the lowest descent is into evil and, so far, into non-being; but to utter nothing, never. When the soul begins again to mount, it comes not to something alien but to its very self."

Before concluding this chapter it is necessary to say a few words about Verses 23, 24 the last two verses, which, with their command to refer all matters to the authority of the *Shastra*, have been and are the delight of orthodoxy. But to take *Shastra* here as meaning the traditional scriptures—or any scriptures, in fact—is to misunderstand the whole tenor of the Gita, with its reiterated counsel to take refuge in the *buddhi* (e.g. chapter ii, verse 49) and its constant teaching that all knowledge is to be found in one's own heart.

The fact is that the word *Shastra* here means the Threefold Ruler (*shasaka traya*),[1] the *manas* united with the *buddhi* and *mahat*, or, in plain language, the inner knowledge that is revealed in the heart by the spiritual intuition. This is the meaning of the Upanishadic counsel to sink the senses in the mind, the mind in *buddhi* and the *buddhi* in the *Mahat Atman* or Great Self, and it is to these Inner Rulers that one should always submit. Following the dictates of that inner Light one should perform all actions in the world, and he who ignores that inner Voice, "to follow the promptings of desire, attains neither success nor happiness nor the highest Goal."

---

[1] It is only fair to state that this is not the accepted etymology of the word *shastra*. I am quite aware that many will consider it a fanciful one.

CHAPTER XVII
THE YOGA OF THE THREEFOLD FAITH

Verse 1   THE seventeenth chapter commences with a question that is often asked: what is the condition of the man who has faith but no knowledge of the commands of the Inner Ruler (for the reference to the ordinances of *Shastra* must be understood in the light of what was said at the end of the last chapter)? But this question, though so common, is based upon a misunderstanding of the nature of faith. Faith is sometimes confused with intellectual belief based upon a weighing of probabilities, and still more often with a blind acceptance of credal orthodoxies rooted for the most part in nothing more than the instinct for social conformity. But the former is more properly termed reasoned opinion, while the latter scarcely merits any mental label at all, being a mere verbal habit based on herd-instinct.

True faith is something of a much higher nature. It is the reflection in the lower mind of *knowledge* already possessed by the higher and the *buddhi*. We read in chapter thirteen, verse twenty-five, of those who on hearing, perhaps for the first time, of higher truths at once give themselves up to them. They are able to do so because of this irradiation of the lower mind by the knowledge of the higher, an irradiation which gives a sense of certainty akin to that which a man feels on understanding a geometrical proposition, the only difference being that, in the case of faith, the grounds for that certainty have not entered the brain-consciousness. Therefore it was that Hermes said:

"My word doth go before thee to the truth. But mighty is the mind, and when it hath been led by word up to a certain point, it hath the power to come before thee to the truth. And having thought over all these things, and found them consonant with those which have already been translated by the reason, it (the mind) hath believed and found its rest in that Fair Faith."

It is important to understand this. The world is full of men seeking to persuade others to believe in this or that doctrine, book, or teacher, but the blind belief which they demand is, if given, nothing but the inert response of a *tamasik* mind and has no connection whatever with the Fair Faith of which Hermes speaks. Blind beliefs are perpetually coming into conflict with ascertained truth and it is for this reason that the believers are so fanatically propagandist, for they seek to silence their own doubts by the shouting of many voices.

The Fair Faith, on the other hand, can never come into conflict with knowledge, for it *is* knowledge even though its grounds have not been realised. Nevertheless, the lower mind is treacherous and many things which have a soul of truth within them may not themselves be true. The mind translates its knowledge in terms of its own concepts. Thus the true faith that there is fundamental justice in the Cosmos may lend its certainty to erroneous notions of a personal God and final Judgment Day in cases where such concepts fill the mind.[1]

Truth must be all-inclusive and harmonious. It cannot form into little eddies and closed systems. The only safe course is, as Hermes says, to think over all things and to accept those which are found to fit in with what is already known in one harmonious whole. If it be asked in what way this differs from the procedure of the so-called rationalist, it must be answered that the latter accepts only the data of the senses and the logical conclusions of the mind upon them, while the follower of the Fair Faith accepts the data coming from above and then proceeds to work over their interpretation until he can express them in a form consonant with reason.

The necessity for this "working over" arises because the Verses mind in which the knowledge is reflected is a thing of many colours, being made up of the *gunas*. "The faith of each is shaped to his own nature." If a man can rise to his true Self he is no more concerned with faith for he has knowledge, but as long as that knowledge has to be reflected in the lower mind it is inevitable that it should take on the colours of that mind.

The true Man is the Knowledge which makes up the higher Self, and when that knowledge has to show itself as faith, that faith is as much of the true Man as is able to manifest within the limits of his personality. Therefore is it said: "A man consists of his faith; that which his faith is, he is even that." That is the reason why those who have accomplished great deeds, whether like Joan of Arc they possessed what is called religion, or whether like Napoleon they believed but in then- own "destiny," have always been filled with faith. Their deeds have been accomplished by the power of their higher Selves, and that power was available to them because those Selves were reflected in their hearts in the form of faith.

Not only is his faith the Man himself; the turn which is given to it by his mind *is* also his lower, personal self, for the expression of his faith depends on which of the three *gunas* is dominant in his personality. A *sattvik* man will give his faith *sattvik* expression, and so with the other

Verses 2, 3

[1] Occasionally, though not often, a man is able to keep his faith uncontaminated by his mental furniture. For instance, the Catholic mystic, Juliana of Norwich, worried about the fate of the heretics and heathen, received from a vision of Christ the assurance that "all manner of things will be well," an assurance that she seems simply to have accepted although it was at utter variance with the teachings of her Church which, doubtless, formed the concepts of her mind. Much more typical, though, is the case of St Teresa, whose Catholicism made her mould the revelations of her vision into the ridiculous statement that in the case of a heretic the mirror of the Soul was irretrievably shattered!

Verse 4

types. This comes out very clearly in the objects of men's worship. The only object of worship to the man of knowledge is the *Atman* in himself and in all beings, but those who live by faith alone will feel that unperceived *Atman* as a wondrous Power, sensed in external things and worshipped accordingly. *Sattvik* men will feel Its presence in the great awe-inspiring forces of Nature, in Sun and Wind and Water, and so will "worship the Gods." As their faith becomes purified they will turn more and more to the spiritual power behind those forces and leave the outer forms.

Rajasik types will sense the same Power as it rushes fiercely in the desire-currents and so will worship *yakshas* and *rakshasas*, the personified consciousness behind desire for wealth and angry violence respectively. Those in whom *tamas* predominates will feel their imagination captivated by the fact of death and so the shades of the dead will draw their worship.

In modern civilisation, too, these types appear in the nature-mysticism of a Wordsworth, in the all too common worship of wealth and power that shows itself in a morbid interest in the lives of the wealthy and powerful, and in the devotion to the so-called spirits of the dead who are the Gods of the spiritist cult, though in this last case there is also an admixture of *rajasik* curiosity.

Verses 7-10

It is not only in the objects of worship that the influences of the *gunas* make themselves felt; they show also in such things as the type of food eaten. Western readers may be inclined to see very little connection between faith and food, and on the other hand, in India, there is a tendency to see only too much connection. The true course, as always, lies in the middle. Since the body is built up of the food that is taken into it, and since, also, the taste of food forms an important and regular portion of our sense-life, it is obvious that both the quality and taste of food will have a significance for him who is trying to follow the Path, though by no means the excessive significance that is sometimes attached to it in India. No amount of merely *sattvik* eating will suffice to make a man spiritual.

Verse 11

The sacrifice (*yajna*) which the Gita mentions next must not be limited to the ceremonial sacrifices of ancient India. The *yajna* of the Gita means sacrificial action in general, the dedication of one's goods and deeds and self to the service of the Life in all. The *sattvik* man will do this, not out of any desire for personal reward, even in the shape of his own salvation, but because his *sattvik* nature reflects the knowledge of the Cosmic Sacrifice and impels him to participate therein.

Verse 12

The sacrifice of the *rajasik* man is, as might be expected, tainted by desire, and so he sacrifices in order to gain some benefit for himself, and usually denies the possibility of action that is free from such desire. In inferior types the mainspring of his action is to be found in the wish to be known as a religious man, philanthropist or patriot.

Verse 13

Tamasik sacrifice is a still lower type, in which only the semblance of sacrifice is shown. It is not governed by any rule or principle (*vidhi*) nor has it any sanction in the inner *Shastra* (*mantra*). No actual giving away is involved (*asrish-tanna*) and the whole performance is carried out without any skill (*dakshinam*). The motivation of such so-called sacrifices is usually mere instinct for social conformity.

It would be tedious to comment at length on the other ways in which a man's faith may manifest. The list is not a mere miscellaneous collection. Worship, food, sacrificial action, self-discipline and charity are all important aspects of the spiritual life, and it is for this reason that the Gita has gone into such detail about them.

Some words must, however, be said about *tapasya*, usually translated as austerity, but better rendered as self-discipline. *Tapasya* does not mean standing on one leg in a forest nor piercing the body with sharp spikes. Such torture of the body, common both in mediaeval Europe and in India, is the *tamasik* man's idea of *tapasya*. Identifying himself with his physical body, he can see no way of making spiritual progress but by forcing that body to be passive under torture,[1] and so he goes about naked or wears hair-shirts, or else he starves himself and then mistakes the hallucinations of a weakened brain for spiritual visions.

Verses 5, 6, 19

Discipline of the body is quite a different tiling from its injury by such practices. The body is the field in which we have to work and, later, will be needed for the service of the One. To weaken or destroy it by injudicious austerities is to destroy a valuable instrument. It is sometimes urged that the body is unreal and transient and that the man of knowledge will not care whether it functions well or badly, whether it lives or dies. But such a view is based on misunderstanding. Those who are practising self-discipline are not men of knowledge but, rather, men trying to gain knowledge. A weakened body, as the *Upanishad* has taught,[2] means a weakened mind, and if the body is unnecessarily abandoned before the Goal is reached, it only means that valuable years will have to be spent in educating a new one and in bringing it to the point at which the Path was left. The true attitude to one's body should be to treat it as one treats a riding horse, something to be intelligently disciplined, adequately cared for and properly used, and not as something either to be allowed to wander off at its own free will or else to be beaten to death or uselessness.

There is a further consideration that is equally powerful. The outer senses are but the manifestations of the inner or mental ones. The mortification of the outer leaves the inner ones quite intact. Indeed, the sense-powers, forcibly suppressed without, are driven inwards and revenge themselves in a riot of imaginative phantasy within, which will disturb the spiritual life far more effectually than ever the outer sense-life could have

---

[1] It is no answer to this to urge that such self-torturers often hold an extremely dualistic theory of the relationship between soul and body. Theory is one thing and perception quite another. It is just because they know nothing but the body that they imagine that bodily torture will liberate the soul.
[2] *Chandogya Upanishad*, vi, 7.

done.

Self-discipline must begin, not with the senses, but with the mind. In the enumeration of the six mental endowments that form part of the fourfold qualification for knowledge of the *Brahman* (see Chapter XV), *shama*, or control of mind, precedes *dama*, the control of sense. The disciple must bend all his energies to the task of controlling his unruly mind, and when that is accomplished he may be sure that the outer senses will offer no serious obstacles to being brought under control. Trying to control the senses without having first subjugated the mind is like trying to bail water out of a sinking ship without first stopping the leak. Even in cases of definitely inappropriate sense-indulgence, the inner phantasying about the objects of enjoyment does far more damage to the inner life than the actual outward gratification.

Another point that must be noted is that the mind cannot, under ordinary conditions, be treated as something separate from and independent of the body. It is true that the mind is the crux of the whole discipline, but it is also true that the ordinary disciple is quite unable to rise to the level of functioning in his true or higher mind and that the mind in which he does live is very closely bound up with the physical body. It is easy to talk about being indifferent to bodily sensations, but nevertheless, to say nothing of severe pains, a few hours in a stuffy room will destroy almost anyone's power of clear thinking, and a few days of overwork or loss of sleep will cause self-control to vanish in gusts of irritability. This being so, it is obviously foolish for the ordinary disciple to attempt a fine disregard of the bodily and external aspects of life when, all the time, his mental life is intimately bound up with them. "The contacts of matter come and go," as we read in chapter two, but while the disciple should "endure them bravely," he will not, in the earlier stages,[1] be able to disregard them altogether without disastrous results.

Verse 14   So much for the negative side of *tapasya*. On the positive side what is needed is an harmonious control of body, speech and mind. The body is to be disciplined by being used for the service of the Gods, the Twice-born (of the genuinely spiritually illumined, that is, not of those who merely arrogate the title to themselves on the strength of outward ceremonies), of Teachers and all Knowers of the Truth, and further, by the practice of cleanliness, straightforwardness, harmlessness to all beings, and *brahmacharya*.

The last word connotes control and not suppression of the sex-forces. A neurotic celibacy with the so-called unconscious mind full of thwarted sex, issuing in a welter of more or less disguised phantasy, is the very worst condition to be in for one who seeks the inner life. Such a condition may, like extreme bodily weakness, give rise to strange experiences and visions, but it will quite effectually prevent any real treading of the Path.

[1] It should be remembered that these last six chapters are inevitably to some extent recapitulatory.

Sex will be transcended; it cannot be suppressed— with impunity.

It is important to note that a mere renunciation of sex by the conscious mind and will is not enough. Many would-be *sanyasis* in India, and I suppose some people in the West, having heard or read of the virtues of *brahmacharya* screw up their wills to a renunciation of all sex. The inevitable result is that the unsatisfied sex-desires are repressed into what psychologists term "the unconscious." From the point of view here adopted the term unconscious is a misnomer, for nothing exists that is not supported by and floating in the consciousness. What is really meant is that the mind-consciousness ceases to pay attention to them. However we may phrase it, the fact remains that these desires, with the psychic energy that is locked up in them, prevent all peace of mind, and, if denied attention, manifest as disturbing dreams and in other ways, such as bad temper. The only remedy is to bring them once more into the focus of attention; but in such cases—namely, where sex-desires have been repressed—this is usually impracticable, since to do so involves tormenting the mind with thoughts of having fallen from the Path or with division in the will.

A mind at peace with itself and a unified will are absolute essentials on the Path. The disciple should therefore be content to grow harmoniously as a flower grows, and not try to force his development by renunciations which spring from the will alone and not from the whole being. The sex-desires must be de-energised by withdrawal and not pushed away by mere will. Only when they are drained of their energy is it safe to "renounce" them and then, indeed, renunciation is no longer needed.[1]

Of harmlessness (*ahinsa*) it is quite sufficient to say that one who seeks to serve the Life in all must certainly abstain from lulling living creatures for his "sport" or even, in ordinary circumstances, for his food. "All beings tremble before punishment; to all life is dear. Judging others by yourself, slay not, neither cause to slay." [2] To cast eyes of greed at the flesh of a fellow-being is no act for a disciple of this Path. Rather will he remember the perhaps legendary story of how the Buddha in a previous life gave his own flesh to feed a starving tigress and her cubs.

In addition to the above-mentioned discipline of the body he will discipline his speech, taking care that it is always truthful and helpful:

" Govern the lips
As they were palace doors, the King within;

---

[1] The above should not be interpreted as urging a free yielding to sex-desire. That too is fatal for the Path. As always, it is the Middle Path which is to be followed. What is meant is that the desires should be kept in the field of attention, *there to be dealt with* by detachment of the Self from them and consequent de-energising of them. To push them out of sight into one of the lumber-rooms of the mind is not to deal with them at all. One of the absolute essentials of the Path is that the disciple should face fearlessly whatever is in him, no matter how much his higher nature resents its presence. Self-ignorance and self-deceit are absolutely fatal.

[2] *Dhammapada*, 130.

Tranquil and fair and courteous be all words
Which from that presence win." [1]

While being truthful he must avoid the common egoistic fault of making his devotion to the truth an excuse for inflicting pain upon his hearers. This control of speech is by no means easy, as all who have tried to practise it are aware. In any case it is not possible to bring it to perfection until the mind is also disciplined.

The mental discipline is in fact the most essential of all, since it is in the raising of the mind to its true nature and in bringing about its union Verse 16 with the *buddhi* that the essence of the inner life is found. The mind must be tranquil, gentle and free from wandering thoughts. The word for the last quality is mauna, which literally means "silent," but, as the context shows, the silence in question is a mental one and signifies the ability to remain calmly still in the face of those outer stimuli which usually make the mind jump about like the monkey to which it is often compared.

In addition, it must be *Self*-controlled, able to direct or check its course of thought by its own inherent power, depending neither on the spur of physical necessity, nor on the lure of some outward gain; in the later stages at least it should not even depend for stillness upon the hypnotic rhythm of mantra repetition. Lastly, it must be pure in feeling too, free from all fear and hatred, filled with love and great compassion for all beings. It need hardly be added that if this discipline is to bear spiritual fruit it must be carried out harmoniously, without any one-sided exaggerations or Verse 17 fanaticisms, and with the *sattvik* characteristic of disregard of any personal gain. Love of the *Atman*, not fear of the world, must be the motive force behind the effort.

Verse 23   The chapter ends with the threefold designation of the *Brahman, Om Tat Sat*. This well-known *mantra* is intended here to show the Path along which a *sattvik* faith will lead the aspirant, thus indirectly answering the initial question of the chapter. *Om*, as is well known, signifies the *Brahman*, but also stands for the three great states of Consciousness [2] which lead up Verse 24 to the Fourth or transcendental state. With *Om* the acts of sacrifice and discipline that constitute the treading of the Path are commenced. That is to say, the attainment of the true Self, the Consciousness, though in its separated, individual form, is the task of the first stage.

Verse 25   The next stage, marked by what we have seen to be the typically *sattvik* characteristic of abandonment of all desire for fruit, is the bringing about of the union of that individual Self with the unindividuated *buddhi*, the cognitive aspect of the *Mahat Atman*, the One great Life. This stage is referred to by the word *Tat* (That) because it is through union with the Light Ocean of the *buddhi* that true knowledge of That, the transcendental

[1] *Light of Asia.*
[2] *Jagrat, swapna* and *sushupti.* See Appendix C.

Reality, is gained.

The last stage is symbolised by *Sat*, which stands for Being, also for *Verse 26* Goodness and Reality. This stage is the attainment of the *Brahman* and this attainment is the "praiseworthy deed" which the text mentions as yet another meaning of the word.

But we have seen in the fourteenth chapter (verse 26) that, instead of withdrawing his Light from the world and merging it in the unmanifested *Brahman*, it is possible for him who has won to the Goal to stay and serve the One, crucified in the countless suffering forms within the bitter Sea. Therefore the Gita adds that steadfastness in sacrifice, austerity and gift is *Verse 27* also *Sat*; meaning thereby that he who maintains his life of Sacrifice and offers up his dearly bought Salvation as a great Gift of Light to those who walk in darkness has no less attained than he who goes beyond to the other Shore. His *Sat* is "action for the sake of That" in all. Hence is it said that by this *mantra* of the triple Path have been brought forth of old the Teachers,[1] *Verse 23* Knowledge and the Sacrifices— the Sacrifices, namely, of those liberated Souls who find *Nirvana* in the very midst of Sorrow.

---

[1] The word *Brahmanas* in this verse is usually taken to refer to the books of that name, rather inferior books from the spiritual point of view. It seems more appropriate to take the word as referring to the *Brahmans* —i.e. Teachers of the Knowledge.

CHAPTER XVIII
THE YOGA OF THE RENUNCIATION OF LIBERATION [1]

THIS chapter commences with a question about the nature of true renunciation which arises out of the conclusion of the last. There it was taught that it is possible for the liberated soul to remain steadfast in service even after its liberation. Current teaching in India, however, taught that *all* action must be renounced. The *karma yoga* might be a useful and necessary preparation but, since all action springs from illusion, it was only intended to lead up to that final renunciation of all action that was known as *sannyasa*. The point is an important one since, if this latter idea is correct, it cuts away all possibility of their being any help for man from his liberated brothers; he who acts is still in bondage and he who is liberated cannot act.

Verse 2   The intention of this chapter is to show that this idea is not correct and accordingly Sri Krishna starts by making a distinction between *sannyasa* (renunciation) and *tyaga*. The former, he says, means the renunciation of desire-prompted actions. The mind, united with the *buddhi*, no longer flows outwards into the desire-currents but acts from the *buddhi*-determined knowledge of what is right. Obviously, though, it is still possible for the *sannyasi* to enjoy the fruits of his right action and when, in the course of time, his knowledge brings him to the threshold of the *Brahma Nirvana* there will be nothing to prevent his taking it and passing for ever from the manifested world.

   Therefore Sri Krishna goes on to teach that there is a further stage which he terms *tyaga*.[2] *Tyaga* consists in the giving up or dedicating to the One Life in all of the fruits which accrue from even right and desireless

Verse 3   actions. In spite of the views of some teachers that all action should be

---

[1] In some editions this chapter is entitled simply *sannyasa yoga*, but that is the title of chapter five. A few also give it as *moksha yoga*, but the full title is *moksha sannyasa yoga*.

[2] In popular usage *sannyasa* and *tyaga* are more or less synonyms, but in addition to the meaning of "relinquishment," *tyaga* has also the meaning of donation, or giving away (see Apte). I cannot think of any one English word which combines the two concepts of renouncing and giving except, perhaps, the word dedication. My friend Pandit J. C. Chatterji pointed out to me that the past participle, *tyakta*, is used of offerings made to the Gods in the sacrificial fire.

abandoned as leading to bondage, He asserts most categorically that acts of sacrifice, discipline and self-giving (the actions of the Path, as was pointed out at the end of the last chapter) should *not* be abandoned, for they are purifiers. Verse 6

Even these actions, though, should be performed without attachment, without, that is, the feeling of doing them for one's own personal purity. The fruit, also, which accrues from such action is to be set free for the service of the One Life, in the spirit that prompted the *Mahayana* followers of the *Bodhisattva* Path to make over the merit of their actions to the welfare of all beings. Some there are who object that such helping of others is mere illusion and would involve an infringement of the law of *Karma*. It will be time to listen to that objection when the objectors themselves deny ever having received any help through the medium of books or living teachers. Others there are who are kept back from this Path by a false humility. It will be time enough, they say, to think of such service when we ourselves are liberated and it becomes a real possibility. But that is a mistake. It is only he who, from the very start, has accustomed himself to the idea of treading the Path for the sake of all who will be able when face to face with the actual bliss of the *Brahma Nirvana* to be certain of being steadfast in sacrifice and of giving up his bliss to serve his suffering brothers.

This is the luminous *sattvik tyaga* as opposed to those other types of renunciation which spring from laziness, sense of inferiority, or desire to avoid the pain and suffering of life. Such "sour-grapes" renunciation is definitely inferior. It is a foul slander (whether ancient or modern) to represent the renunciation of the Buddha as having been of that sort. Truer insight was shown by the author of *The Light of Asia* when he made him say when about to leave his home: Verses 6, 7, 8

> "This will I do because the woeful cry
> Of life and all flesh living cometh up
> Into my ears, and all my soul is full
> Of pity for the sickness of the world;
> Which I will heal, if healing may be found
> By uttermost renouncing and great strife."

Love, not fear, is the mainspring of all true renunciation.

The doing of actions because they are in harmony with the Cosmic process as revealed by the *buddhi*, and so are "what ought to be done," but without the pride of agency and without the desire for personal fruit, is the highest renunciation. The abandonment of the actions themselves is impossible as long as the would-be renouncer has a body and is unnecessary under any circumstances, for the actions that are performed without any desire for fruit can bring no bondage to the Soul at any time. Verse 9 Verses 11, 12

When desire has been renounced and also personal gain there is

Verse 14 nothing left in action which can bind. To show that this is no dogma, but a plain fact, the Gita proceeds to give an analysis of the five factors that are involved in all action, whether bodily, verbal, or mental. These are the physical body, the "doer," that false self which is produced by the union of the Light with the psycho-physical vehicle, the various sense-organs, the vital energies (*cheshta*) within the body and, lastly, the forces accumulated by the *karma* of one's past lives (*daiva*).

Verses 16, 17 That being so, he who, through not having united himself with the *buddhi* (*akritabuddhi*) sees himself, the *Atman*, as bound up in actions is quite deluded. If the Self does not project itself into the forms by the notion "I am the doer," it can no more be affected by actions than the moon can be entangled in the ripples of a lake. As a Chinese sage has expressed it: "The moon is serenely reflected on the stream, the breeze passes softly through the pines. . . . When this is understood, the *karma* bonds are by nature empty. When not understood, we all pay for the past debts we have contracted." [1]

Verse 19 To further elucidate the point, the Gita shows that besides the nature of the action itself we must consider the actor and his knowledge. All these factors are shown to be threefold according to the *guna* that is predominant.

Verse 26 If the action is not to bind the Soul, all three of these must be *sattvik*. The actor must be one who is unattached and free from the sense of "I"; his knowledge must be that pure knowledge which sees one indestructible

Verse 22 Essence pervading all, "undivided in the separate beings," and the action itself must be appropriate, sanctioned by the inner Ruler and skilfully

Verses 23, 25 performed with regard to the actor's capacity and to the consequences for others.

This last statement is sufficient to show that, in advocating renunciation of the fruit of action, the Gita is not sanctioning irresponsible acts. The consequences of actions upon others must always be looked to; it is only the personal gains that are to be renounced. It is true that there are certain verses in the *Puranas* and elsewhere which represent liberated souls while still on earth as going about laughing and crying and behaving irresponsibly "like children or idiots." But these verses must not be taken literally. The man of Knowledge is not an idiot, nor does he manifest his liberation by childish behaviour. It is true that personal thinking will have come to an end in him, but in its place the Cosmic Ideation manifests through him, and though his acts may not accord with established social conventions they are in harmony with the great Cosmic Order.

Verses 29-32 It is not necessary to follow through in detail the threefold nature of reason (*buddhi*), firmness and pleasure, as the account verses given in verses 29 to 39 is perfectly straightforward and needs no comment, except to say that the word *buddhi* here signifies the ordinary intellect and not the higher *buddhi* of which so much mention has been made. The latter

---

1 *Yoka Daishi.* Quoted from Suzuki's *Manual of Zen Buddhism.*

is *sattvik* in nature and is beyond the mind, while the former comes under the influence of all of the gunas and is a mental function. It has, however, this in common with the higher *buddhi* that, when *sattvik*, it is able to determine truth upon its own level and, in so far as intellectual truth is one, it is the same in all.

With verse forty-one, as Shankara has pointed out, a new section begins. Up to this point the chapter has formed an integral part of the last block of six chapters and has been concerned with setting forth in detail the principles underlying Sri Krishna's teaching in the earlier chapters. From the point of view of the disciple they represent the effort to assimilate and express in intellectual terms the Divine Knowledge revealed in the Vision of the Cosmic Form. From verse forty-one onwards the Gita turns to the task of summing up the whole.

Reference has already been made (chapter iv, v. 13) to the fourfold order of society. The Divine foundation there claimed for the classification of men into *Brahmans, Kshattriyas, Vaishyas* and *Shudras* must not be interpreted as sanctioning the injustices and prejudices of the orthodox Hindu caste system. It is not necessary to point out that there is plenty of evidence that the caste system itself in ancient India was not always the rigid and lifeless institution that it now is.

In any case, what the Gita is concerned with is not any particular sociological system, however ancient, but something far more universal. It is expressly stated that the classification in question depends upon the *gunas* manifested in the natures of the men concerned. Not only in India, but all over the world there are four great types of men. There is the *Brahman*, the teaching, priestly, legal, or "professional" type; the *Kshattriya*, the ruling, warrior, statesman type, the "hunting and shooting man" of the West; the *Vaishya*, or banking, merchant, agricultural type, and, lastly, the *Shudra*, the servant, manual labourer type. Each of these great types has certain well-defined characteristics, sometimes, though not at all necessarily, inherited by their offspring, and, though some overlapping undoubtedly occurs, they are at least as well-marked throughout the world and in all ages as, say, the modern psychological division into introverts and extroverts.

It must be noted that the qualities by which a man is classified under one of these types are, in the cases of the *Brahman* and *Kshattriya* at least, of a moral and intellectual nature. A man is not a *Brahman* because he is the son of a *Brahman*, nor even because he performs professional priestly functions. He is a *Brahman* if he possesses certain qualities, such as control of mind and senses, self-discipline, forgiveness, straightforwardness and wisdom. In this the Gita agrees with the Buddha, who also said: "Not by matted hair, nor by lineage, nor by birth is one a *Brahman*. He is a *Brahman* in whom there are truth and righteousness." [1]

Verse 42

[1] *Dhammapada*, 393.

The four types have also an important symbolic significance for the inner life. The *Brahman*, detached and pure, seeing the One in all, stands for the *sattvik buddhi*. The *Kshattriya*, ruler, fearless and much-enduring, is the pure *rajasik manas*, the higher mind. That is why Arjuna, the individual Self, is represented as a *Kshattriya*. The *Vaishya*, concerned with the getting of wealth, symbolises the desire-nature (*rajas* mixed with *tamas*), always flowing outwards, while the *Shudra*, born to serve, stands for the *tamasik* physical body, instrument of all.

Verse 45   The verses which follow describe how perfection is to be won by being intent on one's own duty (*dharma*). The word *dharma* signifies the quality or natural function of a thing or person. Thus, the *dharma* of fire is to burn and the *dharma* of a *Kshattriya* is to manifest the qualities mentioned in verse 43. In these verses we must bear in mind the inner as well as the outer significance of the fourfold system.

Verses 46, 47   Perfection is to be attained by using one's own characteristic functions in the service of That "from which this manifestation has proceeded." The attempt to perform the *dharma* of another is fraught with danger since it will be an attempt to build one's life on the basis of an undeveloped, and so inferior, function. It is like the successful comedian who aspires to take a tragic part, the result being usually a complete failure. The *dharma* to which one is called may seem by human standards a defective or inferior one but, on deeper analysis, it will be found that the same is true of all *dharmas*, just because they are relative and perfection is only in the Whole. Nevertheless, all are necessary to the working of the Cosmos and one can "see Infinity within a grain of sand."

From the inner point of view an equally important meaning attaches to this performance of duty without regard for the fruits, this worship of the One through one's own natural function. Man is not a creature of this physical plane alone, and perfection will be attained when all the various levels of his being, as symbolised by the four types, fulfil their natural functions in perfection. Even the desire-nature, the most troublesome part of man, has its work to perform in the Cosmos and, once again, the Gita is teaching that instead of the Light's being withdrawn from the manifested universe, in the manner of the *Sankhyas*, it should function free and unattached on all the levels. The *tamasik* inertia of the physical body and the fierce rush of the desire-mind are to be transmitted by non-attachment into stability and energy respectively. Thus controlled and mastered they, no less than the luminous *buddhi*, are fit instruments for the service of the One.

Verse 51   This *yoga* by which all the levels are transmuted is the Path to mastery of the Cosmos. The disciple must be united to the One Life by the pure *buddhi*, the wasteful rush of the mind (*atmanam*) must be checked by firmness so that it moves by its own power and is no longer pulled and pushed by the blind forces of attraction and repulsion. The objects of the senses, no longer considered as objects of personal enjoyment, must be dedicated[1] to the service of the One Life. Studiously detaching himself (*vivikta sevi*) from the forms, constant in that inner meditation which needs no special time or place or posture, he will cut the knot of egoism so that the distorted movements of lust, hate, violence and greed to which that knot gives birth will cease and die. Verse 52

Then is the disciple ripe for becoming the Eternal *Brahman*. He who was human has become the Cosmic Man, his feet— no more of clay—firm based on earth, his head high in the cloudless sky above. Of all the levels of the manifested world he is the master. Nowhere is anything he need reject, for all that is, is verily the *Brahman*. Himself the calm eternal *Atman* far beyond all sorrow, he now, if he has come along the Path of Love, attains to that supreme devotion which consists in sacrificing his own immediate bliss to serve that same Eternal in the world of gloom and darkness. Verse 54

By that great Love he knows the One in its essential nature. He is the true *advaiti* (non-dualist) for he knows that there is no need to flee from "this" into "That." He knows the meaning of the *Mahayana* phrase, "*Nirvana* and *Sansara* are the same," and thus through love he throws away salvation, to find it where he stands.[2] He may and does perform all actions freely, but all the time his heart is fixed on the Eternal and through Its grace,[3] Its calm enlightening power, wherever he may be, whatever he may do, he dwells eternally within the Great Abode. Verse 55 Verse 56

At this point Sri Krishna drops the general exposition and speaks direct to His disciple's heart. He promises him that if he puts aside all selfish fear and clings to the Light within, Its power will carry him past all the obstacles and dangers that confront him on the way. At the same time, He adds the warning that the treading of the Path, the fight against the embattled Powers of Darkness, is, in the end, inevitable. His egoistic desire for enjoyment and fear of suffering may hold him back from the fight for the time, but in the end the remorseless pressure of cosmic evolution will force his feet along the Path he shrinks from now, and that same egoism that held him back, fatted like an ox for the sacrifice, will be remorselessly destroyed. Verses 58, 59

For that great Ruling Power which guides the Cosmos is seated in the heart of every being. Whirling as though upon a potter's wheel, none can escape "the Spirit's plastic stress." However much man may proclaim himself an independent ego existing for and in himself, the Ruling Power of Spirit is within him and will not let him rest. Man is, as it were, bound Verse 61

---

[1] *Tyakta.* The sense of dedication is dominant here.
[2] This is the meaning underlying the *Vaishnava* rejection of *mukti* (liberation) in order to serve Krishna. It is obvious that it is also the *Bodhisattva* doctrine of the Buddhists.
[3] The word *prasad* means grace and also tranquil clarity. In using the former meaning one must guard against the introduction of any of the theistic sentimentalities that cluster round the term. It is not in any way like the capricious favours of a Maharaja, but more like the power inherent in a magnet to make magnets of any bits of iron that adhere to it.

to the Centre of his being by an elastic cord; the more he strains at it, the greater will be the reaction. This is why an exaggerated movement of materialism is followed by an equally exaggerated religiosity, an age of licence by an age of Puritan restraint.

Sooner or later, all must tread the Path; but in the meanwhile there is no compulsion. The will of man, a spark of the Divine willing, is ineluctably free, and no true Teacher ever forces his disciple even for the latter's good. Verse 63 Having revealed the Secret Path of Wisdom, all that He says is, "having reflected on it fully, do as thou wishest." The Path is free to all; each has the right to enter but none will ever compel him or trespass in the least upon his will.

But why await the age-long grinding of the cycles, when all the while the Middle Path exists, and may be trodden by whoever will? Avoiding the Verse 62 lures of sensual desire on the one hand, and of reactionary asceticism on the other, let the disciple consecrate his *whole being* to the service of the Divine Power dwelling in his heart. Prefacing His words by the statement that what He is about to say is the ultimate Mystery, the supreme teaching, Krishna repeats the verse with which He had concluded chapter nine:

"Fix thy mind on Me, give thy heart's love to Me, consecrate all thy Verse 65 actions to My service, hold thine own self as nothing before Me. To Me then shalt thou come; truly I promise for thou art dear to Me."

Krishna stands here for the Eternal One manifesting as the boundless Life in all, but His words are also true as applied to the human Teacher. If the disciple consecrates his life, actions, feelings and thoughts, without exception, to the loved Teacher, and if he meditates upon Him *as being within his heart*, His form will come to be a symbol of his own diviner Self and speak with that Self's voice to guide him through the fight.

This method is an easier one for most because the human form draws forth most easily the love of man. Love is the easiest way to self-transcendence; urged on by love, man holds himself as naught. The disciple must still undertake the actual fighting; Krishna is charioteer and bears no arms. Nevertheless, his inexhaustible power will flow through the dedicated vehicles, and with Him as guide the victory is sure.

As the disciple proceeds, the beloved Form becomes more and more the heart and focus of his life, until no thought or action is performed except in relationship to Him. Gradually as He becomes the Ruling Power of the disciple's life, and the latter's vision turns increasingly inwards, the Form will recede and grow unimportant, leaving in its place that which is both in Teacher and disciple, "the Light that lighteth every man that cometh into the world," the one great Life that streams throughout all beings. This is the moment when the Teacher whispers in the ear of his disciple the mystic words of the *Upanishad*: "That art thou" ; and, having whispered, retires for ever, leaving his pupil an Enlightened One who is himself the Teacher and the Goal.

This is what is meant by that taking refuge in Krishna which, when Verse 66 accomplished, frees the disciple from all other duties. The latter has no longer to think of any duties of his own to be fulfilled nor any mastery of his separate vehicles, for his whole life on all levels is consecrated to Him. When, as described above, he reaches the level of union with the One Life, all "sins" drop from him in Its pure and stainless Light. The statement "I will liberate thee from all sins" is no cheap theological promise but a plain statement of the fact that in losing self all sins are lost as well. Henceforth the free. Divine, pervading Life alone acts through what men in ignorance will still call "him."

The Gita adds a warning against communicating this Mystery to anyone Verse 67 who is undisciplined, without love, without desire to serve (*ashushrushu*), or who speaks evil of the Teacher. This prohibition is not prompted by any spirit of exclusiveness but by the desire to prevent harm being done. The above-mentioned types would assuredly fail to understand its inner meaning and, grasping at the letter of such promises as that in verse 66, would harm themselves and others.[1]

The next two verses make this entirely clear, for they set forth the praises of those who impart the mystic teaching to such as are ready to profit by it. They are the renouncers of personal salvation to whom the chapter title refers, they who out of transcendent devotion (*para bhakti*, cf. verse 54) set aside their bliss till every living being can share it with them. It is for this great Sacrifice that Krishna says of them, that none either are Verse 69 or ever will be dearer to Him. They are the calm Great Ones [2] spoken of by *Shankaracharya* who, having themselves crossed over the Ocean, devote themselves unselfishly to helping other to cross.

Little remains to say.[3] The Path, the Goal and the Great Sacrifice have been set forth and understood and the Soul breaks out in triumphant ecstasy:

"Destroyed is my delusion. Memory has been regained. By Thy grace, Verse 73 O Unfallen One, my doubts are gone. Thy bidding I will do."

Once before,[4] after the first inner perception of the spiritual Pervading Powers, Arjuna has proclaimed the vanishing of his delusion, but now the further steps have been accomplished. He is established in Reality; he has regained his Memory of That Eternal One from which he came, to which he now returns. All Knowledge now is his and, with the alternatives before him of eternal changeless bliss or of unwearying service of his suffering

---

[1] The use of the Gita to justify bomb outrages and the futilities of sentimental pietism are instances of what can result from a disregard of this prohibition.

[2] *Shanta Mahantah*—i.e. those who, though realising their nature as the *Shanta Atman*, beyond all manifestation, yet remain on the level of the *Mahat Atman*, the cosmic Ideation or Divine Wisdom (*Viveka Chudamani*, verse 39).

[3] The reference to the results of simply hearing with faith (verse 71) must be understood in the light of what has been said about faith in the previous chapter.

[4] Gita, xi, I.

brother-men, he chooses the latter and cries out to the Unfallen Changeless Being that he will do His bidding and will serve Him to the end.

Thus ends the dialogue between the Soul and its eternal Source. It is the Soul itself that is enlightened, but the illumination is brought down to the level of the ordinary waking personality by the mediation of Sanjaya, the link between the two. "Remembering, remembering" the glories of that Divine Enlightenment, he floods the heart with joy and proclaims the undying truth, that when the human Soul is united with the Divine, victory, welfare and righteousness are eternally assured.

Verses 76-78

APPENDICES

APPENDIX A
NOTE ON THE TERMS CONSCIOUSNESS AND FORM

THE two terms, consciousness and form, are in constant use throughout this book and an understanding of the sense in which they are used is of vital importance.

If any experience is analysed—say, for example, the visual experience of a blue disc—two aspects can be distinguished. There is the content, a round blue shape in this instance, and the "awareness" of that shape. The content is what I have termed *form* and the awareness *consciousness*.

It must be carefully noted that form does not here mean outline, but filled-in content-shape, and the term must also be understood in the same way of other elements of experience, sensuous or non-sensuous. For instance we have the "form" of a sound, a taste, a feeling, or a thought, which must be understood by analogy with the forms of visual experience.

In contrast with these forms, which are all different both as regards individual forms within one class and as regards different classes of forms, there is the awareness or consciousness, which is of the same sort throughout.

There are many drawbacks to the use of the word consciousness. In the first place it is used in half a dozen different senses by philosophers and psychologists, and in the second place it suffers from the great drawback that it has no active verbal form. One can say "to be conscious of" but not "to conscious" such-and-such an object. There is the word "awareness" and the dubious coined derivative "awaring," which I have also occasionally pressed into service, but it is ugly and not very current. The best term is one that was coined by E. D. Fawcett in his *The World as Imagination, Zermatt Dialogues*, etc. The term in question is *consciring*— *i.e.* "knowing together"—and has as its correlative, for the content-form, the word *conscitum* (plural, *conscita*) I should certainly have availed myself of these coinages but, unfortunately, they are not as yet sufficiently widely current to be generally understood and, moreover, a great deal of the book had been written before I came across Fawcett's writings.

It should be clear from introspective meditation that all forms are sustained in consciousness, and that, apart from consciousness, we know nothing and can know nothing of forms. It is in fact meaningless to talk of forms as existing apart from consciousness.[1] The objects supposed by some to exist behind the forms are mere mental constructs devised for dealing with experience in practice. No one knows them, no one can ever know them; to believe in their existence is a pure and quite uncalled-for act of faith.

It should not be supposed that by the forms are meant sensations, camera pictures of reality located somewhere in the brain. The brain itself (as an "object") is one of the constructs of which mention has just been made. The usefulness of such constructs in certain realms of thought and study is not at all denied, but they are irrelevant here.

The primary bedrock of experience is not sensations in the eye, ear, or brain, but visual and other forms *in space*. All the rest is inference and construction. Materialistic science begins by abstracting consciousness from the forms in order to deal with them more objectively and impersonally and then, when analysis fails to reveal any life or conscious principle in those forms, triumphantly exclaims that all is mechanism, nowhere is there anything of a spiritual nature. Behaviourist psychology is an example of the same procedure applied to mental life. If you start by abstracting consciousness from phenomena it is obviously absurd to expect to find it as a term in your concluded analysis. For this reason no one should feel disappointed that science (as nowadays practised) does not know anything of the existence of "the soul." It is the old story of looking for one's spectacles when they are on one's nose.

To go into this subject fully would require a volume and not an appendix. Here I am only concerned to indicate the sense in which the word consciousness has been used in this book. It follows from that sense that the modern term "unconscious" mind can have no meaning. There is not the slightest reason for supposing that anything whatever, physical or mental, exists or can exist save as the content of consciousness. Hence we can talk of a sub- or a superconscious mind, meaning by those terms mental processes that are sustained in consciousness below or above the level at which it is normally focused, processes which are not attended to by normal consciousness, but we cannot talk of an unconscious mind, for that would have no meaning.

It only remains to add that the Sanskrit term for what is here termed consciousness is *chit*, as distinct from *chitta*, which means the mind. The Buddhists, on the other hand, speak of *Vijnana* (Pali—*vinnana*). Thus consciousness illuminating visual forms is called *caksuh-vijnana*

---

[1] This position must by no means be confused with that of subjective idealism. The consciousness spoken of is not "your" or "my" consciousness, in fact "you" and "I" exist only as constellated form-sequences brought to foci in that consciousness which, in itself, is neither human nor individualised, but a pervading Light.

(eye-consciousness), illuminating thoughts, *mano-vijnana* (mind-consciousness), and so on. Beyond the sense and mind consciousness (at least in *Mahayana* systems) is the *Alaya Vijnana* or store-consciousness, corresponding to the *Mahat Atman* as used in this book. The Mahayanists also use the word *chitta* to do duty for consciousness as well as for mind. For instance they will speak indifferently of *chitta-matra* or *Vijnana-matra*, meaning by both terms pure consciousness.

APPENDIX B
NOTE ON THE WORDS SOUL AND MATTER

THE word Soul as used in this book does not refer to a separate entity within the body but to the inner centre of the linked streams of experience that make up a personality. That centre is a focus in consciousness, not any individual's consciousness but the all-pervading sea of Light. As such it is not a separate "entity" any more than the focus to which light is brought by a lens is a separate entity. That focus primarily exists on the level of the higher or pure manas, but a projection of it is to be found functioning as the desire-mind or personality lower down. It is that lower or projected centre that is the core of the empirical personality. It does not exist in any objective way, but comes into being as a centre to which our experiences are referred. That is why a very young child has no sense of self and that, too, is why, when in certain pathological states the experience-content gets organised into two instead of one constellation, we get two selves instead of one—the so-called dissociation of a personality.

As for the higher Self, the true ego, that too is not a "thing-in-itself." It is however a focus which lasts through ages. Itself not born, it yet emanates that projection which forms the self of any given life. Its own content when outward-looking is the accumulated fruit of the experiences gained by its repeated projections, and when inward-looking the universal knowledge of the *buddhi*.

In a still higher sense the Self is the One Life in all (*Mahat Atman*), seeing through all the foci but beyond them all. In the highest sense it is the transcendental Self, the *Shanta Atman*. Beyond that is the *Parabrahman*, no self at all.

It will be seen that Soul and Self have been used synonymously. When the former word has been used it was because the context needed a warmer emotional tone than is conveyed by the more philosophic term Self. In particular it refers to what has been termed the true Ego, backed by the feeling-knowledge of the *buddhi*.

The Sanskrit word *Atman*, of which self is a translation, is used in just the same way of any level with which the Light is identified.

Sometimes the body, more often the mind (*e.g.* Gita, vi, 5), sometimes the *buddhi* (*e.g. jnanatman* in *Kathopanishad*), sometimes the One Life, the Cosmic Ideation (*Mahat Atman*), sometimes the transcendental Self (*Shanta Atman*), sometimes, though only symbolically, the *Parabrahman* (*Paramatman—e.g.* Gita, xv, 18). In this last case the term should be taken as signifying That which is the reality behind all self. It will be seen from this that *Atman* is not a thing, but a Light or, as was perhaps the earliest meaning of the word, a "breath."

Throughout this book self with a small "s" signifies the empirical or personal self, Self with a capital the true ego or higher Self. Qualifying adjectives are added to denote the still higher levels.

Turning now to the word "matter" it is necessary to point out that it is *not* used in the sense of "stuff" existing in its own right. It has been shown in the course of the book that there is not the slightest reason to suppose that any such " stuff" exists at all. It is a mental construction and under the eye of modern physics it is evaporating more and more with each new advance. There is nothing beyond or behind the sense-data— except the *Brahman*, which, if the word must be used, is the only "stuff" that exists. The billiard-ball atoms of the nineteenth century, the miniature solar systems of the early twentieth and the waves of probability of the present are all alike pure mental constructions evolved for the explaining, measuring and predicting of experience, and have no more reality in themselves than mathematical concepts such as the square root of minus one.

Where the word matter has been used in this book it is in the sense of objectivity, of content standing over against the Light, of self-projection into that content and of the Self-loss, separation and pluralism that result. The descent of the Soul into Matter signifies the going-out of the Light into its content, its self-identification with it and the consequent increasing objectification of the latter. This should be borne in mind throughout.

APPENDIX C
NOTE ON THE FOUR STATES OF CONSCIOUSNESS

THROUGHOUT Hindu philosophic and symbolic writings frequent references are made to the three states of Consciousness, *Jagrat, Swapna, Sushupti,* and the fourth transcendent state known simply as *Turiya,* or "the fourth." Translated as the waking, dreaming and deep-sleep states, this scheme seems to many merely a rather naive attempt at classification of psychological states. To those who have more vision it is a key to unlock many locks. The "dreaming" and "deep-sleep" states are not to be identified with the states commonly known as such. Rather, the latter are species of those genera. The *Jagrat* or "waking" state is that of ordinary consciousness, a state in which the Consciousness illuminates the field of outer sense-data. It is the world of outer objectivity, or, more strictly speaking, it is the world in which the division of subject and object is most clearly apparent. In this state we think of the "world" as something quite outside us and quite independent of ourselves. It would exist, we feel, even if we did not. That is why *The Voice of the Silence* refers to it as the *Hall of Ignorance.*

The second or *Swapna* (literally, dreaming) state is felt as an inner world. Its content is made up of the data of the *inner* senses and of the thoughts, and it reaches up as high as the *manas.* Though the distinction between subject and object is not felt to be so hard and fast it still persists, as, of course, does the illusion of plurality. In the *Jagrat* state the world was felt as a hostile or at best neutral environment in which we are arbitrarily plunged, but in the *Swapna* state it is felt even by us that the content of that world is a projection of our own psyche. However unpleasant we may find the environment of a dream, or the universe of thought in which we are absorbed, we recognise (at least afterwards) that it was our own creation. Its unpleasantness is due to something unpleasant in us. This is the world of inner, often hidden, desire and of psychic forms. *The Voice of the Silence* calls it the *Hall of Learning* because it is through experience of that state that we learn, first, that we are not the physical body, and secondly, that environment is self-created and is an outer manifestation of our own past acts and thoughts (*karma*). "What is to be learnt from it is that all that happens to us is the inevitable result of what we have thought, and in that plastic world this can be readily seen and grasped. If one's thoughts have been harmonious our *Swapna* environment, whether in day-time phantasy, at night, or after death, will be a pleasant one (*cf.* the heaven worlds of mythology and spiritualism), which may tempt us to linger enjoying vivid pleasures. How often for example would we not like to prolong those vivid dreams in which, though we have a body, it no longer clogs us with its inert weight and we fly and do all manner of pleasant things with an unheard-of ease?"

Nevertheless "under every flower a serpent is coiled," the serpent of desire. However pleasant it may be, this world is still a world of desire and plurality, and, as the *Upanishad* says, "As long as there is plurality there is fear."

The disciple must therefore pass on to the third state, the state of *Sushupti* (dreamless sleep), termed in *The Voice of the Silence* the *Hall of Wisdom*. This is the level of *buddhi-mahat* and is termed the hall of wisdom because in it plurality, the great illusion, has vanished: all is one living Unity of Light. It may be wondered why the dark state of dreamless sleep should be taken to typify this state if it is One of Light. The reason for the darkness of the state as known to most men is that they are centred in the personality (lower *manas*) and cannot rise to their own true Selves, still less to union with the *buddhi* above. The result is that when the pluralistic vision of the lower self is transcended nothing is left except a dark blank, retaining of the true *Sushupti* nothing except its unity.

As Gaudapada puts it in his *Karikas* on the *Mandukya Upanishad* (iii, 34 and 35): "The condition of the mind of a wise man in *samadhi* (trance on the *Sushupti*-level), free from imaginations, is to be distinguished from that of dreamless sleep for it is not the same. In sleep the mind is simply overpowered, but not so in *samadhi*, for then it is the fearless *Brahman* blazing with the light of Knowledge." And Shankara comments: "For the condition of the mind immersed, during sleep, in the torpidity of ignorance (*avidya*—i.e. the idea of plurality), and still full of the potential impressions of the cause of experience, is quite distinct from that absolutely independent and perfectly tranquil condition of *samadhi*, all light."

The above explains why it is that the *Upanishads* declare that the Soul goes to the *Brahman* every night in sleep and also why modern readers are apt to feel that, if that is so, going to *Brahman* can be no very great affair! Again, when the *Upanishads* declare that the waking feeling "happy I slept" is the memory of the bliss of *Brahman* (more exactly of the *Mahat Atman*) they are not referring to a physical feeling of refreshment after sleep but to a phenomenon well known on the Path. In early stages it will happen that, though the personal consciousness of the disciple is not able to unite properly with the *buddhi*, yet *Sushupti* experience is able to be reflected in his personal mind, and he may be aware of it in his waking consciousness either as a memory of a peculiarly vivid dream felt to be charged with spiritual meaning or simply as a feeling of inner bliss felt equally to be of intense significance, though of what it was about he has no knowledge.

The *Turiya* (fourth) state is that of sheer transcendence, the unmanifested Consciousness of the *Shanta Atman*. It is the Goal and is best left in silence.

It may be added that the *Mandukya Upanishad*, which deals with these four states, though in a very compressed manner, states that the *Mantra Om* can be considered as split up into the three elements, A, U and M. Of these A signifies the *Jagrat* state, U the *Swapna* and M the *Sushupti*, while the *Om*, taken as a single unity, stands for the "Fourth."

The repeated counsel to meditate on the *Om* has no reference to setting up "vibrations" in the subtle body but to raising the consciousness through the three stages into the Fourth. See also the verses from *Mundaka Upanishad* quoted on the fly-leaf of this book.

APPENDIX D
NOTE ON AVATARAS

As chapter four (particularly verses 6 to 8) is the main authority for the doctrine of Avataras or Divine Incarnations it is perhaps desirable to say a word or two on the subject. According to orthodox tradition certain times in the history of the world have been marked by direct Divine "descents." Besides less-known ones, Rama Chandra, Sri Krishna, Buddha and, by the more liberal-minded, Christ are usually considered as such. There is a well-known list of ten which is generally accepted, though the Bhagavata has a less widely known list of twenty-four. The doctrine is accepted as a relative truth by the *Advaita Vedanta* school, though in strict accuracy it can find little place in *Advaita* thought, for which all forms and all births are due to ignorance. In reality the teaching belongs to the theistic *Vaishnava* schools and it is notable that, practically speaking, all *avataras* are descents of *Vishnu*. The general doctrine is that *Vishnu*, conceived as a personal God, from time to time takes birth among men in forms which are sometimes considered material *ad hoc* creations, sometimes as beneficent illusions created by Him (*cf.* Docetism), sometimes as eternal, spiritual forms projected into the ken of ordinary mortals on special occasions.

The first theory is altogether naif and is that of the unreflecting man in the street. It involves an arbitrary interference with the laws of causation and postulates a psycho-physical complex with no *karmik* antecedents whatever.

The third theory was evolved to meet the emotional requirements of devotees but is also exposed to various difficulties. First, it assumes the existence of eternal forms; second, it assumes that such forms exactly resemble familiar material forms except in the undefined adjective "spiritual"; thirdly, it has to fall back upon mystery to explain why such forms should be perceptible at some times and not at others.

The " Docetism" of the second theory is apt to repel both the common sense of the man in the street and the emotions of the devotee. Nevertheless it conceals profounder doctrines than appear at first sight, for the real Krishna, Buddha, or Christ is not the outer form which, *like all other forms*, is illusory, but the birthless and invisible *Atman* within, known to Buddhist tradition as the *Dharmakaya*.

The best way of stating the position seems to be as follows. When after countless lives of suffering followed by the mystical seven lives of effort a man has climbed the ladder and stands upon the edge of the Goal, two possibilities exist. If his past struggles have been motivated only by the wish for his personal salvation then he may, and in all probability will, merge himself within the white eternal Light and vanish for ever from the world of men. If on the other hand his efforts have been dominated by love and compassion for his fellows, instead of merging in the Light he may manifest that Light through his perfected but still existing lower vehicles of mind and body, thus bringing about a "descent" of that Light into the world of men. Thereafter "he" is no more a man as we understand the term but a mere vehicle for the manifestation of the Eternal. This is the true meaning of the *avatarana*, or descent.

The first type may be compared to a man who climbs a tree and plucks and eats the fruits; the second to one who, having plucked, descends with them to distribute to his fellows.

The matter has been beautifully expressed in the *Gnostic Crucifixion*, translated by Mead from the *Acts of John*:

"But this is not the cross of wood that thou shalt see . . . nor am I [Christ] he that is upon the cross. I was held to be what I was not, not being what I was to many others; nay, they will call me something else, abject and not worthy of Me. As then the Place of Rest is neither seen nor spoken of, much more shall I, the Lord of it, be neither seen nor spoken of. . . . Pay no attention then, to the many and them that are without the mystery think little of; for know that I am wholly with the Father and the Father with Me. . . . What thou art, thou seest; this did I show unto thee. But what I am, this I alone know, and none else. . . . Thou hearest that I suffered; yet I did not suffer. . . . And thus I speak separating off the man. First then understand the Logos (*Atman*), then shalt thou understand the Lord (*Brahman*), and in the third place only the man (the "human" teacher) and what he suffered."

One other point remains to be noticed. It will be remembered that in connection with chapter four it was stated that where the tension in the inner worlds becomes sufficiently acute, a manifestation would take place. Just as the lightning strikes the highest object so, in the absence of a man who has climbed to the top of the Ladder, the spiritual flash will strike the most spiritually evolved man of the time and so produce, according to his stature, one of those partial manifestations known to Hindu tradition as *ansha avataras*.

APPENDIX E
DIAGRAM OF THE COSMIC LEVELS

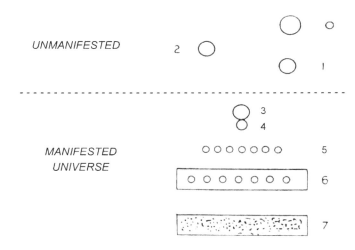

Number 0. *Parabrahman, Purushottama*, beyond all levels.
    „   1. *Shanta Atman*, Pure Consciousness, Unmanifested Self, *Adhyatma, Swabhava*.
    „   2. *Mula-prakriti*, the Matrix, Unmanifested Object, *Avyakta*.
    „   3. *Mahat Atman, Mahat*, the One Life, Great Self, *adhi-daivata*, Cosmic Ideation, Divine Wisdom.
    „   4. *Buddhi*, knowledge of Number 3, also the faculty by which that knowledge is acquired, *jnana atman*.
    „   5. *Manas*, higher Mind, *Ahankara*, Individual Egos, the "point of view," *jiva, Adhiyajna*.
    „   6. Lower *manas*—i.e. *manas* united with the desire-nature; personalities; also the Indriyas (senses) and their inner objects, *Adhibhuta*.
    „   7. The outer world, objects of the outer senses, *Adhibhuta*.

Numbers 0 and 1 are often taken as one, and so are Numbers 3 and 4. Number 6 is sometimes split into two when the lower *manas* is differentiated from the pure desire-nature. Where the five levels of consciousness are spoken of Number 2 is omitted as on the same level as Number 1, and Numbers 6 and 7 are taken together, as both are brought to a focus in the lower mind. It will be noticed that, while Number 7 is purely objective, Number 6 has two aspects, subjective and objective. It is the level of the desire-mind and also of the objects of the inner senses.

APPENDIX F
NOTE ON THE PROCESS OF COSMIC MANIFESTATION

The manifestation of a Cosmos depends on the polarisation of the One, the *Parabrahman*, into the transcendental Subject, the *Shanta Atman*, and the transcendental Object, the *Mula-prakriti*. While it would be obviously absurd to attempt to explain how that polarisation actually occurs, it may be useful to make a few suggestions as to how we may conceive it as occurring.

Let us take as a basis the sublime Creation Hymn of the *Rig-Veda* (x, 129, Griffith's translation):

> 1) "There was not non-existent nor existent;
> there was no realm of air, no sky beyond it.
> What covered in, and where? and what gave shelter?
> Was water there, unfathomed depth of water?"

"Existent" (*sat*) must here be taken in the sense of ex-istent, something which "stands forth." Note that while *air* (the moving world of *manas* and plurality) and *sky* (the calmly shining Cosmic Ideation, *Mahat*) are negated, that which covered in (the all-enfolding consciousness or *Shanta Atman*) and the *depth of water* (the Matrix or *Mula-prakriti*) are not negated but questioned. It cannot be said of them that they are not, though neither can it be said that they are.

> 2) "Death was not there, nor was there aught immortal:
> No sign was there, the day's and night's divider.
> That One Thing, breathless, breathed by Its own nature:
> Apart from It was nothing whatsoever."

The *mortal* personalities and the *immortal* Egos had not come into existence nor was there any division between the *dark* or lower half of the Cosmos and the *light* upper half. The One however was not in a static death-like state, but was characterised by a rhythmic process which will be discussed later.

> 3) "Darkness there was: at first concealed in Darkness
> the All was indiscriminated chaos.
> All that existed then was void and formless:
> by the great power of warmth (*tapas*) was born that Unit."

So far beyond all thought or imagination is that One that It is only to be conceived as Darkness. In that Darkness was buried the potentiality of all existence. By the power of *tapas* or self-limitation arose the Unit, the *Shanta Atman*, or One Consciousness.

> 4) " Thereafter rose Desire (*kama*) in the beginning.
> Desire the primal seed and germ of *Manas*.
> Sages who searched with their heart's thought discovered
> the existent's kinship in the non-existent."

With the arising of the unitary Consciousness the other aspect of the One becomes the Object (*Mula-prakriti*) and, attracting the attention of the Consciousness, causes an outpouring of energy which is here termed Desire and which is the root of the individual Self (*manas*). The second half of the verse tells how, by searching within the heart (*manas*), the original undifferentiated Reality is to be found.

> 5) "Transversely was their severing line extended:
> What was above it then, and what below it?
> There were begetters, there were mighty forces,
> free action here and energy up yonder."

Below these two is a great gulf, the "abyss" of the *Kabala*, which divides the manifested below from the unmanifested above. Above was the massive energy and "here" (*i.e.* below) the *begetters*, mighty forces of "desire" spiralling downwards and referred to in Gita (xi, 15) as the Divine Serpents.

> 6) "Who verily knows and who can here declare it,
> whence it was born and whence comes this creation?
> The Gods are later than this world's production.
> Who knows then whence it first came into being?"

The actual first impulse to creation is for ever hidden in the Darkness, and that is why the Buddha kept silent on the subject and refused to go beyond Desire. The Gods who are the levels of manifested consciousness came into being later. In other words, Consciousness cannot penetrate to its own root.

> 7) "He, the first origin of this creation,
> whether He formed it all or did not form it,
> Whose eye controls this world in highest heaven,
> He verily knows it, or perhaps He knows not."

The proximate origin of the creation is *He*, the *Shanta Atman*, the One Consciousness, whose *eye controls this world in highest heaven*, all the forms being drawn forth and sustained by and in that Consciousness. The ultimate root is, however, even beyond that *Atman*. Not even for the *Shanta Atman* can It be an object of knowledge, for to know It is to merge in It and in that merging the separate Knower comes to an end.

One point remains to be noticed. The second verse states that in the One (even during the period of *pralaya*) there is a certain rhythmic process symbolised as breathing. Within the One exist in potentiality the two poles of Subject and Object (which, it will be remembered, were not entirely negated in verse one). We may conceive that "breath" as a rhythmic alternation of polarity between these two. When the pendulum swing has attained a certain amplitude we may conceive something happening analogous to what takes place in ourselves when mental processes that have been going on below the threshold of consciousness rise into the light and emerge as "I am experiencing such-and-such."

Incidentally it may be mentioned that some accounts treat the emergence of the *Mula-prakriti* as prior to that of the *Shanta Atman*. The contradiction is not so much real as apparent. It must be remembered that we are in a region beyond time as we know it and the stages are more logical than temporal ones. When the emergence of the *Mula-prakriti* is taken as prior it is because, from one point of view, consciousness *manifests* only when there is something there to be conscious of, just as light becomes manifest only when there is something to be illuminated. The two (Subject and Object) are two poles of the One Reality and priority in manifestation is largely a matter of viewpoint.

As an illustration of the identity of the inner teaching in the different schools, the following quotation from the *Zohar* may be of interest. The identifications in brackets are somewhat tentative as I have not made an adequate study of the Kabalistic version. The translation is Sperling and Simon's:

"What is within the Thought [the *Shanta Atman*] none can conceive, much less can one know the *En Soph* [the *Brahman*], of which no trace can be found and to which thought cannot reach by any means. But from the midst of the unpenetrable mystery, from the first descent of the *En Soph*, there glimmers a faint undiscernible light like the point of a needle, the hidden recess of thought [the *Shanta Atman*], which even yet is not knowable until there extends from it a light in a place where there is some imprint of letters [the *Mula-prakriti*], and from which they all issue. First of all is *Aleph* [the *Mahat Atman*], the beginning and end of all grades [the levels], that on which all the grades are imprinted and which yet is always called 'one' to show that though the Godhead contains many forms [the Cosmic Form] it is still one. This is the letter on which depend both the lower and the upper entities" (Zohar, i, 21A).

APPENDIX G
NOTE ON THE AFTER-DEATH PATHS

Popular Hinduism has sometimes taken the "times" of death mentioned in chapter eight, verses 23-26, literally, and the *Mahabharata* relates how Bhishma held off death for several months in order that the sun might enter on the Northern Path—*i.e.* till the winter solstice was over. Taken literally, however, contradictions are involved. For instance, what would happen to a man dying in the light fortnight of the month of November—*i.e.* during the Southern Path? Shankaracharya emphatically affirms that the Path taken after death depends on *jnana* alone and that the time of death makes no difference whatever. He goes on to say that the various "times" mentioned are symbols for the Gods who are the stages on the Path, a statement which is perfectly comprehensible if we remember that the "Gods" mean the levels of consciousness.

The two Paths are in fact the paths taken, the one by the man who identifies himself with die consciousness, the Light of the *Atman*, and the other by him who identifies himself with the passing forms that are illumined by that Light.

On the first path the Yogi passes from the consciousness on the desire-level (withdrawn from the objects of desire and symbolised by fire and light—these two are given as one in the Upanishadic version) to the "day" of the higher mind (which persists as a focus throughout the Cosmic Day unless, indeed, destroyed by passing Beyond); thence he passes to the bright fortnight, the waxing moon of *buddhi*, and to the sunlight of eternal summer (in the *Mahat Atman*).

On the other path the traveller is absorbed in the "smoky" contents of the desire-consciousness and so, failing to see the "day" of the higher *manas*, is lost in the "night." It goes without saying that for him the moon of *buddhi* wanes (the dark fortnight) and that, though the Light of the Great *Atman* is within him all the time, he sees it not and is left in the darkness of an almost Arctic winter (the six months of the sun's southern path) and sees only the "moonlight"—here not the Light of "*buddhi*" but the Light that is entangled in the moon of forms (see *Prashna Upanishad*, i, 5).

Perhaps it should be added that these two paths are in the nature of "limiting paths," they represent the two extremes. The ordinary man will find himself somewhere between the two. After death he will find himself in his desire-body, a subtle body resembling the body in which even now he finds himself in dreams, a body which can experience pleasure and pain but which cannot be injured. All in him that is of real worth will then ascend to the higher, though in many cases it will not be conscious of that Ego but will live in it much as a dissociated personality may live within the psyche of a man on the earth. That is called in the symbolism "going to the night" instead of to the "day" of the Ego.

There within the Ego it will experience subjectively the fruits of its good deeds (which the Gita terms enjoying the wide heaven world), culminating in a flash of expanded consciousness as it unites with the Ego. In the ordinary man this flash of union is the immediate precursor of the raying-out of energy that will form the new personality and, inheriting the *karma* of its predecessor, will be reborn on earth.

It is thus seen that there is a gap between the personalities of two successive incarnations, which explains the lack of memory of the former life. The few cases of memory of a former life that occur sporadically (a well-authenticated case occurred in Delhi during the past year or two) are usually ones where, through some strong desire, the ascent to the Ego has not been made and rebirth takes place almost at once, the subtle desire-body remaining unchanged.

In the *Tibetan Book of the Dead*, edited by Dr Evans Wentz, it is taught that: "After death thy own consciousness, shining, void, and inseparable from the Great Body of Radiance, hath no birth and death and is the immutable Light—*Buddha Amitabha*." It is stated that the mentality of the dying person momentarily enjoys a condition of balance which is compared to that of a needle balanced laterally on a thread. But it is added that, owing to unfamiliarity with such a state, the consciousness principle of the average human being lacks the power to function in it; "*karmik* propensities becloud the consciousness principle with thoughts of personality . . . and, losing equilibrium, it falls away from the Clear Light" (*Tibetan Book of the Dead*, pp. 96 and 97). It is after this that the visions, pleasant or terrifying, of the after-death state commence.

Students of the Buddhist tradition may find that the above explanation throws light on the well-known difficulty in stating from a Buddhist viewpoint what it is that passes from one life to another. Obviously the personal self cannot transmigrate, since a new one is projected for each life. On the other hand, the higher Self is not really born at all and so cannot be said to transmigrate either. Consciousness cannot be said to transmigrate as it is all-pervading and motionless. All that can be said to pass over from one life to the next is karma, and this, at least by some, has been said to be the Buddhist answer. I am quite aware that most Buddhists would not accept the idea of the existence of the higher Self. This is not the place to go into the reasons for such non-acceptance but it should be pointed out that what the Buddhists object to is a permanent self-entity, while what has in this book been termed the higher Self is not a permanent entity, not, in fact, an entity at all.

The same teaching of the two paths occurs in the Orphic tradition. Speaking of the mystic Y and the path which leads to filth and oblivion the Orphic poem *The Descent into Hades* reads:

"Thou shalt find to the left of the House of Hades a wellspring and by the side thereof a white cypress. To this well approach not near. But thou shalt find another cypress and by this the Lake of Memory, cold water flowing forth. Guardians will be before it. Say unto them: 'I am a child of Earth and Starry Heaven, but my Race is of Heaven alone. This ye know yourselves. Quickly give me the cold water flowing forth from Memory's Lake.' And of themselves will they give thee to drink from the holy well-spring and thereafter shalt thou have lordship together with the rest of the heroes" (from Eisler's *Orpheus the Fisher*).

APPENDIX H
NOTE ON THE FIVE ELEMENTS

It must not be supposed that the *Mahabhutas*, the so-called five elements, are elements of matter in the sense of the chemist's elements (though even the latter have now vanished as ultimate entities). Indian philosophic thought is concerned with the analysis of experience, not of "matter." The Hindu view has been excellently stated by Pandit J. C. Chatterji (on page 40 of his *India's Outlook on Life*) as follows:—

"These are collectively the five *Bhutas* and are produced by the five sensation-generals called *Bhuta-matras* (later *Tanmatras*), inasmuch as they have no other meaning except the inferred, *i.e.* the imagined origins or concomitants, moving or stationary, of the sensations of Odour, Flavour ["taste" would be better here.—K.P.], Colour, Temperature and Sound as they are actually perceived by means of the senses operating in the physical body, *i.e.* as varieties in these sensations as distinguished from the general ones. And they are produced in the following manner."

The author then goes on to explain in a manner which, whether altogether sound or not, is very interesting, the details of their arising. In the end he sums up as follows:—

"Thus from the experience of variation in the five general objects of perception there are produced also the five important factors of the physical, namely Ethereal Space (*Akasha*) and the four others technically and symbolically called Air (*Vayu*), Fire (*Agni*), Water (*Ap*) and Earth (*Prithivi*)—ingredients collectively designated in Sanskrit by the technical name of *Bhutas*, *i.e.* the ever-passing Have-beens (never the ares) which are but Ghosts (*Bhuta* also means 'ghost') of the Real, the one ever-abiding Being that is the inmost self of them all, as of the universe."

Buddhist tradition is also quite explicit. The *Abhidharma Kosha* (i, 13) explains that the "earth" of common speech merely means a coloured shape, while the philosophical earth, water, fire and air signify forces of firmness (in some accounts repulsion or that which causes extension), cohesion, maturing (energising?) and flowing-forth or motion. (Note that even the earth of common speech is held quite correctly to be a "coloured shape" and not a solid substance.)

Some may detect a slight flavour of artificiality (almost of apologetic) in this account of the five elements. Perhaps they are not entirely wrong. In still older times, older than what we call philosophic thought, the five elements were earth, water, etc., in their natural sense, the sense we still use in such a phrase as "exposed to the elements." But, at the *same time*, they were used in mystical teaching as *symbols* of various levels of being. Later the symbolic reference to the higher levels was forgotten by teachers who had no knowledge of them and they came to be regarded as just physical-plane realities. The list of five remained, however, sacrosanct and so there was a need for a reinterpretation on philosophical lines. Hence the flavour of artificiality adhering to such interpretations. The Gita, a work which preserves the older mystical symbolisms as well as the newer philosophic thought, uses the elements sometimes in one sense, sometimes in the other. When we read of the earth and fire in chapter fifteen (verses 13 and 14) it is in the symbolic sense that they are used, but in such a verse as Gita, xiii, 5, the sense is "philosophic," and the term should be understood along the general lines set forth above.

In any case, as Chatterji has observed, the five *Mahabhutas* are inferred, not perceived, and the real elements are the elements of sensation (what we should nowadays term sense-data), smell, taste, colour-shape, touch and sound. Even these are elements only in the psychological sense. They represent the elements into which our experience can be analysed and, even if considered "atomic," the atoms must be regarded as psychological irreducibles and not as "material" atoms.

GLOSSARY

Adityas: A class of Vedic Gods, six, seven, or eight in number, the sons of *Aditi*, the Infinite. They are golden, many-eyed, unwinking, sleepless, and they support all that moves or is stationary (Macdonnell's *Vedic Mythology*). They represent the levels of consciousness. Later they became twelve in number and were affiliated to the twelve months.

Akasha: Space—rather in the sense of a continuum than of mere emptiness. We read also of *chid-akasha*, the space of consciousness.

Ananda: Bliss as distinguished from mere hedonic pleasure.

Asura: Originally a title of the great Gods, *Indra, Agni* and *Varuna*, but later, by a different etymology, it came to mean not-divine, and so a Titanic enemy of the Gods. The *Rig-Veda* has both meanings, the later *Atharva-Veda* only the latter. Used in the Gita of the "dark" path of *pravritti*, q.v.

Atman: Originally (perhaps) meaning breath, the word came to stand for self, or anything that may be considered self, from the body up to the highest Reality. Particularly it signifies the higher Self (*jivatman*), the manifested cosmic Self (*Mahat Atman*) and the Unmanifested transcendent Self (*Shanta Atman*). It is the consciousness, particularly on the higher levels.

Avyakta: The Unmanifested, especially *Mula-prakriti*, but also (*e.g.* Gita, viii, 20) the *Parabrahman* and the *Shanta Atman*.

Bhakti: Service motivated by love and worship. Also used for the emotions of love or worship themselves.

Bhishma: A hero in the *Mahabharata*, the adviser of King *Dhritarashtra* and a devotee of Krishna though fighting on the other side. In the Gita he stands for blind faith.

Bodhisattva: In *Mahayana* Buddhism one who treads the Path not for his own salvation alone but for the salvation of all. In the highest sense it is used of one who reaches the Goal, but instead of entering the transcendent *Nirvana* preserves an apparent individuality in order to help others on the Path.

Brahmacharya: Originally the study of the sacred tradition under a *guru*. Later, since the period of study, as contrasted with the following period of life as a householder, was characterised by sexual continence, the word came to have this restricted sense of chastity. Whence *Brahmachari*, one who practises sexual restraint. In the Gita the emphasis is an inner one.

Brahman: The name given in the *Upanishads* for the Supreme Reality. Especially used of the *Parabrahman* but also of the *Shanta Atman* and sometimes for the *Mula-prakriti* (*e.g.* Gita, xiv, 3). Discussion of the etymology would take us too far afield, but it may be taken as the Greatness (*brih*). It must not be confused with *Brahma*, the four-headed God, who symbolises the creative Power of desire, nor with *Brahman*, a member of the priestly caste, nor *Brahmana*, a class of scriptures.

Buddhi: An impersonal spiritual faculty giving knowledge of the Cosmic Unity. Also used of the knowledge itself. See Appendix E. It is also the root of such higher emotions as love. In a lower sense it is used for the purely intellectual aspect of our empirical personalities.

Daivi: Bright, the adjective from *Deva*, a shining power or "God." Used in Gita xvi of the path of *nivritti*, q.v.

Dehi: Literally, the dweller in the body; more exactly, the consciousness focused therein.

Dharma: A difficult word to translate and one having many meanings. Leaving aside meanings which do not occur in the Gita we may take it as the Cosmic Order. Micro-cosmically it is the law or principle which governs the development of the individual. Secondly, it can be rendered as duty. *Dharma* and *karma* were the two aspects into which the *Vedic rita* (the Cosmic Order) was split up.

Dhritarashtra: The blind king of the *Kauravas*—see Prolegomena, p. xix; literally, "he who has seized the kingdom."

Drona: A Brahman who lived as a Kshattriya and was the teacher of military arts to both *Kauravas* and *Pandavas*. In the Gita he stands for the power of ancient tradition, which has to be slain.

Duryodhana: Eldest son of *Dhritarashtra* : literally, "he who is hard to overcome," the desire-nature.

Ganga: The River Ganges, which traditionally rises from the feet of *Narayana* and flows through the three worlds purifying all who bathe in its water. From the inner point of view the stream of consciousness flowing through the three states. See Appendix C.

Guna: Literally, quality or "strand"; a technical term for the three moments of the *Mula-prakriti*—namely, *sattva* —reflecting power, manifesting as brightness, harmony, purity; *rajas*—transmitting power, manifesting as desire, energy, mobility; *tamas*—absorbing power, manifesting as darkness, stagnation, inertia. See Chapter

XIV. The interplay of these three forces makes up all the content of the universe whether physical or mental.

Jagrat: Literally, waking consciousness. See Appendix C.

Jiva: The individual Self. The Light focused in the higher *manas*; also called *jivatman*. See under *Atman*.

Jnana: Knowledge in all senses, from the purely worldly knowledge to gnosis, the intuitional knowledge of the *buddhi*. In the Gita usually in the latter sense.

Kapila: The original teacher of the *Sankhya* philosophy. In the Gita (chapter x) he is taken as the archetypal *siddha* (perfected *yogi*).

Karma: Literally, action. Expecially actions as the elements that manifest the aspect of the Cosmic Order that we know as causal sequence (see also under *Dharma*). Hence also the law by which actions inevitably bear their fruit.

Karna: In reality a half-brother of the *Pandavas*, being the son of their mother by the Sun-God. He was abandoned at birth and became the friend and ally of the *Kauravas*. He was actuated by intense rivalry against Arjuna and the *Kauravas* placed great reliance on his prowess. In the Gita he signifies the power which genuinely worships ideals but places them in the physical life of the senses, believing there to be no other. In this he may be contrasted with *Jayadrath* (Gita, xi, 34), who is a genuine *Kaurava*, and who typifies the belief that the sense-life is itself good.

Kauravas: Dhritarashtra and his sons. The *Asurik* tendencies of *pravritti*, q.v.

Loka: Literally, "that which is seen" (*lokyate*). This and higher worlds. The levels of consciousness. The *lokas* are sometimes classified as three (in which case they correspond to *Jagrat, Swapna* and *Sushupti*, see Appendix C), sometimes as seven, corresponding to the seven levels (see Appendix E).

Mahat: Same as *Mahat Atman* but with emphasis on the objective aspect.

Mahatma: One who has identified himself completely with the One Self (*Mahat Atman*). Nowadays the term is applied to any holy body.

Manas: The mind in its two aspects of the true Thinker or individual Self (higher *manas*) and the empirical thoughtsystem or personality (lower *manas*). In the higher sense it is symbolised by Arjuna and is that which persists from life to life. The two aspects are symbolised by twin *Ashwins* in the *Vedas*.

Manu: An ancient lawgiver and king. In the Gita used in the plural to signify the higher Selves of men as the true lawgivers, rulers and progenitors of personalities.

Maruts: A class of Vedic warrior-gods. They are the "heroes," the "sons of heaven" by *Vayu*, the moving power of air. They are brothers, equal in age, having one birthplace, one mind and one abode. They have grown on earth, in air and in heaven (the three worlds). They are self-luminous fires, ride on chariots and strike downwards with golden spears. See Macdonnell's *Vedic Mythology*. They represent the higher Selves. Their occasional hostile nature is to be understood from Gita, vi, 6.

Mula-prakriti: See *Prakriti*.

Nara: Literally, man; Arjuna, the higher Self.

Narayana: He who dwells in the Cosmic Waters. The supreme Self. Mythologically the Supreme God who sleeps on the Serpent of Eternity in the Causal Ocean, the *Shanta Atman* in the *Mula-prakriti*. From his navel comes forth a lotus on which is born *Brahma* (*Mahat*) and from the latter the whole universe. Identified with Krishna.

Nirvana: The final Goal; extinction of all selfhood and separateness. Called in the Gita *Brahma-Nirvana*, indicating that it is not annihilation but extinction of selfhood in the Real (*Brahman*).

Nivritti: Fulfilment, completion, fruition. Technically the Path of Return, the ascent from "matter" to Spirit, the fulfilment of the Cosmic Play.

Parabrahman: The Supreme Reality. See *Brahman*, which is also used in the same sense.

Prajna: Wisdom, a synonym of *buddhi*, especially considered as the Wisdom content of *buddhi*, Illumination.

Prakriti: The source, original, or material cause of anything. The objective moment of the *Parabrahman*, the great unmanifested Matrix which is the source of all forms. Often termed *Mula* (root) *Prakriti* to distinguish it from its evolutes which, as material causes, are also called *prakritis*.

Pranava: That which sounds forth. The symbol *Om*. See Appendix C.

Pravritti: Continued advance, flow, the outward-flowing Cosmic movement, the correlative of *Nivritti*, q.v.

Purusha: Said to mean "he who dwells in the city" (of the body or the universe). The pure witnessing consciousness. Said in the Gita to be threefold, the perishable purusha or individual Self, the imperishable (the *Shanta Atman*) and the *Purushottama* (highest *Purusha*), the *Parabrahman*.

Rajas: See *Guna*.

Sanjaya: The charioteer and adviser of Dhritarashtra. Turning of the thought-system of the lower *manas* towards the true Thinker (higher *manas*). Conscience. See Prolegomena.

Sankalpa: A bringing-together by the will or imagination. Use of the personal will to formulate some end for oneself.

Sankhya: A system of philosophy said to have been founded by the sage Kapila. Its essence is the discrimination between *purusha* and *prakriti*, q.v. The early forms of *Sankhya* seem to have been monistic and must be distinguished from the later scholastic form that we have in the *Sankhya karikas*. See Gita, ii.

Sanskara: An impression or memory-trace. These impressions of past acts and thoughts serve as causative forces for bringing about further developments. A man's knowledge of a foreign language is not always manifested in his mind, but it is always there in a latent form and will issue in actual words under suitable circumstances. Such latent knowledge is a *sanskara*. There are also *sanskaras* in the higher Ego and in the Cosmic Mind. The word has other meanings not relevant here.

Sannyasi: One who has renounced the household life to wander about as an ascetic. The *sannyasi* abandons all the ceremonial observances of the brahmans, including the worship of the sacred fires, hence he is said to be without fire and without rites. The Gita gives an inner meaning to the conception. See Gita, vi, I.

Sattva: One of the *gunas*, q.v.

Shastra: An order or command. Usually applied to the scriptural books, also to any science or art. In the Gita it signifies *shasak traya*, the threefold inner Ruler.

Tamas: One of the *gunas*, q.v.

Tapasvi: One who practises *tapasya* (religious austerities). The word tapas means heat, or glow, and was used of the severe penances performed by Hindu ascetics. In the Gita it stands for self-discipline. It is also said that the Cosmic process was caused by the *tapas* of the *Parabrahman*; here *tapas* means self-limitation.

Tattva: A principle or element of existence, or rather of experience. Any of the "levels" of the Cosmos.

Upadhi: "Limitation, condition (as of time or space)" (Apte's *Dictionary*). A vehicle. That in which the consciousness works, by which its manifestation is limited. The thought-system of the lower *manas* is the *upadhi* of the true Thinker or higher *manas*. The latter is limited and conditioned by the former.

Vedanta: Literally, the conclusion of the *Vedas*—the *Upanishads*. Any system of philosophy claiming to be based on the *Upanishads*, the Gita and the *Brahma-Sutras*. Expecially used of the monistic system formulated by Shankaracharya (8th century A.D.?), but this system should strictly be called *advaita* (non-dualist) *Vedanta* as there are other claimants to the *Vedantic* title, such as the semi-dualistic and dualistic systems of Ramanuja and Madhva. In the Gita it signifies the final Knowledge, to impart which was the purpose of the *Vedas*, as of all other traditions.

Virata: A king in the *Mahabharata*. During the thirteenth year of exile, in which the *Pandavas* had to remain unrecognised by anyone, they took refuge in various disguised capacities in Virata's service. Arjuna, who had disguised himself as a woman, repaid the debt by acting as charioteer to the young prince and routed single-handed an army of the *Kauravas* who were attempting to drive away Virata's cattle.

Vyasa: A Seer who is credited with having classified the *Vedas* and with being the author of the *Mahabharata* and all the *Puranas*. It was by his blessing that Sanjaya was able to "overhear" the dialogue between Krishna and Arjuna. One of the meanings of the word is diffusion, extension, and we may consider Vyasa as symbolising the power of inspiration, the power which diffuses and extends downwards the higher knowledge.

Yajna: The ritual sacrifices of the *Vedas*. In the Gita it means sacrifice in the more general sense.

Yoga: Union, joining. The Path on which the self is united to the Self and the Self to the All. Teaching about that Path. Also (as the Sovereign Yoga, Gita, ix, 5) the union of the *Shanta Atman* with the *Mula-prakriti* which brings about the Cosmic process.

Yukta: Joined, united; also fit, right, or suitable.

More Bhagavad Gita Books by Alight Publications

The Bhagavad Gita Reference Guide
by Rudra Shivananada

The Bhagavad Gita and the Light of Asia
by Edwin Arnold

Bhagavad Gita and Ten Principal Upanishads
by Purohit Swami

Alight Publications

Books by Yoigiraj Gurunath Siddhanath

Dew Drops of the Soul
Earth Peace through Self Peace
Wings to Freedom
The Reality of Kriya Yoga

Books by Rudra Shivananda

Chakra self Healing by the Power of Om
Breathe like your Life depends on it
In the Light of Kriya Yoga
Healing Postures of the 18 Siddhas
Yoga Purification and Transformation
Insight and Guidance for Spiritual Seekers
Breathe Better Live Longer
Practical Mantra Yoga
Living a Spiritual Life in a Material World
Transformed by the Presence

Printed in the USA
CPSIA information can be obtained
at www.ICGtesting.com
LVHW021458211223
766988LV00093B/4815